DEVOLUTION AND CHOICE

IN EDUCATION

THE SCHOOL,

THE STATE

AND THE MARKET

**Geoff Whitty,
Sally Power** and
David Halpin

Open University Press
Buckingham · Philadelphia

Open University Press
Celtic Court
22 Ballmoor
Buckingham
MK18 1XW

and
1900 Frost Road, Suite 101
Bristol, PA 19007, USA

First Published 1998

A catalogue record of this book is available from the British Library

ISBN   0 335 19711 6 (pb)   0 335 19712 4 (hb)

Library of Congress Cataloging-in-Publication Data
Whitty, Geoff.
    Devolution and choice in education : the school, the state, and
the market / Geoff Whitty, Sally Power, and David Halpin.
        p.   cm.
    Includes bibliographical references (p.) and index.
    ISBN 0-335-19712-4. — ISBN 0-335-19711-6 (pbk.)
    1. School-based management—Cross-cultural studies.   2. School
choice—Cross-cultural studies.   3. School management and
organization—Cross-cultural studies.   4. Politics and education—
Cross-cultural studies.   5. Education and state—Cross-cultural
studies.   6. Educational change—Cross-cultural studies.   I. Power,
Sally.   II. Halpin, David.   III. Title.
LB2806.35.W55   1997
371.2—dc21   97-8654
                                                                 CIP

Typeset by Type Study, Scarborough
Printed in Great Britain by Biddles Ltd, Guildford and King's Lynn

CONTENTS

PREFACE AND
ACKNOWLEDGEMENTS

This book arose from an invitation from the Australian Council for Educational Research (ACER) to review the emergent research evidence on the effects of devolved systems of schooling. We are grateful to ACER for providing us with the stimulus for the writing of the book. Its origins in their invitation will still be obvious to readers.

In undertaking the review, however, the nature of our project changed somewhat. We soon realized that it was quite impossible to study devolved systems of schooling in isolation from other reforms and wider changes in the nature of modern societies. Otherwise, it might have appeared that the predominantly negative findings of the research, particularly on the equity effects of the reforms, resulted from the failings of the individual institutions and teachers that the reforms had apparently been intended to 'empower'. Whatever the rhetoric might have suggested, devolution was clearly not a simple matter of governments handing power to professionals and local communities.

It was particularly clear that, in many countries, devolution had become linked with attempts to create markets, or rather 'quasi-markets', in education. Our title therefore became *Devolution and Choice in Education*. But we were also aware of the apparent paradox that, in many contexts, devolution of responsibilities to individual schools was accompanied by increased powers of surveillance on the part of central and state governments. Hence our sub-title *The School, the State and the Market*. The book now combines a review of research findings with an attempt to make sense of the 'bigger picture' that might help us to understand those findings. At the end of the book, we have also tried to consider some possible alternatives to quasi-market forms of devolution.

We are grateful to the Economic and Social Research Council for funding our own research on education reform in England and Wales (project nos C00230036, C00232462, L20825201001, R000232810, R00234185,

R000231899, R00023391501). We would like to thank colleagues who worked with us on these projects, in particular, Tony Edwards, John Fitz, Sharon Gewirtz, Peter Aggleton, Gabrielle Rowe, Elizabeth Barrett, Len Barton, John Furlong, Sheila Miles and Caroline Whiting.

The University of Wisconsin-Madison and the University of Southern California in the USA and the University of Canterbury in New Zealand provided visiting fellowships that enabled us to study the reforms in those countries. We are also indebted to numerous individuals whom we met on visits to the USA, New Zealand, Australia and Sweden and to those whom we have subsequently bombarded with e-mails asking for clarification on particular points of policy. We would particularly like to thank the following people: Richard Bates, Jill Blackmore, Kevin Harris, Bob Lingard, Susan Robertson, Roger Slee, Richard Smith, Victor Soucek, Jim Walker and Lynn Yates in relation to Australia; Michael Apple, Bill Boyd, Tony Bryk, John Chubb, Jim Cibulka, Bruce Cooper, Stephen Dreyer, Fred Hess, Diane Hirshberg, Allan Odden, Roz Mickelson, Alex Molnar, Kent Peterson, Tom Popkewitz, Penny Sebring, Amy Stuart Wells, John Witte and Penny Wohlstetter in relation to the USA; Roger Dale, Liz Gordon, Michael Irwin, Hugh Lauder, Patrick Lynch, Martin Thrupp and Cathy Wylie in relation to New Zealand; and Inger Andersson, Monica Bergman, Tomas Englund, Ulf Lundgren and Gary Miron in relation to Sweden. None of those named should, however, be held responsible for the ways in which we have interpreted their comments. Last but not least, we have learnt a great deal from our colleagues in the 'Parental Choice and Market Forces' seminar at King's College London. In addition to those we have already mentioned, these include Stephen Ball, Richard Bowe, Miriam David, Diane Reay, Carol Vincent and Anne West.

Acknowledgement is also due to the following publishers for permission to reproduce the following extracts within this book:

Table 3.1 reproduced from OECD (1995) *Decision-making in 14 OECD Education Systems*, by permission of OECD (Organisation for Economic Cooperation and Development), 2 rue André-Pascal, 7577 Paris, France.

Table 3.2 reproduced from J. D. Chapman, W. L. Boyd, R. Lander and D. Reynolds (eds) (1996) *The Reconstruction of Education: Quality, Equality and Control*, by permission of Cassell Plc, Wellington House, 125 The Strand, London, England.

Table 4.1 reproduced from S. Gewirtz, S. J. Ball and R. Bowe (1995) *Markets, Choice and Equity in Education*, by permission of Open University Press, Celtic Court, 22 Ballmoor, Buckingham, England.

Table 5.1 reproduced from J. Codd (1995) Evaluation reform and the contradictory discourse of evaluation, in *Evaluation and Research in Education*, 8(172), 41–54, by permission of Multilingual Matters Ltd, Frankfurt Lodge, Clevedon Hall, Victoria Road, Clevedon, England.

Part I

MAPPING EDUCATION

REFORM

1 INTRODUCTION

The past decade has seen an increasing number of attempts in various parts of the world to restructure and deregulate state schooling. Central to these initiatives are moves to dismantle centralized educational bureaucracies and to create in their place devolved systems of education entailing significant degrees of institutional autonomy and a variety of forms of school-based management and administration. In many cases, these changes have been linked to enhanced parental choice or an increased emphasis on community involvement in schools. Such policy initiatives often introduce a 'market' element into the provision of educational services even though they continue to be paid for largely out of taxation. This may involve 'privatizing' them both by involving private sector providers and by handing over to individuals and families decisions that were previously a matter of public policy. Most often, it entails making public services behave more like the private sector. The term 'quasi-market' is increasingly being used to characterize such attempts to introduce market forces and private decision-making into the provision of education and welfare (Le Grand and Bartlett 1993).

Levačić (1995: 167) suggests that the distinguishing characteristics of a quasi-market for a public service are 'the separation of purchaser from provider and an element of user choice between providers'. In other words, provision of a service is separated from its finance, so that different providers, including sometimes private and voluntary sector bodies, can compete to deliver the service. She adds that a quasi-market frequently remains highly regulated, with the government controlling 'such matters as entry by new providers, investment, the quality of service . . . and price, which is often zero to the user'. The lack of a conventional cash nexus and the strength of government intervention distinguish quasi-markets from the idealized view of a 'free' market, though few contemporary markets in any field are actually free from government regulation and many of them involve some element of overt or covert subsidy.

In the compulsory phases of education, with which we are primarily concerned in this book, the introduction of quasi-markets usually involves a combination of parental choice and school autonomy, together with a considerable degree of public accountability and government regulation. Parental choice in this context refers to attempts to enhance opportunities for choice among publicly maintained schools and sometimes the use of public funds to extend choice into the private sector. School autonomy involves moves to devolve various aspects of decision-making from regional and district offices to individual public schools and thus to enable their site-based professionals or community-based councils to operate more like those responsible for private schools. Such moves are often justified by reference to the claims of Chubb and Moe (1990) about the reasons for the supposedly superior academic performance of private schools.

Advocates of quasi-market policies argue that they will lead to increased diversity of provision, more efficient management, enhanced professionalism and more effective schools. Some proponents, such as Moe (1994) in the United States and Pollard (1995) in the United Kingdom, have argued that such reforms will bring particular benefits for families from disadvantaged communities, who have been ill-served by more conventional bureaucratic arrangements. However, critics suggest that even if these reforms do enhance efficiency, responsiveness, choice and diversity (and even that they regard as questionable), they will increase inequality between schools.

School autonomy is not necessarily linked to parental choice. It is quite possible to have one without the other and there have been many examples of this in the past. Especially in some parts of the USA and Australia, the provenance of the two reforms has been somewhat different and, in some respects, they have remained competing reform strategies. However, they are increasingly being seen as linked in the context of marketization. For example, although Moe (1994) suggests that choice is a far more potent reform measure than school self-management, school autonomy is seen as necessary to free schools to respond positively to market forces. Similarly, while Domanico (1990) states that 'public school choice is not an alternative to school-based management; it is the most effective way of instituting school-based management' (p. 1), he also regards school-based management as 'the most promising supply-side educational reform' (p. 2). As in many other countries, the linking of school self-management and parental choice to create 'quasi-markets' seems to have become the 'big idea' in education reform.

The detail and the bigger picture

Despite the current popularity of devolving responsibility to schools, and increasing the scope for parental choice, there have been very few attempts to evaluate the more enthusiastic claims of the proponents of these policies that they can transform the nature of education on a significant scale. In part, this can be explained in terms of the newness of the reforms. But it is also the case, as Ozga (1990) has pointed out, that specific policies – and sometimes individual schools – tend to be investigated in relative isolation from one another. There is certainly a divide in the relevant literature between research that focuses on the detail of educational self-management and its institutional application and that which concentrates on the 'bigger picture' of system-wide or even global restructuring.

This division is not only academically unsatisfactory, it can also have damaging practical consequences. In discussing urban education studies of the 1970s, Grace (1984: xii) pointed out that 'those who have engaged with the close detail of policy and practice in urban education abstracted from wider issues' are open to the charge of 'producing school-centred solutions with no sense of the structural, the political and the historical as constraints'. They are thus liable to raise false hopes among those seeking to overcome educational disadvantage. A similar charge might be directed towards much of the school management and school improvement literature of the 1990s.

The issue of self-governance has dominated the field of education management and administration over the past few years. Based on the assumption, implicit or explicit, that giving more control to those with 'hands on' involvement in the running of the schools is a 'good thing', the 'how to' literature concerns itself with identifying the mechanisms and procedures through which schools might become more efficient, effective and responsive to the needs of their staff, students and parents. Educational reform tends to be seen in terms of getting educational aims and objectives right – ignoring the wider political dimensions of change. Focusing on the mechanics of school management means that system-wide issues, let alone the international dimensions of educational restructuring, are often lost from view. The isolation of much writing on education management from social scientific research and theories contributes to its sociological naïvety.

For Grace, such work would be an example of 'policy science', which excludes consideration of wider contextual relations 'by its sharply focused concern with the specifics of a particular set of policy initiatives . . . and is seductive in its concreteness, its apparently value-free and objective stance and its direct relation to action'. What risks being lost to view from this perspective is 'the examination of the politics and ideologies and interest groups of the policy making process; the making visible of internal contradictions within policy formulations, and the wider structuring and constraining effects of the social and economic relations within which policy making is taking place' (Grace 1991: 3). This requires what he terms 'policy scholarship'.

But if the numerous practical treatises on self-managing schools concentrate on institutional and organizational specifics, sociological critiques of current educational reform are sometimes guilty of ignoring detail and complexity. Within these accounts, there is a dangerous tendency to interpret education policy only in terms of economic forces and multinational, even global, shifts. Such arguments are often highly conjectural and not sustained, perhaps even unsustainable, by recourse to empirical evidence (Power 1995). Here we have nothing but the 'bigger picture', with very little illuminating detail.

This book attempts the difficult task of bridging the conceptual gulf which divides these two bodies of literature. It seeks to bring together work that might be characterized as 'policy science' with writings in the tradition of 'policy scholarship'. Seeking to integrate the one with the other inevitably means that theoretical clarity will sometimes be partially obscured by empirical messiness, while what appear to be significant details in particular institutional and national contexts may get lost in the attempt to make broader generalizations. But until an attempt is made to connect the empirical detail and the theoretical bigger picture, it is hard to see how we can understand the complexity of current education restructuring and develop sociologically informed alternatives for the future.

Possibilities and problems of comparison

In order to capture both the detail and the bigger picture, we will look at devolution projects under way in five different national contexts: Australia, England and Wales, New Zealand, Sweden and the United States. Comparative research has always been important in understanding education systems – not just for learning about other countries, but also for generating critical understanding of domestic developments. It is a means by which we can begin to find out more about ourselves (Dale 1992). However, a comparative dimension not only enhances our understanding of the contextual features of education systems, it is increasingly becoming important for *explaining* education processes. Although the extent and nature of globalization are hotly contested (Hirst and Thompson 1995), there is little doubt that some countries are having to respond to similar pressures and introducing education policies which look remarkably alike.

McLean (1992) argues that, despite a variety of perspectives within comparative education, international comparison is generally concerned with examining the interaction between global change and national resistance. But within this broad objective, analyses can have at least two different inflections. On the one hand, comparisons can be used to develop more sophisticated understandings of the peculiarities of national arrangements – focusing on the issue of resistance. On the other, the emphasis can be placed on the search for common characteristics – perhaps indicative of more global change. Neither approach can stand alone, and both need to acknowledge that national education systems are both like and unlike each other in a number of ways. However, in this book, we have chosen to place more emphasis on the similarities between countries rather than the distinctiveness of national policy developments. To some extent this approach is justified by the apparent convergence of policy developments in our five countries, connected with arguments that we are entering a period of 'intensifying globalization' (Giddens 1994).

Yet McLean also points out that comparative research has perils as well as promises. In particular, he claims that it is difficult, if not impossible, to reconcile the requirements of comparison with the retention of authenticity. Our own backgrounds will inevitably lead to instances of omission or misinterpretation when we compare across countries. However, these may be no worse than those which occur when making any form of comparison. As Hirsch (1997: 159) argues, the 'raft of contextual qualifications' that often surround international comparisons tends to ignore the fact that societies themselves change, and that particular cultural characteristics which are often seen to militate against any form of authentic comparison are historically, not just geographically, specific.

Nevertheless, we do need to be aware of the dangers of superficial comparison. Thus, while in some senses the current interest in devolution and choice may be indicative of tendencies of global proportions, we have to understand the working out of those tendencies in very different social and cultural contexts. This means we have to be especially careful about using the experience of one context and applying it to others. Education systems have particular structures and embody particular assumptions which are deeply imbedded in their time and place. Knowledge of the fine-grain detail of their implementation is necessary before reforms in one context can be used as models for policy-making in another, and much the same might be said about the lessons that can be learnt from them. As Seddon *et al.* (1991: 32) point out in an Australian contribution to the literature on school-based management, 'decisions at proximal (or school) level are circumscribed by decisions at higher levels'. We would add that these higher level frames may differ significantly from context to context. Not only will the political background of reform vary across countries, as Robertson and Waltman (1993: 39–40) point out, 'even if the policy is adopted in a semblance of its original form, it may produce surprising and unintended results when torn from its native habitat of institutional structure and political culture.'

Moreover, in reviewing the evidence about reform from different countries, we need to bear in mind contextual differences in research methods and priorities. In each country, some aspects of the reforms have received more attention than others. There is also variation in the mode of investigation. Research from the USA draws on a strong quantitative tradition lacking in much recent work elsewhere. Often it is based on the analysis and reanalysis of large-scale datasets. In England and Wales, the commonly used case study approach has yielded more qualitative data on within-school processes, but few statistically supported generalizable outcomes. Research from New Zealand and Sweden combines qualitative and quantitative approaches, while much of that in Australia tends to be qualitative in nature, and increasingly informed by theories of postmodernism and postmodernity.

Finally, in any study which draws on a range of research projects, it is necessary to take on board the agenda of the researchers and their funders. Some of the research to which we refer has been commissioned by agencies representing particular stakeholders in the education system, and where we are aware that this is the case we have drawn attention to it. But none of those engaged in developing and promoting policies or investigating their consequences can claim to be value-free – whether their position is explicit or implicit, acknowledged or unacknowledged. As we commented above, much of the school management and administration literature is based on the assumption that delegating power to schools is a move in the right direction. Much of the sociological writing, on the other hand, is underpinned by a conviction that current forms of devolution represent a step in the wrong direction. As Lauglo (1996: 21) points out, 'those with faith in a government's good intentions, and the cynics who believe that governments are driven only by self-interest, will have rather different interpretations of such decentralization measures as "privatization" or "community participation".'

While scepticism concerning the motives and consequences of policy is a necessary feature of critical policy analysis, there is always a danger that positions of hostility lead to inconsistency or exaggeration. We are comparing across countries, but when we discuss how things have changed we are also, at least implicitly, comparing over time. In making judgements about the consequences of restructuring we need to be particularly careful not to rewrite the history of education systems in ways which overplay the impact of current developments or ignore the inequities of previous arrangements (Power 1992).

Choice of countries

Comparing across countries and continents will, we hope, enable us to illuminate the various ways in which governments in different parts of the world have attempted to remodel national and local systems of education and to increase the autonomy of individual schools. This in turn will help us to address the question of the extent to which the emergence of similar policies may be interpreted as a universalizing tendency in educational reform, articulating with a specific ideological standpoint or a set of identifiable political and economic conditions. We have chosen our five countries for a number of reasons, some of which are pragmatic and some more principled. We have all undertaken extensive research into recent developments in education policy in England and Wales. Our work has focused on policy formulation, implementation and outcomes in a number of areas, including the changing relationship between public and private education (Edwards *et al.* 1989), the future of the comprehensive school (Halpin 1997) and the emergence of new forms of schools, such as city technology colleges (CTCs) (Whitty *et al.* 1993) and grant-maintained (GM) schools (Power *et al.* 1994). Because of our background, we draw very heavily on the English experience. However, this is more than opportunism. English education policies, and the 1988 Education Reform Act in particular, are often held up as an exemplar to other countries. In the USA, they have been seen by Chubb and Moe (1992) as offering a lesson in school reform that America would be wise to follow, though a recent study for the Carnegie Foundation (Stearns 1996) argues that some aspects of the English reforms should serve as a 'warning bell' to their would-be emulators on the other side of the Atlantic.

The 'special relationship' between these two countries, cemented further through the neo-liberal ideological affinity between Margaret Thatcher and Ronald Reagan in the 1980s, makes the United States a particularly important country for British researchers to investigate. Similarly 'close', yet distant, are Australia and New Zealand. Both these countries have experienced what they tend to call 'economic rationalism' – arguably a peculiarly antipodean variant of neo-liberalism – initially introduced by Labor governments but subsequently extended by governments with more in common with Thatcher's Conservatism or Reagan's Republicanism. It will not have escaped notice that these four countries are anglophone. This clearly enables us to access the key issues and current research much more easily, and we have all been engaged in dialogue with academics and policy-makers in each of these countries. Indeed, the shared language is also likely to be one factor behind the rapid spread of the policies themselves. The fifth country, Sweden, provides an important example of an education system which is undergoing restructuring but coming from a rather different non-anglophone context and tradition. For many of us, Swedish education has often been upheld as a shining example of a public education system in which collective responsibility, progressivism and equality of opportunity and outcome have been effectively reconciled. Yet here too fundamental changes began to be implemented in the 1990s.

We have concentrated on recent education reform in five 'Western' industrialized nations, and while we can make a good case for including each of them, the extent of the move towards more devolved and marketized systems of governance is such that there are many others that could have been selected. Countries with quite different histories, such as Chile, South Africa, Russia and the newly independent states of Eastern Europe, are all in the process of altering and often diversifying existing systems of provision. Examination of any of these would have given us new insights into what is happening at national and international levels. We believe, though, that our five countries offer a limited range of administrative arrangements and political traditions which will allow us to note significant differences while also making meaningful comparisons and even generalizations.

While the contextual differences make cross-national comparison particularly interesting, they also make it complicated. Not only do the various reforms have different origins and antecedents, they are linked together in complex combinations. Indeed, investigating the consequences of reform in just one country is hard enough. In England and Wales, for instance, various forms of self-management came in at the same time as a whole range of other reforms and are intimately linked to a national curriculum and nationwide system of testing. As we shall see, it is virtually impossible to separate out the specific effects of any one of these policies. Such difficulties are magnified when one tries to look across national borders for common or contrasting experiences.

Terminology

Another difficult issue in making comparisons concerns terminology. Within the professional literature, there is a proliferation of terms associated with devolving responsibility to schools, hardly any of which lend themselves to precise definition. Indeed, the very concept of devolution is problematic, and some writers prefer to use terms such as 'decentralization' and 'deconcentration'. But, while such terms may be adequate to describe the dominant 'top-down' mode of initiation of many current reforms, they can be misleading when used to characterize attempts to seize responsibility 'from below'. There are also difficulties with the term 'choice', which Epstein and Kenway (1996: 302) suggest actually embraces the concept of 'devolution', along with 'deregulation', 'dezoning' and what they rather confusingly call 'desegregation', meaning the replacement of collegiality, collectivity and cooperation with competitive individualism. In different contexts, choice can signify any, all or even none of these processes.

Even apparently narrower terms are not without their problems. In a review of relevant literature, Ogawa and White (1994) write of the difficulty of defining the concept of 'school-based management'. It is probably one of the most widely used terms, particularly in the USA, but it is also one of the most elusive (Murphy and Beck 1995). For some of its advocates, it is a proposal to decentralize and deregulate school control; for others, it is also a proposal for shared decision-making within schools; and for others still, it is a method of increasing the influence of parents in school decision-making. But this is only one term among many. Take the example of the term 'self-governing school', which, in England and Wales, is officially linked with policies that encourage alternative forms of autonomous status. Thus, both local education authority (LEA) funded schools operating under the aegis of the local management of schools (LMS) policy and grant-maintained (GM) schools, which are funded by the central state after having 'opted out' of LEA control, are called 'self-governing' institutions, although they enjoy rather different degrees of freedom from external influence. Other terms that predominate in this area, and that are equally open to semantic slippage, include 'school-site autonomy', 'decentralized management' and 'site-based management'. Except where we refer to a specific discourse, we have chosen to use 'self-managing school' as our umbrella concept for such tendencies. Although it too is ambiguous, it seems to represent the appropriate balance between the wide range of responsibilities which might be devolved and the limits of that autonomy.

Finally, we use the term 'public schools' in the North American sense of publicly funded and publicly provided schools, rather than in the English sense of elite private schools.

The focus of our inquiry

Terminology aside, the extent and nature of the reforms varies widely both between and within our five countries. Some programmes have been in operation longer than others, making the various research findings more or less reliable. However, even those reforms which have been under way the longest are still relatively recent, and we should remember that any conclusions can only be indicative of the 'early experience'. In England, the political left has often attacked the right for declaring comprehensive education a failure before it had a chance to get established, but that is now what the left sometimes does in attacking the right's reforms. The right, not unreasonably, replies that you cannot effect a culture shift overnight and that schools and their communities will only really reap the benefits once they have escaped from the welfare state dependency culture. Even so, the fact that new policies are nevertheless being justified by reference to the supposed success of current ones (e.g. DfE 1992a) makes it important to undertake an interim evaluation on the basis of the available evidence.

In reading our book it is important to bear in mind that we write about these issues from the perspective of sociologists of education with a particular interest in the relationship between education and equity. We do not entirely accept recent criticisms of work in this tradition (Foster *et al*. 1996), but we do recognize that this perspective on reform will have influenced the way in which we look at the evidence and the issues we choose to emphasize. Thus, while we are interested in changes in school administration, we are particularly concerned with how these are affecting the nature and range of educational opportunities – although we extend the notion of opportunity to consider the implications of the changes not only for students but also for those who work in schools and members of the surrounding community. In addition, as indicated earlier, we regard it as vital to look at the impact of recent reforms on education systems as a whole. While not denying that school autonomy can bring benefits to individual schools and students, and even have their progressive moments, we surely also need to consider the implications of this for schools that are less advantaged through the new found 'freedoms'.

Our inquiry is divided into three sections. The first section sets the scene by outlining and exploring the various policies which seek to restructure public education systems through devolution of decision-making. Following on from this introductory chapter, Chapter 2 provides an account of recent education reforms which have been put in place in each of our five countries. Initially, this appeared to be the most straightforward writing task, but the pace of education reform made the exercise one of trying to hit a moving target. Although the education policy arena has never been static, the heightened activity of recent years is such that, within each country, no sooner has a policy been announced than it is supplemented, extended or supplanted. Therefore, no claims are made about the definitive or comprehensive nature of this overview.

Chapter 3 attempts to make sense of these policies and their cross-national character. It begins by asking whether the policies we have identified are indeed comparable. Some policies which display striking similarities may have quite different origins and purposes. Similarly, policies which at first sight appear to be divergent may, on closer examination, share many common features. The danger of taking policies out of context arises as a problem not only for those involved in policy formulation, but also for those undertaking comparative research. We argue that, while we should not overlook the ways in which socio-historical circumstances lend different nuances to the various devolutionary reforms, there does appear to have been a convergence of policies, at least in our five national settings. These involve an apparently paradoxical combination of state control and market forces or, to put it more specifically, a combination of an 'evaluative state' and 'quasi-markets'. While devolutionary measures appear to hand responsibility to individual insti- tutions, they have often been set alongside others which tie education providers even closer to the state. Sometimes it appears that it is blame for fail- ure, rather than the freedom to succeed, that has been devolved. Various explanations of convergence, ranging from policy borrowing to developments characterized by terms such as post-Fordism and postmodernity, are con- sidered. While education policies have clearly been influenced by changes of global proportions, we argue that these may not be as apocalyptic as suggested by some commentators and that they have not yet entailed a substantial demise of the role of the nation state in education policy. Our five nations have responded to the changes that have taken place with different combi- nations of neo-liberal and neo-conservative measures. The possibility of developing alternatives to these particular reorderings of central–local relations of governance and public welfare provision is raised and then returned to in the final section of the book.

The second section of the book looks at the consequences of the recent restructuring. Drawing on empirical research findings from each of our five countries, it attempts to identify any early conclusions that can be made about the effects of devolved systems on key educational stakeholders. Chapter 4 focuses on the changing role of school leaders. The headteacher or principal is often seen as the central figure in the self-managing school and the nature and requisites of 'leadership' dominate many of the new management texts. How- ever, despite the apparent neutrality of these ideas, their practical application is often less benign. As principals take on increasing responsibility for finan- cial and administrative issues, heightened by the need to ensure survival within the education market place, they often move away from roles embody- ing academic leadership and collegiality towards ones which more closely resemble corporate director, business executive and even entrepreneur. The discourse of 'new managerialism' may talk of flatter structures and facilitative encounters, but much of the evidence thus far suggests that, as the role of the school principal is reformulated, the gap between the manager and the man- aged grows. These principals are having to take on board new and onerous responsibilities which require them to move into hitherto uncharted territory. But, whatever the costs in terms of time and energy, there is little doubt they are consolidating their power. Current reforms may thus be in danger of cre- ating a new form of 'producer capture' – that of principal control – although in the context of the evaluative state this may be more illusory than real.

Chapter 5 concentrates on the ways in which teachers' work is being affected by the reforms. It is perhaps in this area that there is the greatest divide between school management texts and empirically informed research. Within the former, it is often assumed that devolving responsibility to schools will enhance teacher autonomy and professionalism, but current evidence suggests that 'ordinary' teachers have yet obviously to benefit from the reforms. Rather, they seem to be experiencing processes of intensification within their working lives. The parallel development of centrally determined curriculum and assessment measures makes it difficult to disentangle the

effects of devolution in isolation. Even so, there can be little doubt that institutional autonomy and the delegation of budgets are eroding the possibilities
for collective bargaining procedures over pay and conditions of service, while
neo-liberal and neo-conservative suspicion of the 'liberal educational establishment' has also led to attacks on the collective power of teacher trade
unions. With reference to the future of the profession, the effects of reform on
approaches to teacher education should not be forgotten. Here, too, we find a
combination of state-mandated standards and deregulation.

Chapter 6 explores the impact of restructuring on classrooms and the curriculum. Despite the claims made about the 'levelling down' effects of democratic and bureaucratic control of education, there is very little evidence that
school self-management increases levels of student attainment. Claims that
self-managing schools outperform other publicly maintained schools need to
be scrutinized carefully, as any alleged academic superiority may well be
accounted for by an academically advantaged student intake. And while it
might be argued that it is premature to expect any sudden turnaround in
school performance, there does not appear to be much evidence that the
often-claimed advantages of school self-management, in particular the more
efficient and effective use of resources, are reaching the classroom. However,
while the disciplinary mechanisms of the market and the imposition of centralized curriculum programmes have thus far failed to lever up standards,
they do appear to be reorientating processes of teaching and learning. The
appearance of outcome-led curricula is leading to a new culture of assessment,
which some fear will narrow the scope of education. More specifically, there is
some evidence that the new assessment regimes are leading to an increasing
fragmentation and unitization of the curriculum, the marginalization of non-
assessed fields of enquiry and a more rigid compartmentalization of students.
Paradoxically, though, the impact of the market place is also leading to a reinvigorated traditionalism, endorsed by the neo-conservative elements inscribed
in some curricula, and an increasing commercial penetration of classrooms.
We speculate whether these complex, and sometimes contradictory, processes
are contributing to a new 'hidden curriculum' of marketization.

Chapter 7 explores changes in the governance of schools in different
national contexts. Many of the reforms are built around the assumption that
the key to reforming public education lies in placing education in the hands
of the people, rather than the planners. Although the notion of 'community'
involvement figures strongly in the discourse surrounding the reforms, the
measures through which it is to be encouraged are more limited. Where they
exist at all, they usually involve representation on the school councils and
boards of governors or trustees of existing schools. But even this involvement
is highly delimited, usually of a managerial or administrative nature, rather
than entailing significant degrees of consultation on matters of policy. The
increasing need for professional, particularly business-related, expertise is
leading to an even greater marginalization of those lay members of boards
who do not have these attributes. Even at the level of parents' involvement
with their own children's education, it is possible to detect the polarizing tendencies of the market place. We suggest that quasi-markets might be leading

to a commodification of parents, who become valued according to the resources, in terms of both time and money, that they can bring to the school.

The third and final section of the book draws together the issues and research of the previous two sections. As we noted earlier, it is all too easy to look at the consequences of recent reforms at an institutional level and miss their system-wide effects. Case studies celebrating the success of individual self-managing schools overlook the impact their success has on neighbouring schools. This is particularly important when self-management is articulated with choice-driven funding mechanisms. In addition to overviewing some of the issues relating to efficiency and effectiveness, Chapter 8 looks at the consequences of choice and devolution for patterns of social differentiation. Although it is early days, recent research suggests that the fragmentation of bureaucratic systems of education is leading to a polarization of provision, with 'good' schools being rewarded and able to choose their students – usually those who are academically and socially advantaged – while 'failing' schools are thrown into a cycle of decline from which they, and their students – usually the least socially advantaged – find it difficult to recover. Moreover, far from contributing to diversity in public education systems, the operation of market forces appears to be leading to a consolidation of traditional academic models of schooling. Thus we conclude that in current circumstances choice is as likely to reinforce hierarchies as to improve educational opportunities and the overall quality of schooling.

The studies reported here would seem to suggest that current policies of devolution and choice are unlikely to produce those benefits for the poor that some of their most vocal supporters suggest. Whatever gains are to be had from handing decision-making to parents and teachers, it seems that, if equity is to remain an important consideration in education policy, new ways have to be found of avoiding the divisive effects of choice and devolution. The key issues, therefore, are likely to remain political ones which need to be pursued in the political arena. Chapter 9 looks at the various ways in which this might be approached. Arguing against moves to atomize education decision-making further, we also highlight the impossibility and undesirability of returning to the largely discredited statist policies of the post-war era. In acknowledging the need to move beyond traditional notions of welfarism and citizenship, we consider how far the 'new times', which so many commentators have identified, might provide the conditions in which more inclusive democratic structures might be developed 'from below'. Although these do embody many productive possibilities, we argue that they do not obviate the need to engage with broader political projects, which actively address the role of the state. While the current combination of the free market and the strong economy might seem to preclude any such developments, there may well be a range of opportunities and spaces for coalition and collective action as the structural limits of current responses become increasingly apparent.

2 RESTRUCTURING PUBLIC EDUCATION IN FIVE COUNTRIES

This chapter examines the different ways in which power is being redistributed between central and local government and individual schools and their 'clients' by considering policies for educational self-management and schools of choice in our five countries: England and Wales (taken together for the purpose of this book), Australia, New Zealand, the USA and Sweden.

In making connections between our five countries, we are conscious of the need to bear in mind differences in the constitutional arrangements relating to education provision. Three of the countries with which we are concerned here – England and Wales, Sweden and New Zealand – have national systems of education, while compulsory education in Australia and the USA is primarily the responsibility of individual states. This means that it is easier, though not necessarily easy, to generalize about education policy in the first three countries under consideration than in the other two. Had we chosen to write about the United Kingdom, rather than just England and Wales, we would also have had to note significant differences in the education systems of Scotland and Northern Ireland. On the other hand, there are likely to be many similarities as well as differences between individual states within federal nations. Indeed, the advocates of devolution and self-management suggest that, prior to recent reforms, the so-called 'one best system' in the USA had produced an unusual degree of uniformity and mediocrity in the public school system as a whole (Chubb and Moe 1990).

We also need to acknowledge, as we do in more detail in Chapter 3, differences in the political complexion of the reforms, which, though they have obvious surface features in common, are sometimes quite different in their ideological pedigree and purpose. To compound the problem of comparative analysis further, it is clear that the articulation of educational self-management with choice and markets is stronger in some countries than in others. Politics and ideology apart, the reforms with which we deal in this book are also being implemented within national contexts with their own distinctive 'traditions' of education, 'sometimes overlapping but ultimately unique' (McLean 1995: v). These traditions, which by their nature must influence the form and content of educational reform, include historic evaluations of the knowledge to which schools should give priority, the personal attributes they should foster and the nature of the access, participation and opportunity they ought to provide.

Also important are basic demographic differences between our countries, which have implications for the form and scope of devolved decision-making each adopts and the manner and time-span of its implementation. These differences also have consequences for the characteristics of particular systems of school choice and the marketization of education generally. Indeed, the couplets 'centre' and 'periphery' and 'state' and 'local', which are often key leitmotifs in discourses around devolution, take on quite different meanings when one considers geographical scale and population distribution. New Zealand, for instance, has fewer than four million people, while Sweden has a population of over twice that number in an area about the size of the US state of California. Australia, on the other hand, has a population of just under 19 million people, but in a land mass larger than the whole of the USA, which has nearly 250 million people. In fact, most of the individual states in Australia are larger than England and Wales, which, together, have a population of about 50 million.

Despite the huge land mass, the Australian population is largely concentrated in urban areas, as is that of England and Wales and Sweden. New Zealand and the USA have significant rural populations, but the scale of urbanization in the latter makes nonsense of easy comparison – the city of New York, for example, has a population of over seven million, about twice that of the whole of New Zealand. The rural–suburban–urban division also has a particular ethnic dimension in the USA. Although only a minority of the American people are classified as black (12 per cent) or Hispanic (9 per cent), they mainly live in inner urban areas, while suburban and rural populations are largely white. It is estimated that there are fewer than two million native Americans living in the USA. The indigenous population of Australia is also relatively small. Aboriginal peoples and Torres Strait Islanders, for instance, account for less than 2 per cent of the total population, although they comprise together over one-fifth of those living in the largely rural Northern Territory. The rest of Australia has become increasingly ethnically diverse. In New Zealand, the Maori and other Pacific Islander population comprises 13 and 5 per cent respectively of the total. Britain has a largely white population, but with around 5 per cent black and Asian people, who, as in the USA, live mainly in urban areas. Sweden, while undoubtedly the most ethnically homogeneous of our five countries, still has a minority Saami (Lapp) population of fewer than twenty thousand and a small proportion (about 1 per cent) of immigrants from Turkey, Greece, the former Yugoslavia, Finland and other Nordic countries.

The ethnic composition of each of our countries influences the conditions and consequences of implementing school reforms of the type examined in this book. Experiences of schooling are likely to be differentially shaped by the varied geographic, economic and cultural locations of different groups. Schools of choice programmes that aim to diversify education provision appear to articulate with the idea of racial pluralism and thus, at first glance, may have considerable appeal to those minority groups whose experience of common forms of school provision has not generally been positive. Yet, as we point up later in the book, the new policies too may have differential outcomes for different ethnic groups.

In the following sections we outline briefly the key policies that have been implemented in each of our countries. In doing this we expose ourselves immediately to the risk of being out of date before even going to press, especially following the May 1997 general election in England and Wales. Some policies, notably the nature of devolution of financial control to schools in New Zealand, are still under development, while others, like the Charter Schools initiative in the USA, are at a relatively early phase of implementation. All this makes it extremely difficult to provide, for each of our countries, a 'state of the art' account of what is going on. Nevertheless, although the details of the legislation may shift, the general direction of the policies shows a considerable degree of consistency.

England and Wales

The nature of state education in England and Wales since the Second World War developed within a framework first established by the 1944 Education Act. That Act introduced a national system of primary, secondary and further education. The system was conceived as a partnership between central and local government. It is often described as 'a national system, locally administered'. Even today, when the central government education department – the Department for Education and Employment (DfEE) – has been given increased powers, most of the education provided by the state takes place in institutions maintained by democratically elected local education authorities (LEAs). Also within the public sector are most church schools, which receive funding from these LEAs and varying degrees of autonomy from them. While there is a thriving private sector, particularly in England, only 7 per cent of children of compulsory school age (5–16 years) attend its schools. However, this relatively low percentage (it is significantly higher in both the USA and Australia, for instance) disguises the private sector's disproportionate significance insofar as it is regarded by many people as providing an education that is both socially and academically 'superior' to that found in the public sector. By contrast, critics of the private sector (e.g. Hutton 1995) argue that it is socially divisive and offers unfair access to a privileged minority to particular elite forms of university education and subsequently to high status employment.

During the 1970s, media attention had become focused on the supposed failings and 'excesses' of state schools and teachers, particularly in inner-city LEAs controlled by left-wing Labour administrations committed to fostering equal opportunities. After the Conservative general election victory of 1979, the Thatcher and Major governments set about trying to break the LEA monopoly of public schooling through the provisions of a series of Education Acts passed in the 1980s and early 1990s. Shortly after taking power, the first Thatcher administration brought in the 1980 Education Act, which contained various measures to increase parental choice of school, including the introduction of an Assisted Places Scheme to provide public funding to enable academically able children from poor homes to attend some of the country's leading academic private schools. Much of the rhetoric that surrounded the introduction of the scheme emphasized the role it might play in the education of able children from inner-city areas.

Although, in retrospect, the Assisted Places Scheme may be seen as one of the first steps along the neo-liberal reform path (Whitty *et al.* 1996), it was not until the latter half of the decade that a major process of restructuring public education began. In the 1986 Education Act, the governing bodies, which publicly maintained schools were required to have, were reformed to remove the in-built majority of allegedly self-serving LEA appointees and to increase the representation of parents and local business interests. At the same time, the government began to create new forms of public school entirely outside the influence of LEAs. City technology colleges (CTCs), announced in 1986, were intended to be new secondary schools for the inner city, run by independent trusts with business sponsors and with a curriculum emphasis on science and technology. Sponsors were expected to provide much of the capital funding, but with recurrent funding coming from central government, though the reluctance of business to fund this experiment meant that the government eventually had to meet most of the capital costs as well (Whitty *et al.* 1993). Although this lack of business investment restricted the number of CTCs, there are currently fifteen of them operating in England.

Subsequently, a clause in the 1988 Education Reform Act allowed existing public schools to opt out of their LEAs after a parental ballot and run themselves as grant-maintained schools with direct funding from central government. Like other maintained schools, a grant-maintained school is run by a governing body, although this no longer contains any local government appointees. In addition, it gains increased powers in relation to admissions, finance and staffing. Further legislation, notably the 1993 Education Act, permitted schools to change their character by varying enrolment schemes, sought to encourage specialist technology, language and sports schools and made it possible for some private schools to 'opt in' to the grant-maintained schools sector. Although the rhetoric has been largely about devolving power to schools, parents and communities, the 1993 Act also created a potentially powerful national Funding Agency for Schools (FAS), which takes over the planning function from LEAs where grant-maintained schools are in the majority.

The first grant-maintained schools opened in September 1989. Since then, over one thousand schools have opted out. The number of schools going down this route has declined dramatically in recent years, and it is unlikely that Margaret Thatcher's confident prediction that most schools would opt out will be realized without further legislative measures. However, while the grant-maintained sector includes only a small proportion of all maintained schools (slightly more than 4 per cent), its significance should not be underestimated. Uptake within secondary provision in particular has been quite considerable, if geographically patchy. For although only about 2 per cent of all primary schools have achieved grant-maintained status, over 16 per cent of English secondary schools have. Its significance can be gauged by reflecting on the statistic that approximately 700,000 pupils, or about 10 per cent of the school-age population in England, are presently educated in the grant-maintained schools sector. Moreover, while the grant-maintained secondary sector comprises mostly non-selective institutions, it includes a disproportionate number of academically selective and single-sex schools. As a result, being 'grant-maintained' often carries with it a considerable social and educational cachet, and some choose to emphasize their 'independent' status. However, while grant-maintained schools are no longer controlled by LEAs, they are not independent of the central state, which requires them to teach a prescribed national curriculum and meet inspection criteria imposed from the centre. To suggest, as one previous Education Secretary did, that grant-maintained schools are free to pursue their own educational objectives is therefore something of an exaggeration.

Institutional autonomy within other maintained schools was meanwhile promoted through the local management of schools (LMS) policy – another aspect of the 1988 Act. LMS gives the governing bodies of those schools that remain with their LEAs increased control over their own budgets and day-to-day management, receiving funds according to a formula which ensures that at least 85 per cent of the LEA's budget is handed down to school and that 80 per cent of each school's budget is determined directly by the number and ages of its pupils. While this has made the manner in which funds are allocated to schools transparent, it severely limits the scope for positive discrimination on the part of the LEA to counter disadvantage. The funding formula includes teachers' salaries and teachers are now *de facto* (though not *de jure*) employees of the governing body.

Open enrolment, also part of the 1988 Act, went much further than the limited enhancement of parental choice introduced in earlier legislation. It allows popular schools to attract as many pupils as possible, at least up to their physical capacity, instead of being kept to lower limits or strict catchment areas in order that other schools can remain open. As the necessary corollary of per capita funding, open enrolment was a key feature of the Conservative government's attempt to create a quasi-market in which schools were expected to be more responsive to their clients or risk going to the wall. However, existing rules on admissions, based chiefly on sibling enrolment and proximity, are retained once schools are full, though these rules are more flexible in some areas than others.

Taken together, these measures were widely expected to reduce the role of LEAs to a marginal and residual one over the next few years. However, because schools proved much more reluctant to opt out of their LEAs than was anticipated, the Conservative government floated the idea of introducing legislation to make all schools grant-maintained or abolishing LEAs altogether. While claiming to have already increased diversity and choice, Prime Minister Major looked forward to the day when all publicly funded schools would be run as free self-governing schools. He believed in 'trusting headmasters [*sic*], teachers and governing bodies to run their schools and in trusting parents to make the right choice for their children' (*The Times* 24 August 1995: 5). Comprehensive schools were also to be permitted to introduce selection for up to 15 per cent of their intake without having to seek approval with grant-maintained schools in particular encouraged to become even more selective and specialist in character. Major himself would have liked to see an increase throughout the country in the number of academically selective grammar schools. Although some of these specific policies, notably the Assisted Places Scheme, will be abandoned by a Labour government, the overall emphasis on devolution, diversity and choice is likely to remain.

Despite Mr Major's assertion of trust in educational professionals, central government reduced their autonomy and enhanced its own powers in a number of significant ways, and thus strengthened its grip over the education service as a whole, a theme to which we shall return to discuss in more detail in the next chapter. The main vehicle for this reassertion of state control is the National Curriculum, again part of the 1988 Education Reform Act, which specifies programmes of study and attainment targets for the 'core' subjects – English, mathematics and science (plus Welsh in Wales) – and seven other 'foundation' subjects. It also requires complex assessment and reporting procedures, making possible the compilation of 'performance' league tables that allegedly improve accountability and encourage schools to enhance achievement. Although the most cumbersome aspects of the National Curriculum were removed after a review in 1993 (Dearing 1994), its central features remain in place.

Central government exerts additional influence and a considerable degree of control over the work of schools and teachers through the mechanism of inspection. The significant expansion of school inspections in England and Wales during the first half of this decade, and particularly since 1992 when primary legislation about it was passed, has increased the public accountability of the education system, but almost entirely on the government's terms rather than the profession's. The 1992 Education (Schools) Act radically changed the procedures for inspecting schools, responsibility for which, until then, was divided between a national team of Her Majesty's Inspectors (HMIs) and the inspectorate services of LEAs. Today, school inspections are carried out by private inspection teams, the work of which is supervised by HMI and coordinated by a new regulatory body, the Office for Standards in Education (Ofsted). All Ofsted inspectors are required to adhere to a document – the so-called *Handbook* – which sets out the scope, criteria and standards for their work in the field. By any standard, Ofsted's programme of inspections is awesome. By the end of 1997 it hoped to have looked at and reported on the work of every school in England. As Wilcox and Gray (1996: 2) observe, it is doubtful 'if any more ambitious programme of school-by-school evaluation and review has ever been mounted anywhere in the world'. Certainly there is, as yet, nothing approaching it in any of our other countries. It constitutes, moreover, an astonishing degree of state surveillance of the English education system at a time when the advocates of the educational reforms reviewed in this book claim that its schools and teachers enjoy the greatest autonomy of action.

New Zealand

By contrast with England and Wales, New Zealand in the 1980s was a somewhat surprising context for a radical experiment in school reform, let alone one associated with a conservative agenda. Unlike in England and the USA, there was no widespread disquiet about educational standards in the public school system. Nor were there the vast discrepancies in school performance that contributed to a 'moral panic' about urban education in those two countries. The initial reforms were introduced by a Labour government, albeit one that had enthusiastically embraced monetarism and 'new public management' techniques in the mid-1980s (Wylie 1995). The education reforms, which were introduced in October 1989, were based on the Picot Report (Picot 1988) and the government's response, *Tomorrow's Schools*. They led to a shift in the responsibility for budget allocation, staff employment and educational outcomes from central government and regional educational boards to individual schools. Schools were given boards of trustees which initially only consisted of parents, but members of the business community later became eligible. The trustees have to negotiate charters with central government, but the original requirement to involve the local community was subsequently dropped. The content of the charter must match closely standards set down in *National Education Guidelines*.

Because boards of trustees were given effective control over their enrolment schemes, the New Zealand reforms have ushered in a much more thoroughgoing experiment in devolution and free parental choice in the public sector than has been the case in England and Wales. However, Wylie (1994: xv) argues that the other New Zealand reforms 'offer a model of school self-management which is more balanced than the English experience'. This is because they put 'a great emphasis on equity . . . on community involvement . . . on parental involvement [and on] partnership: between parents and professionals'. Furthermore, neither the costs of teacher salaries nor those of some central support services were devolved to individual school budgets, though there have subsequently been moves in this direction since the election of an overtly conservative National Party administration in 1990. Initially, only 3 per cent of New Zealand schools – about seventy in all – were in a pilot scheme for 'bulk funding' (or devolution of 100 per cent of their funding, including teachers' salaries), but a 'direct resourcing' option has now been opened up to all schools for a trial period of three years. At the time of writing, just over 200 primary and nearly forty secondary schools (the equivalent of about 9 per cent of all schools in New Zealand) have taken up this option. Unlike the English funding formulae, which allocate money to schools on the basis of average teacher salaries, the New Zealand scheme is based on actual teacher salaries and a given teacher–student ratio.

As well as devolving increased amounts of financial decision-making to schools, the government has tried to diversify further the types of school available. A significant innovation here, and one that connects with both the notion of affirmative action and the principle of educational pluralism, has been the funding since 1989 of *Kura Kaupapa Maori* ('schools with a Maori charter'), which aim to preserve and promote the Maori language and to support Maori culture generally. At the time of writing, about thirty *Kura* are operating, most of them in the primary phase and involving just over one thousand pupils. This alternative choice within New Zealand education, however, is not expressed in quasi-market terms. Instead, and this may be significant for analyses of alternative ways of managing local education systems, the *Kura* have been developed in response to a need felt and expressed by a minority constituency within New Zealand society dissatisfied with mainstream education provision. It stresses collective rather than just individual needs. As Hirsch (OECD 1994: 131) states, 'it is in the nature of this initiative that it is run by groups with a strong sense of their mission, rather than by educational entrepreneurs trying to sell to a wide market.' To that extent it represents an interesting example of how grass-roots movements can sometimes take advantage of school reforms that have not been introduced with them especially in mind.

The extension of publicly financed choice into the private sector, which caters for about 4 per cent of children in New Zealand, has recently begun with the announcement of a three-year pilot of an equivalent of the English Assisted Places Scheme, termed Targeted Individual Entitlement. Although the trial is small scale, with only 160 students from low-income families being allocated to 46 of New Zealand's total of 129 private schools each year, it has led to claims that 'it marks the start of a move towards a voucher system in which schools compete for parents' education dollar' (*Wellington Evening Post* 28 September 1995). Students, who are selected by individual schools rather than through random balloting as recommended by the Treasury, must come from families earning NZ$25,000 or less per annum. Applications for places on the scheme are running annually at around 800.

Alongside these reforms, a New Zealand Curriculum Framework has been introduced, but this, as its name indicates, is far less detailed and prescriptive than the English model and pays more attention to minority Maori interests. On the other hand, an outcome-based approach to national assessment is being phased in, which potentially could provide central government and employers with a highly controversial alternative mode of accountability and control. Relatedly, an Education Review Office (ERO) – New Zealand's equivalent of Ofsted – has been set up to investigate and report publicly on the performance of schools. However, unlike Ofsted, the ERO does not evaluate the work of schools in the light of fixed standards. Rather, to use its own publicity, the ERO is concerned 'to discover, analyse critically, adjudge and then publicly report on the quality of pre-tertiary education in terms of what the consumers and those who directly represent their interests consider appropriate and of acceptable quality' (quoted in Brooks and Hirsch 1995: 101). Although the ERO appears anxious to evaluate and report on the work of individual schools in terms of the aims and objectives which underpin their institutional charters, it has to be remembered that charters are only granted to schools that can demonstrate they have educational programmes that articulate sensitively with the government's *National Education Guidelines*. Accordingly, while the role of the ERO appears less draconian than the English model of inspections, its implications for state control of educational activity may in practice be little different.

Australia

Not surprisingly, given its geographic proximity, there are many similarities between New Zealand educational reforms and some of those which have been implemented in Australia. There are, though, significant differences. Many of these stem from Australia's federal constitution. With the exception of a few small external territories, education provision is mainly the responsibility of the six states and the Northern Territory. The federal (Commonwealth) government does have some influence on education, most notably by providing subsidies to all private, non-government schools, developing nationwide policies and distributing special grants to offset regional disadvantages. However, the individual states and territory retain all significant responsibility for administering education services and provide the major proportion of funding – at least at primary and secondary level.

Devolution has been a feature of Australian government reform since the 1970s, when many powers were delegated to individual states. Since the mid-1980s, however, there has been a new state-initiated wave of decentralizing reforms. Although these reforms vary in emphasis and detail across the country, and although they need to be understood against the backdrop of attempts by the federal government to centralize aspects of education policy – notably in the areas of higher education provision and the content of school curricula – they share many common features. As M. Angus (1995: 8) comments 'the core ideas spread like an epidemic across systems and state boundaries'. This process was assisted by the highly influential Australians Brian Caldwell and Jim Spinks. Their book, *The Self-managing School* (1988), has become a key text in the field and they have also been employed as consultants by various state education departments in the process of remodelling public education (Brennan 1993).

The 'blueprints' for restructuring began to appear in the late 1980s as a series of key reports outlining the direction of future developments. In 1987, Western Australia saw the publication of the *Better Schools* report, which devolved many administrative responsibilities to schools. The state determined each school's block grant and basic staffing entitlement, but schools were given responsibility for teacher selection and non-staff budgets. *Better Schools* also introduced the 'unit' curriculum and mechanisms for monitoring performance. Also in 1987, the Northern Territory government brought out its own plans, *Towards the 90s*, in many ways similar to the *Better Schools* report, but holding more functions at the centre. South Australia, too, has recently seen the installation of a new administrative structure which delegates significant powers to principals and outlines new teacher competences (Ryan 1993). Queensland, similarly, has been restructuring its education system with the publication of *Focus on Schools* (1990), while at the same time introducing curriculum and competency testing. The *Student Performance Standards* (1992) policy, for instance, requires students to be assessed in various subjects against pre-established levels of competency.

New South Wales implemented its first decentralization programme with the publication of the first Scott report, *Schools Renewal* (1989). This promoted more thoroughgoing devolution and choice – not only restructuring school management along corporate principles but deregulating school zones to stimulate competition between schools (L. Angus 1993a). The New South Wales government has also sought to introduce specialization by creating new kinds of school. These include specialized high schools – languages and technology being the most common specialisms – and a gradual return to academic selection. By 1994, the 19 selective high schools catered for 5 per cent of new entrants (Hirsch 1994). Despite a change of government from the conservative Liberal–National Party coalition back to Labor in 1994, these policies remain intact – even strengthened (Crump and Nytell 1996).

But it is Victoria that is considered to be the 'bell-wether' state (M. Angus 1995: 18). Victoria was a leading proponent of devolution throughout the 1980s. By the end of 1992, all schools were governed by a school council that had budgetary control for all items except teaching staff salaries. Although these early 'noble but flawed' reforms (L. Angus 1993a: 14) were couched in terms of democratic citizenship rather than competition and efficiency, they provided fertile ground for the introduction of quasi-market mechanisms embodied within a framework entitled *Schools of the Future* (1993). In 1993, the newly elected Liberal–National Party coalition government invited applications to place 100 schools into a pilot programme which would give them almost full control over budget and personnel. Over 700 schools applied and 320 entered the programme in its first phase. Successive expansions have meant that all but two Victorian schools are now in the programme. Nearly all intermediate levels of government have been removed and the state department of education is only a quarter of its original size.

Under the *Schools of the Future* framework, each school is governed by a school council of up to 15 members, of whom no more than one-third can be education system employees. Working alongside the school council, but in an advisory capacity only, have been two kinds of 'representative committee'. Originally legitimized through local industrial agreements, one kind deliberated 'administrative' issues (local administrative committees) and the other monitored 'curriculum' initiatives (curriculum committees). The school council, however, became the chief executive body – it recruits the principal, who then takes responsibility for staff and resources. Although Odden (1995: 10) claims that the programme 'represents one of the world's most comprehensive, well-designed, promising and professional approaches to decentralized management of schools', the reforms need to be seen against a background of sharp reductions in the level of resourcing from the state. During 1993–4 over 600 schools were closed and there was a 20 per cent reduction in the number of teachers employed as result. Moreover, the present government in Victoria has abandoned the representative committee structure, which only survives here and there on an *ad hoc* and delegitimized basis. This has allowed the state department to increase its direct control over the curriculum. In common with other states, and the other countries featured in this book, Victoria has developed a curriculum and standards framework, determining curriculum content and assessment requirements across subjects. Again, these are outcome-based, outlining expected performance against pre-established standards.

A full picture of school choice and educational self-management in Australia is not possible without considering the size and role of the private school sector in that country. Its private sector is the largest of any of our five countries, accounting for almost one-third of student enrolments. Seventy per cent of Australian private schools are Catholic, mostly charging low fees and serving families of low and middle incomes. The remainder chiefly comprise schools that adhere to other Christian denominations, in particular Anglican. These non-Catholic schools tend to be attended by pupils from more privileged backgrounds and include among their number institutions with high academic reputations. The federal government subsidizes all private schools using a sliding formula which divides institutions into different bands on the basis of 'need', which is linked to individual schools' private resources from fees and donations. Some private schools serving relatively less well off communities, therefore, receive the highest subsidy – nearly half the average cost of educating a pupil in the state sector – while the more elite establishments, which tend not to be Catholic, enjoy much less, the lowest being about 12 per cent of average costs. In each case, the state government tops up the subsidy.

United States of America

While over five million American children attend private schools, which is equivalent to 11 per cent of the total, these institutions do not, as in Australia, receive significant public financial support. The involvement of the Catholic Church in private education in Australia, however, is mirrored in the United States, where roughly one-half of all private enrolments are at schools of this sort. Only about 20 per cent of all US private schools have secular foundations, but this type of minority private school features strongly in a significant experiment in public support for private education which has been under way in Milwaukee, Wisconsin, since 1990. There, public funds have enabled children from poor backgrounds to attend non-religious private schools. An attempt to extend this policy to religious private schools is presently the subject of a legal challenge.

However, experiments of this sort have hitherto reflected a minority interest among America's educational reformers, whose chief preoccupation in the 1990s has been to seek ways to improve the quality of public education via various forms of restructuring. Newmann (1993) includes parental choice, greater school autonomy and shared decision-making as among the eleven most popular restructuring reforms. One recent account claims that three-quarters of America's school districts have introduced school self-management (Ogawa and White 1994). One of the first big city school districts to embark upon systemic reform of this kind is Chicago, where, since 1985, great efforts have been made to improve public school education. The Illinois legislature has passed three major education bills, each promoting a particular set of policy strategies for school improvement in Chicago. The first of these increased state-directed accountability by requiring Chicago schools to produce an annual report card on student performance, to meet various prespecified targets and to implement particular categorical programmes. This expansion of the monitoring role of the state was complemented in 1988 by a measure to increase parental power through the mechanism of site-based management. This included the requirement that each school be governed by a local school council. This elected body, which is made up mostly of parents and community representatives, has the power to hire and fire the school principal, set budgetary priorities and develop a curricular focus. More recently, in 1995, and in the wake of analyses which indicated that the reforms up to that point had not impacted positively on student achievement, the Governor of Illinois signed into law legislation placing the Chicago school system under mayoral control and instituting a corporate management model in all Chicago's public schools.

Chicago's school reforms, which stress community empowerment and state-directed accountability rather than the marketization of education provision, are very particular to that city, even within the state of Illinois. They should certainly not be seen as representative of what is happening in other states and cities. But, given the limited role of the federal government in relation to education, it is hard in any event to generalize about the nature and provenance of attempts under way elsewhere to enhance parental choice and devolve decision-making to schools. Even in the context of *America 2000* (1991) and *Goals 2000* (1994), which exhibit something of the same tension between centralizing and decentralizing measures to be found in England and Wales and New Zealand, the role of the federal Department of Education has had to be largely one of exhortation. Cookson (1995: 409) suggests that, during the 1980s, President Reagan used it as 'a "bully pulpit" for espousing his beliefs in school choice and local educational autonomy', while George Bush 'went further . . . in attempting to reorganize the public school system according to what he believed were sound market principles'.

During the Clinton years, earlier work on voluntary national standards and accountability measures has been taken further and some support provided for state and local educational improvement efforts designed to help all students attain high academic standards. School self-management is still seen as one way of contributing to this aim, as is parental and community involvement. Choice, though, has been rather less in evidence in the federal rhetoric, at least under the first Clinton administration.

Meanwhile, the more significant decisions continue to be taken at state and district levels. Wells (1993a) demonstrates the huge variety in origins and likely effects of the various choice plans that have been mooted or implemented in the US over the past few years. Similarly, Raywid (1994a) includes among the specialist or 'focus' schools which she advocates a whole variety of institutions with very different origins and purposes. These include long-standing speciality schools, such as the Boston Latin School and New York's highly academic Stuyvesant High School, magnet schools associated with desegregation plans, alternative schools, sometimes based on progressive pedagogic principles, and private Catholic schools.

Nowhere is the localized nature of much of this reform better reflected than in the US charter school initiative. Although the policy enjoys cross-party support and is underwritten financially by a new programme of federal grants, charter school legislation has to be adopted on a state-by-state basis, with the result that there is a degree of variability in the way it is interpreted and implemented on the ground. These differences articulate with the way in which individual states determine for what purposes charter schools may be established, how many schools may apply for and be granted charters and the educational goals which must be met by particular charter schools before renewal. Wohlstetter *et al.*'s (1995) analysis of charter school policies reveals that autonomy may be granted along one dimension, but not along others. And, while charter schools are often seen as a populist reform, the policy tends to build on professional concerns. Across the eleven states which had charter school legislation in place by 1994, nine spoke of facilitating innovative teaching, only three stressed community involvement and others (e.g. Minnesota) stressed the importance of catering for at-risk students (Wohlstetter *et al.* 1995). As Wells *et al.* (1996: 8) argue, 'charter schools reflect the unique political struggles over the meaning of this reform in each state and local community.' However, the reform is increasingly being championed by the national leaders of free-market education in the USA, often at the expense discursively of regular public schools, the work of which is frequently defamed (Nathan 1996).

Accurately generalizing about the charter school reform, even so, remains very difficult. What can be safely written is that it is a policy which is being taken up in an increasing number of places and has popular support among politicians – albeit some of conservative persuasion – and many education administrators. By 1996, twenty-five states had authorized charter school programmes and over 200 schools across the USA had been granted charters. The greater number of these represent public schools which have converted to charter status, the remainder being newly created institutions. The agreement, or 'charter', is drawn up between a group of individuals who want to operate a school – which normally include teachers, parents and community leaders – and a charter-granting authority – usually a school district or the state. Charter schools are vested with decision-making authority in such areas as the budget, staffing and the curriculum, in exchange for which they are held accountable for agreed upon standards of performance.

Mention of 'accountability' in this context anticipates a further strand of education policy deliberation in the USA in recent times: the fervour of activity to identify clear performance indicators to monitor and evaluate the work of individual schools. Attempts to meet this need, not surprisingly, are many and varied, thus making generalization risky. One thing is clear, however: educational self-management is regarded as a key resource in fostering greater accountability and helping to increase the quality of public schooling. The charter school experiment is a critical case here, for it facilitates the creation of new schools on the understanding that they will work hard to achieve their prespecified educational objectives. In other words, the initial granting and renewal of autonomous status, in this experiment as in others like it, is made conditional upon education professionals successfully meeting previously agreed targets. Outcomes are thus what matter; and self-managing schools 'police' themselves rather than satisfy the requirements of a team of visiting inspectors, a mode of surveillance which, in any event, is very little used in the United States except on a voluntary basis, as in New York's 'New Compact for Learning' scheme. However, a possible foretaste of what tighter, prescriptive control of schools operating under devolved management might look like is provided by the California Learning Assessment System (CLAS), first piloted in 1992. This system monitors closely individual school performance and, using data collected through questionnaires, interviews and classroom observation, compares and contrasts educational outcomes. While it is too early to assess CLAS's impact, its ideological significance resides in the fact that it is a further embodiment and example of the way in which government, despite the advent of educational self-management, seeks to give with one hand and take back with another.

Sweden

While the 'one best system' may have been deemed to have failed in the USA, it is considered by many educationists to have been the hallmark of success within Sweden, where a highly regulated comprehensive system of education seemed to have contributed to remarkably little between-school variation and standards which compared favourably with those of other countries. However, despite this long-standing presumption in favour of public education and a strong tradition of centralism, Sweden too is in the process of restructuring through devolution and choice.

Hirsch (1994) identifies a two-stage process of devolution. From the mid-1970s onwards, a process of decentralization took place which involved transfer of responsibility from central government to municipalities or local *kommuns*. In 1991, the central state ceased to regulate teaching appointments and headships and the 288 municipalities eventually took over full responsibility for organizing and implementing school activities (Swedish Institute 1996). From 1996, each municipality is given a single grant with which to fund obligatory services, including education, and then decides how to allocate this money and organize schooling.

The Swedish reforms thus appear to differ from those in our other countries by enhancing rather than reducing local democratic influence over education policy. However, Englund (1993) has identified a gradual shift from collectivism to individualism within the Swedish school system during the 1980s, with education increasingly being regarded as a private rather than a public good. Indeed, even before it lost power in the election of 1991, the Social Democratic government approved proposals to distribute funds to private schools. With the return of centre/right coalition government, a 'free choice revolution' took place which emphasized 'competition and choice' through supporting private provision and encouraging various forms of 'voucher'. Municipalities were required to provide vouchers worth at least 85 per cent of the average cost of education in municipal schools in respect of students attending approved independent schools. The reform began with compulsory level schools and was extended to upper secondary and special schools. The shift towards choice and devolution was strengthened at local level, where the right also made electoral gains – with three-quarters of the municipalities obtaining a 'burger' party majority (Chapman *et al.* 1996). Schools were encouraged to develop specialisms within the national curriculum and some municipalities have encouraged competition among their own schools (in place of traditional catchment arrangements). Schemes, similar to that of LMS in the UK, where the money follows the pupil, are also being put in place. The municipality of Nacka, for instance, allocates 85 per cent of its education budget directly to schools on the basis of pupil numbers (Chapman *et al.* 1996).

Miron (1993) believes that the move towards quasi-markets in Sweden was largely driven by economic pressures and accelerated through the political and ideological motivation of the centre/right government. The reforms, though philosophically appealing in libertarian terms, did not really reflect widespread dissatisfaction with the previous system. The number of independent schools has grown but, although attendance in them doubled in four years, they still constitute only 2 per cent of all enrolments. Nevertheless, they have had a significant impact in some of the urban areas, to which they are almost entirely restricted.

When the Social Democrats were returned to power in 1994, they modified, but did not abandon, most of these policy developments. For example, although they have not removed the voucher scheme as pledged, they have reduced its value (to 75 per cent). New proposals are currently under discussion which will change the basis of support to independent schools, deny support when it would be damaging to overall provision in the municipality and require independent schools to adhere more closely to the national curriculum. These recognize a need to 'balance collective and individual interests' (Miron 1993).

As elsewhere, while the trend may be one of devolving managerial and financial responsibility, the central government has maintained a significant measure of control over curriculum content and evaluation of performance. Sweden's 1985 Education Act outlined a highly specified national curriculum, which detailed the structure and components of each year of schooling down to 60-minute teaching units. Since 1993, the detail of this curriculum has been slimmed down and the emphasis changed from control of input to control of output. While there is more space for influence at the lower levels of the system, there is also increased emphasis on the 'basics' (Swedish, English and mathematics), reinforced by standardized achievement tests in all subjects for grades 5 and 9. Accordingly, the OECD (1995a: 188) identifies 'a clear move away from a pupil centred approach to schooling and the social and personal development functions towards their purely educational purposes based on subject knowledge and, in general, a reinforcement of the academic component of education at all levels.' Assessment of the National Curriculum and evaluation of the education system has been put under the control of a National Agency of Education, which replaced national and regional boards of education in 1991.

Overall, there has been a shift away from traditional bureaucratic control to control via 'frame' laws setting goals and objectives. Lundgren (undated: 1) says that the reforms can be 'characterized as a deregulation, but . . . also a sharpening of rules and demands'.

Summary

Within each of our five countries a range of policies has been implemented that attempt to restructure public education. A common theme is the devolution of financial and managerial control to more local levels, either to municipalities and schools, as in Sweden, or more commonly away from regional and district levels to individual schools, as in the LMS policy in England and Wales, the 'direct resourcing' experiment in New Zealand and the USA Charter Schools initiative. Another common characteristic is the promotion of parental rights to choose schools, sometimes articulating with changes in funding formulae, where the money follows the pupils, resulting in a move towards quasi-markets in education. One aspect of this is the introduction of policies that allocate public funds to be spent on private education. Such policies, especially when combined with formula funding for public schools, help to create a 'virtual voucher' system of the sort advocated by some New Right politicians, such as Sexton (1987). The concept of diversity of provision, whether within the private or public sector, is also a key aspect of current policy discourse. However, it is evident that these liberalizing reforms are being implemented alongside others which consolidate power within central governments, at national or state level. In particular, centrally defined goals concerning what schools should teach, and how their performance should be assessed, are becoming commonplace. This theme – the change in the role of governments – is taken further in the next chapter, which will cast a critical eye over the key characteristics of reforms in our five countries and consider whether they represent a common and coherent trend in the reformulation of the relationship between schools and the state.

3 DEVOLUTION AND CHOICE: A GLOBAL PHENOMENON?

This book is premised upon the assumption that useful comparisons can be made about the educational reforms being implemented in our five national contexts. It is clear from the preceding two chapters that public education systems in England and Wales, the USA, Australia, New Zealand and Sweden are in a period of transition. In each, a range of policies has been introduced that seeks to reformulate the relationship between government, schools and parents. But to what extent are these policies comparable? Can they be said to constitute a coherent trend? And, if so, what does it signify? Is the widespread emergence of devolutionary policies nothing more than a series of local responses to local crises, or does it indicate a more profound restructuring of local–government relations on an international scale?

The almost simultaneous emergence of similar reforms across continents has led some to suggest that the current restructuring of education needs to be understood as a global phenomenon. Indeed, it has been argued that this trend is part of a broader economic, political and cultural process of globalization in which national differences are eroded, state bureaucracies fragment and the notion of mass systems of public welfare, including education, disappears. But, rather than embracing such grand theories wholeheartedly, we need to consider whether contextual specifities are at least as significant as any broader cross-national developments. This chapter, therefore, explores the degree of commonality and coherence within the education reforms of our five countries before going on to consider the extent to which we are witnessing a fundamental change in the governance of national systems of education.

Contrasts and convergence

Policy-makers are often criticized for looking overseas for solutions to domestic problems in the naive belief that policies designed in one context can be unproblematically transported elsewhere. Those involved with analysing these policies also need to be wary of decontextualizing reforms. To compare across countries without recognizing the distinctive historical and cultural dimensions of policies is to risk 'false universalism' (Rose 1991), whereby similarities are spotted without reference to the context in which they were developed.

Certainly, as we saw in the previous two chapters, any cross-national comparison needs to acknowledge the differences in the degree and manner in which education is being restructured. The extent to which responsibility has been devolved downwards differs greatly both between and within countries. For instance, Hirsch (1995) claims that in New Zealand school autonomy has gone so far that the notion of a public education 'system' is fast becoming an oxymoron. This is a far cry from other places, such as the American state of New Mexico, where any such measures are highly delimited (Wohlstetter *et al*. 1995). Lawton (1990) developed a three-point scale in order to differentiate policies according to the degree of devolution entailed. He found wide variation, with the New Zealand reforms scoring the most points, while measures in Rochester, New York, devolved the least.

However, given the national differences in administrative arrangements and the complex ways in which authority can be redistributed, single scales along which to measure degrees of devolution are bound to provide only partial indices of change. As a recent OECD (1995b) study of education decision-making reveals, it is certainly far too simplistic to make a straightforward distinction between centralized or decentralized systems. Its study of 14 countries, which include New Zealand, Sweden and the USA, distinguishes four levels of decision-making to take into account countries with federal constitutions. The numbers of powers at each level were compared, together with the mode of decision-making at each of these levels in relation to a range of responsibilities. Although they identify the decision-making structures of an 'average' education system (where schools would take 38 per cent of the decisions), there are huge variations between countries. With reference to three of the countries that we are considering, Table 3.1 reveals that decision-making powers in relation to secondary level public education are distributed in quite different ways.

As we have seen, recent reforms in New Zealand have eliminated all intermediate levels of decision-making. This has resulted in a situation where extensive powers have been delegated to schools, but have also been retained by, even consolidated within, central government. Recent reforms in England and Wales have been less dramatic, but are probably closest to this mode of devolution. Grant-maintained schools in particular by-pass the intermediate level influence of LEAs and stand in an unmediated relationship with central government. While schools in New Zealand have more powers than any of the other fourteen countries, mainstream public schools in the USA have the second fewest. Federal government there is deemed to have no decision-making power, while even state agencies (at upper intermediate level) appear to have relatively little. Decision-making is concentrated at local levels, but principally within the district rather than the school. In the Australian federal

Table 3.1   Decision-making in New Zealand, Sweden and the USA (percentages)

	School	Lower intermediate	Upper intermediate	Central government
New Zealand	71	0	0	29
Sweden	48	48	0	4
USA	26	71	3	0

Source: OECD (1995b: 40)

model, though, the state level has been more powerful. Within the Swedish public education system, decision-making is now concentrated at the local levels, but, unlike in the USA, it is divided evenly between the school and the district.

We also need to acknowledge differences in the political complexion of reforms which may look similar. In England and Wales, New Zealand, Sweden, Australia and the USA, or at least in individual states within these last two countries, devolution, institutional autonomy and school choice have often become associated with a conservative agenda for education. Yet support for at least some aspects of these policies is by no means limited to New Right politicians who argue that social affairs are best organized according to the general principle of consumer sovereignty. Indeed, some of the earliest moves to devolution in Victoria, Australia, in the early 1980s were talked of in terms of professional and community empowerment, even though more recent policies there have been associated with the New Right. This was also the case with some of the devolution initiatives in New Zealand in the 1980s, despite the fact that subsequent reforms there too have been more concerned with fostering market freedom than with equity (Grace 1991; Gordon 1992). In both countries, governments of different political complexions have supported reform, albeit with somewhat different emphases. In the United States, the Chicago reforms were originally supported by a curious alliance of black groups seeking to establish community control of their local schools, white old-style liberals who had become disillusioned with the performance of the school board, New Right advocates of school choice and some former student radicals of the 1960s. Similarly, radical reformers of many shades of opinion are currently looking to the charter school movement as the way to create their own 'educational spaces' (Wells *et al.* 1996). In Sweden, while the balance has shifted back to a concern with equity issues with the return of a Social Democratic government, there has been cross-party support for the general direction of the reforms. And even in England and Wales, where the reforms have been most closely and consistently associated with a New Right government, the key elements are likely to be kept in place by an incoming Labour administration.

Much of this confusing complexity derives from the many shades of meaning behind devolution and choice. Not only do the two concepts enter into different relationships with each other, they are both 'multi-accented'

Table 3.2 Implications of different forms of decentralization

Alternatives to bureaucratic centralism	Emphasis in the distribution of decision-making authority	Means of evaluating and monitoring institutions and educational practice
Political rationale		
Liberalism	Wide dispersal, e.g. strong local government in fairly 'large' units; private provision; market mechanism; professional autonomy	Market forces or professional self-regulation; weak state control
Federalism	The federal authority is weak; no further prescription	No implications
Populist localism	Strong local government at 'community' level; parental control	Informal feedbacks through local transparency
Participatory democracy	Weak 'outside' control; collective 'inside' decisions; flat internal structure	Only 'inside' participation; collective process; control from 'below'
Quality and efficiency		
Pedagogic professionalism	Individual teacher autonomy; weak 'non-professional' autonomy	Professional self-regulation; peer review
Management by objectives	Strong school management; outside scrutiny of results and expenditures	Performance indicators compared with objectives and budgets
Market mechanism	Competition; strong school management	Customer demand; accreditation of schools
Deconcentration	Strong state agents at regional level; regionally unified sector planning	Management information systems

Source: Lauglo (1996: 40)

concepts in their own right. As Lauglo (1996) points out, what he calls 'decentralization' should not be thought of as a unitary concept. Indeed, he identifies eight alternatives to the conventional bureaucratic centralism of mass education systems, of which four reflect different political legitimations for redistributing authority and four reflect different arguments concerning the quality of education provision and the efficient use of resources (see Table 3.2). These alternatives are variously, and often simultaneously, emphasized within each of our countries. Liberalism, or more accurately neo-liberalism, is evident within all of them, but perhaps most particularly in England and Wales, where it has become closely articulated with the so-called 'new public management', combining what Lauglo terms 'market mechanisms' and 'management by objectives'. Such developments are also strongly in evidence in New Zealand and in some states in the USA and Australia. However, justifications for decentralization within some American districts, such as Dade County, Florida, can be seen as being related to pedagogic professionalism – at least within the reforms of the 1980s – while professional control was also an aspect of Swedish reforms at that time.

A further feature of some justifications surrounding restructuring has been references to the democracy of local participation. However, local democratic control of education has been called into question in England and Wales and the United States, though somewhat strengthened in Sweden. In other cases, pressure for local participation often takes the form of local populism, rather than either representative or participatory democracy. Within local populism the rights of the 'common people' are set against the dominance of established elites – the education profession in many cases. But, as Lauglo (1996: 27) argues, it would be misleading to represent such populism as having the radical implications of participatory democracy, 'for while it may be radical in its rejection of elite dominance, it tends towards conservatism in relation to the cultural values of ordinary folk'. The extent to which such localism is a real, rather than rhetorical, element of recent reforms is questionable given the diminution of local government in most contexts and the increasing formalization of feedback mechanisms within some of our examples.

Clearly, then, any cross-national discussion of educational restructuring needs to bear in mind a wide range of variance. Educational reform is being conducted within contexts with different histories, different constitutional and administrative arrangements and different political complexions. Moreover, the nature and extent of devolution, and the ways in which policies are interconnected, vary both within and between countries.

However, while such variance needs to be acknowledged, it should not obscure the common factors. It is clear from the above discussions that there are common trends across our five countries. As Fowler (1994) comments, despite the large body of 'exceptionality literature', 'important variations among institutions and cultures do not erase deeper similarities' – particularly between advanced industrial democracies. The above discussion of Lauglo's table (our Table 3.2) suggests considerable congruence in the policies we are considering. Within the range of political rationales, it is the neoliberal alternative which dominates, as does a particular emphasis on market-type mechanisms. This decentralization via the market is also articulated with justifications of quality and efficiency, drawing on the discourse of the new public management with its emphasis on strong school management and external scrutiny – made possible by the development of performance indicators and competency-based assessment procedures, reinforced in many cases by external inspection. These developments in education policy reflect a broader tendency for liberal democracies to develop along the lines of what Gamble (1988) has called the 'strong state' and the 'free economy'. This strong state, which in federal systems may embrace state as well as federal levels of government, increasingly steers at a distance, while the notion of the free economy is extended to a marketized 'civil society' in which education and welfare services are offered to individual consumers by competing providers rather than provided collectively by the state for all citizens. Using the terminology we introduced in Chapter 1, bureaucratically provided welfare is being replaced by welfare distributed through 'quasi-markets'.

This approach reflects a shift from conventional techniques of coordination and control on the part of large-scale bureaucratic state forms and their replacement by a set of 'discursive, legislative, fiscal, organisational and other resources' (Rose and Miller 1992: 189). But, although these devices may appear to offer considerable scope for local discretion compared to the 'dead hand' of centralized bureaucracies, they also entail some fairly direct modes of control. For example, the devolution of funding to schools on a per capita basis requires schools to attempt to maximize their rolls. Schools which do not attract students are penalized in a direct fashion by the withdrawal of funding and staffing resources. And the publication of test results and school inspection reports potentially provides a powerful link between the requirements of the 'strong state' and the actions of individual schools and parents in the market place.

The evaluative state and market forces

Particularly helpful in understanding how the state remains strong while appearing to devolve power to individuals and autonomous institutions competing in the market is Neave's (1988) concept of the 'evaluative state'. Neave's own conception of the rise of the evaluative state was developed from a comparative analysis of recent trends in higher education reforms in Western Europe. However, the trends he identifies are also applicable to the compulsory phase of education in the countries we are considering – as well as other areas of social policy, such as health and social care. He argues that policies, which were initially little more than a short-term response to financial difficulties in the early 1980s, have since developed into a long-term strategic thrust. This has two principal components. One is the reformulation of the relationship between education and the government, which he identifies in terms of the rise of the evaluative state. The second dimension is the reformulation of the relationship between education and society, which is 'an attempt to insert a particular form of externally defined "competitive ethic" as the prime driving force for institutional, and thus system, development' in education (Neave 1988: 7–8).

The state has always undertaken evaluations of those areas for which it has primary responsibility, but Neave argues that it is important to distinguish evaluation for system maintenance and evaluation for strategic change. What we are seeing currently is the growth of strategic evaluation – but of a particular sort. Earlier forms of strategic evaluation were undertaken on an *a priori* basis. Governments drew up long-term goals, allocated resources and put in place procedures by which they could assess whether these goals had been achieved – and if not, why not. As Neave (1988: 9) puts it, 'strategic evaluation sought to remedy the visible shortcomings of a system in a steady state by revising the targets within which the subsequently reformed system would operate.' It is possible to argue that this form of governmental intervention and monitoring carries all the hallmarks of the modernizing enterprise.

In the evaluative state, however, the role and timing of evaluation is different. Instead of *a priori* evaluation, we have *a posteriori* evaluation. What matters is not the process by which goals might be achieved, but the output. Neave argues that this shift of emphasis from process to product, from input to output, indicates a significant new development in the relationship between the state and education system. First, it replaces the predominant concerns of quality of provision and equity of access and opportunity. Second, by focusing on output, it redefines the purpose of education in terms of the economy rather than individual demand. Third, it provides a powerful instrument for steering individual institutions.

There is, then, 'a rationalization and wholesale redistribution of functions between centre and periphery such that the centre maintains overall strategic control through fewer, but more precise, policy levers, contained in overall "mission statements", the setting of system goals and the operationalization of criteria relating to "output quality" ' (Neave 1988: 11). Rather than leading to a withering away of the state, the state withdraws 'from the murky plain of overwhelming detail, the better to take refuge in the clear and commanding heights of strategic "profiling" ' (Neave 1988: 12). In some cases, this brings about the emergence of new intermediary bodies – trusts, agencies and quangos – which are directly appointed by and responsible to government ministers rather under local democratic control. In England, the Funding Agency for Schools, which directs government funds to grant-maintained schools and takes over the planning of local provision once a substantial number of schools in an area have opted out of their LEA, is a prime example, as is Ofsted. Such agencies are often headed by a new breed of government appointees, who tend to have a higher public profile than conventional state bureaucrats and have had a significant role in setting new political agendas through close contacts with the media. The evaluative state also requires significant changes to be made at the institutional level. Schools have to develop new modes of response which require new structures and patterns of authority. In particular, it seems to encourage strong goal-oriented leadership at the institutional level, involving a shift from the traditional collegial model to that of the 'chief executive', and the growing importance of 'senior management teams' or 'cabinets' in schools.

Neave (1988) suggests that the evaluative state does not represent any one ideological viewpoint. Its key characteristic is a move away from government by 'bureaucratic fiat'. Yet there are close links between what he describes and Pusey's (1991) concept of economic rationalism, in which education is framed as a commodity and education policy becomes the means by which it can be more efficiently and effectively regulated and distributed. As Marginson (1993) outlines, economic rationalism in education has three components. First, there is an overriding concern with economic objectives. Second, the market becomes the ascendant metaphor. Although political advocacy of markets may be downplayed in some contexts, there is a clear permeation of business values and vocabulary in educational discourse. The third component of economic rationalism is the central administration of the system, whereby education is brought more directly and effectively under the control of central government agencies. Sweden, England and Wales and New Zealand, and many states in America and Australia, have introduced competency-based performance indicators as a means of measuring educational output. Although justified in terms of consumer information and public accountability, these programmes enable government to scrutinize more effectively educational expenditure and productivity, while at the same time blocking alternative definitions of what counts as appropriate learning.

Marginson (1993) claims that the emphasis on economic objectives entails a distancing of education from social and cultural domains. In practice, though, there is often another component to current policies that needs to be taken into consideration. The New Right in many countries is a coalition of neo-liberal advocates of market forces and neo-conservative proponents of a return to 'traditional' values (Gamble 1983). The balance between the neo-liberal and neo-conservative aspects of contemporary conservatism varies between and within the countries we are considering here. However, where neo-conservatives are strong, they expect the education system to foster particular values, especially among those whose adherence to them is considered suspect. The criteria of evaluation employed are thus not only those of economic rationalism, but also those of cultural preferences. This is particularly the case where there is perceived to be a threat to national identity and hegemonic values either from globalization or from supposed 'enemies within', who are sometimes seen to include 'bureau-professionals' and members of the 'liberal educational establishment'.

McKenzie (1993: 17) argues that British governments have 'actually increased their claims to knowledge and authority over the education system whilst promoting a theoretical and superficial movement towards consumer sovereignty'. Although other countries have not been as prescriptive as Britain, many governments at state or national level have tightened their control over the curriculum in terms of what is taught and how this is to be assessed. This central regulation of the curriculum is not only geared towards standardizing performance criteria in order to facilitate professional accountability and consumer choice within the education market place; it is also about creating, or re-creating, forms of national identity.

In England and Wales, the formulation of the National Curriculum has been underlain by a consistent requirement that schools concentrate on British history, British geography and 'classic' English literature. During its development, the influential Hillgate Group (1987: 4) expressed concern about pressure for a multicultural curriculum and argued for 'the traditional values of western societies' underlying British culture, which 'must not be sacrificed for the sake of a misguided relativism, or out of a misplaced concern for those who might not yet be aware of its strengths and weaknesses'. This privileging of one narrow and partial version of national culture is less visible in Australia and New Zealand, although the importance of 'knowledge of Australia's history' has sometimes been a key element in ministerial pronouncements on the objectives of the nation's schools (Slattery 1989), and in both countries there have been attempts to generate a distinctive national identity (Fiske *et al.* 1987). In Australia, a powerful consortium of 'back-to-basics' groups representing Christian fundamentalists and conservative business interests is attempting to influence curricula 'hearkening back to a simpler and more certain mythic world of yesteryear, in which values were monolithic, unchanging and unchallenged' (Welch 1996: 103). The issue of a national curriculum has attracted considerable controversy within the USA, but individual states can legislate on curricula and for many years have controlled the selection of school textbooks. Texas, for instance, has a policy of excluding publications which do not promote 'traditional' lifestyles and values (Delfattore 1992). The general shift rightwards, and the influence of powerful fundamentalist and conservative lobbyists, make it increasingly likely that any legislated curriculum, whether at state or national level, will draw on a partial and narrow selection of American culture (Apple 1996).

In short, schools may have been given new responsibilities for institutional finance and administration, but have lost ground in other areas, especially in relation to the curriculum. In each of our five countries, national or state governments have taken on new powers in defining what counts as school knowledge, how performance should be assessed and to whom it must be reported.

Accounting for policy convergence

Even though these directions in education policy have not penetrated all countries (Green 1994), and they have been mediated differently by the traditions of different nation states and different political parties, the similarity between the broad trends in many parts of the world suggests that education policy may be witnessing something more significant than passing political fashion. In seeking to understand the similarities between policies in our different countries, a range of explanations can be invoked. At one end of the continuum are those that highlight the role of individual policy-carriers, and at the other end are theories of globalization and postmodernism where the traditional role of the nation state is overridden by multifaceted international restructuring. Of course, these various explanations may not be mutually exclusive, but each emphasizes different loci of change which have important implications for generating potential alternatives to current policies.

One form of explanation is that ideas developed in one context have been copied in another. To some extent, neo-liberal policies have been actively fostered by international organizations; for example, by the IMF and the World Bank in Latin America and Eastern Europe (Arnove 1996). But informal modes of transmission are probably more common. There is certainly evidence to suggest that when education policy-makers formulate proposed reforms they look to other countries for inspiration and justification. An Education Secretary in the Thatcher administration, Kenneth Baker, used reports about and personal visits to specialist schools in New York City and elsewhere in the United States to support the city technology colleges experiment. Conversely,

England and Wales' grant-maintained schools' policy has apparently inspired some charter school legislation in the United States, notably in California, where Bill Honig, the state superintendent, was said to have been impressed by opting out following a brief visit to the United Kingdom. Moreover, some of the principals of the first schools to opt out in England have 'carried' the policy across the Atlantic in the course of attending programmes of study at the University of Southern California as part of their work for an MBA degree. With reference to Australia and New Zealand, Smyth (1993a: 5) claims that Victoria's *Schools for the Future* framework bears an 'even plagiaristic' resemblance to New Zealand's policy blueprint *Tomorrow's Schools*, which, he suggests, was 'hijacked directly from Thatcher's England'. Seddon (1994: 4) argues that Australia in general has displayed 'a dependent and subservient preoccupation with developments in the UK and USA'. The flow of ideas between Australasia and Britain has not been one-way, however. The lack of sustained interest in opting out within England and Wales has led policy-makers to suggest that the requirement for a parental ballot be waived in line with New Zealand's model for 'bulk-funded' schools (Catherall 1995). Finally, Miron (1993) suggests that the centre-right coalition in Sweden looked to Thatcherite England for its inspiration, but itself sought to become a 'world leader' in fostering choice policies in education.

While policy-borrowing has clearly been a factor in the move towards choice within devolved systems of schooling, it only begs more questions. What gives these particular policies such widespread appeal across different countries and different political parties? To what extent does their appeal stem from a disillusionment with existing modes of education provision, or does it rather reflect a more general crisis within the state or even a shift of global proportions?

It is sometimes suggested that these shifts in the ways in which education is organized reflect broader, even global, changes in the nature of advanced industrial societies, characterized by some commentators as post-Fordism and by others as postmodernity. Thus, some observers suggest that the reforms can be understood in terms of the transportation of changing modes of regulation from the sphere of production into other arenas, such as schooling and welfare services. They point to a correspondence between the establishment of differentiated markets in welfare and a shift in the economy away from Fordism towards a post-Fordist mode of accumulation which 'places a lower value on mass individual and collective consumption and creates pressures for a more differentiated production and distribution of health, education, transport and housing' (Jessop *et al.* 1987: 109). Ball (1990), for example, has claimed to see in new forms of schooling a move away from the 'Fordist' school towards a 'post-Fordist' one – the educational equivalent of flexible specialization driven by the imperatives of differentiated consumption replacing the old assembly-line world of mass production. These 'post-Fordist schools' are designed 'not only to produce the post-Fordist, multi-skilled, innovative worker but to behave in post-Fordist ways themselves; moving away from mass production and mass markets to niche markets and "flexible specialization" ... a post-Fordist mind-set is thus having implications in schools for management styles, curriculum, pedagogy and assessment' (Kenway 1993: 115).

However, Kenway (1993) regards the rapid rise of the market form in education as something much more significant than post-Fordism; she therefore terms it a 'postmodern' phenomenon, accentuating the nexus between the 'global' and the 'local'. Although notoriously difficult to define, within the realm of social relations, postmodernity is usually associated with processes of globalization, the rise of new technologies, commodification across all realms of social and cultural production, the breakdown of old collectivities and hierarchies and an increase in social reflexivity. In her own pessimistic version of postmodernity, 'transnational corporations and their myriad subsidiaries . . . shape and reshape our individual and collective identities as we plug in . . . to their cultural and economic communications networks' (Kenway 1993: 119). Her picture is one in which notions of 'difference', far from being eradicated by the 'globalization of culture', are assembled, displayed, celebrated, commodified and exploited (Robins 1991). Such trends can be detected in the current emphasis on both tradition and diversity in education policy.

In other accounts the rhetoric of 'new times' seems to offer more positive images of choice and diversity, reflecting the needs of communities and interest groups brought into prominence as a result of complex contemporary patterns of political, economic and cultural differentiation, which intersect the traditional class divisions upon which common systems of mass education were predicated. From this perspective, it is possible to contrast postmodernity to the oppressive uniformity of much modernist thinking – as 'a form of liberation, in which the fragmentation and plurality of cultures and social groups allow a hundred flowers to bloom' (Thompson 1992: 225–6). Some feminists, for example, have seen attractions in the shift towards the pluralist models of society and culture associated with postmodernism and postmodernity (Flax 1987). The real possibilities for community-based welfare, rather than bureaucratically controlled welfare, are also viewed positively by some minority ethnic groups (Wells *et al.* 1996), while (as we have already noted) many of the leading advocates of quasi-market systems of public education claim they will be particularly beneficial for the urban poor (Moe 1994; Pollard 1995).

Part of the appeal of the recent education reforms thus lies in their declared intention to encourage the growth of different types of school, responsive to needs of particular communities and interest groups. They also link to concepts of multiple identities and radical pluralism and can thus seem more attractive than unidimensional notions of comprehensive schooling and, indeed, unidimensional notions of citizenship. Some aspects of the rhetoric of the new policies thus seem to connect to the aspirations of groups who have found little to identify with in the 'grand narratives' associated with class-based politics. In this sense, the reforms might be viewed as a rejection of all totalizing narratives and their replacement by 'a set of cultural projects united [only] by a self-proclaimed commitment to heterogeneity, fragmentation and difference' (Boyne and Rattansi 1990: 9). In other words, support for schools run on a variety of principles reflects a broader shift from the assumptions of modernity to those of postmodernity.

However, there are various problems with these 'new times' theses. They are not only 'notoriously vague' (Hickox 1995) but also tend to exaggerate the extent to which we have moved to a new regime of accumulation and signification. Moreover, in the field of education, it is certainly difficult to establish a sharp distinction between mass and marketized systems. For example, the so-called 'common school' in the USA or the 'comprehensive system' in Britain were never as homogeneous as many commentators claim. Nor have there been decisive changes in the prevailing character of schools as institutions. Insofar as recent changes in management practices represent an '*adjustment* to the problems of Fordism' rather than signifying an entirely new direction, neo-Fordism may be a more appropriate term than post-Fordism (Allen 1992). In terms of broader developments, Giddens's concept of 'high modernity' (Giddens 1991) probably captures the combination of change and continuity rather better than that of 'postmodernity'.

Although the changes may thus not be as momentous as Kenway and others suggest, her pessimistic analysis of what changes have taken place has rather more credibility than an optimistic one. There does seem to have been an intensification of social differences and a celebration of them in a new rhetoric of legitimation. As we shall see later in this book, there is a growing body of empirical evidence that, rather than benefiting the disadvantaged, the emphasis on parental choice and school autonomy is further disadvantaging those least able to compete in the market (Gewirtz *et al.* 1995; Lauder *et al.* 1995; Smith and Noble 1995). At the same time, it is increasing the differences between popular and less popular schools on a linear scale – reinforcing a vertical hierarchy of schooling types rather than producing the promised horizontal diversity. For most members of disadvantaged groups, as opposed to the few individuals who escape from schools at the bottom of the status hierarchy, the new arrangements seem to be just a more sophisticated way of reproducing traditional distinctions between different types of school and between the people who attend them.

So, to regard the current espousal of heterogeneity, pluralism and local narratives as indicative of a new social order may be to mistake phenomenal forms for structural relations. Marxist critics of theories of postmodernism and postmodernity, such as Callinicos (1989), who reassert the primacy of the class struggle, certainly take this view. Even Harvey, who does recognize significant changes, suggests that postmodernist cultural forms and more flexible modes of capital accumulation may be shifts in surface appearance, rather than signs of the emergence of some entirely new post-capitalist or even post-industrial society (Harvey 1989). At most, current reforms would seem to relate to a version of postmodernity that emphasizes 'distinction' and 'hierarchy' within a fragmented social order, rather than one that positively celebrates 'difference' and 'heterogeneity' (Lash 1990). Thus, despite new forms of accumulation, together with some limited changes in patterns of social and cultural differentiation, the continuities seem as striking as the discontinuities.

Exporting the 'crisis'

Even if current policies are new ways of dealing with old problems, there clearly have been changes in the state's mode of regulation in all our countries. With the progressive removal or changes in the role of tiers of government or administration between the central state and individual institutions, conventional political and bureaucratic control by public bodies is replaced by quasi-autonomous institutions with devolved budgets competing for clients in the market place – a system of market accountability often regulated by so-called non-governmental agencies. Such quasi-autonomous institutions, state-funded but with considerable private and voluntary involvement in their operation, appear to make education less of a political issue. The political rhetoric accompanying the educational reforms in Britain certainly sought to suggest that education had been taken out of politics as normally understood (Riddell 1992).

For Chubb and Moe (1990) in the United States, the removal of schools from the local political arena is a *sine qua non* of their success. This is consistent with the common sense explanation for the plethora of similar education reforms, which is that they have emerged in response to a crisis within public education systems. To various degrees, many of the reforms have been prefaced with allegations that bureaucratically controlled education is both inefficient and unproductive. Systems of 'mass' schooling were seen to have 'failed' on a number of counts. They have disappointed those who see education as a route to a more equitable society as differences in educational outcomes continue to reflect differences in socio-economic status. Mass systems of public education are also deemed to have been unproductive in terms of economic returns, as is evident in frequently aired concerns about educational standards and international competitiveness.

It is difficult to argue against claims that mass schooling has failed to overcome social disadvantage or be particularly responsive to criticism from business and industry, but there is some evidence to suggest that the recent discourses of derision reflect more than the groundswell of public discontent. As Gordon and Pearce (1993) point out, there are marked differences in how and when the 'blame' for educational failure was allocated. In New Zealand, for instance, they claim that there was little publicly expressed discontent about educational effectiveness prior to 1987 when the 'neo-liberal blueprint' was put forward. As Grace (1991) documents, the crisis was 'manufactured' by treasury officials, the conservative National Party in opposition, the media and the business roundtable. While concerns about educational standards have been voiced in Britain and the USA for much longer, it is not easy to link them closely with the changes we are currently witnessing. Berliner and Biddle (1995) claim that recent criticisms of American public education are themselves part of a 'manufactured crisis'. They argue that there is insufficient evidence to support any of the widely quoted claims concerning diminishing performance, relative to either that of previous students or those from other countries. Also with reference to the USA, Mickelson (1996) highlights the false premises of Gerstner *et al.*'s influential book, *Reinventing Education: Entrepreneurship in America's Public Schools* (1994). She claims that 'Although many of the book's arguments are founded on factual errors and its proposed solutions are dubious, the authors' high public profile, their bully pulpit, and the resources available to disseminate the book to the public and to decision-makers, unduly weights the influence of their thinly veiled ideological treatise in support of market-based reforms and privatisation' (Mickelson 1996: 6). And even if it is possible to explain recent restructuring in the USA and Britain as a response to public disillusionment, such an argument can hardly be applied to Sweden, which is often considered to have one of the most effective, and equitable, national education systems. So, although there can be little doubt that some groups who have traditionally been disadvantaged by the 'one best school' approach may welcome reforms which seem, at least initially, to offer more responsivity to their agenda, it is unconvincing to explain the recent restructuring in terms of educational failings alone.

Rather more convincing is the argument that these new arrangements for managing education and other public services can be seen as new ways of tackling the problems of accumulation and legitimation facing the state in a situation where the traditional Keynesian 'welfare state' is no longer deemed viable. According to Dale (1989), the state has a permanent set of problems which derive from the needs of capital. First, there is the need to support the capital accumulation process. Second, the state must guarantee a context for capital's continued expansion. Finally, the state needs to legitimate the capitalist mode of production, including the state's own part in it. The restructuring of education can be seen as a response on the part of the state to shifting economic conditions which require it to revise the way in which it attempts to tackle these core problems.

There are at least two directions along which the state needs to secure legitimacy. One relates to the need to conceal, or at least displace responsibility for, the shortcomings and inherent inequities of capitalism itself. The second relates to the requirement that it legitimates its own activities; for instance, disguising its relationship with capital through a position of benign neutrality. As capitalism fails to bring prosperity and opportunity, there is a danger that people will 'see through' not just the structural problems of education systems, but the basis of the mode of production. For all our countries, the 1980s saw rising unemployment rates and, while some groups prospered throughout the decade, the gap between rich and poor grew wider.

Through explaining economic decline and enduring poverty in terms of failures within the state infrastructure, attention is deflected away from the essential injustices and contradictions of capitalism. The management of the public sector is called into question and the demands for reform prevail. The generation of policy alone becomes part of the solution. As Apple (1996: 88) argues, governments 'must *be seen* to be doing something . . . Reforming education is not only widely acceptable and relatively unthreatening, but just as crucially, "its success or failure will not be obvious in the short-term"' (his emphasis). But, whereas in the past the attempts to restore legitimacy may have involved increasing bureaucratization and greater 'expert' intervention, these processes are now seen as the problem rather than the solution. Bureaucratic control of education, it is suggested, stifles responsivity to the needs of business and industry.

With reference to the need to legitimate its own activities, it is possible to argue that the current move towards school decentralization arises from the state's inability convincingly to present public education as a means of promoting a more equitable society and redistributing real opportunities. Such a position is taken by Weiss (1993), who draws on the work of Weiler (1983) to suggest that, in Germany, devolution is the latest in a series of strategies used by the state to legitimate its policies and practices. He suggests that policies of school autonomy and parent empowerment leave conflict to be dealt with at lower levels of the system, with the higher administrative structures uninvolved, and therefore, above reproach. Malen (1994) uses concepts drawn from Weiler's (1989) work on decentralization to suggest that site-based management in the United States may have considerable political utility for managing conflict and maintaining legitimacy.

Devolution can be seen as a complete abdication of responsibility by the state, 'a deliberate process of subterfuge, distortion, concealment and wilful neglect as the state seeks to retreat in a rather undignified fashion from its historical responsibility for providing quality public education' (Smyth 1993b: 2), or as a selective withdrawal from areas in which it has difficulty succeeding, such as equality of opportunity (Nash 1989). Either way, making educational decision-making the responsibility of individual institutions and families is an effective strategy for 'shifting the blame'. The failure of individual schools to flourish as 'stand alone' institutions can be attributed to poor leadership or teaching quality. Similarly, unequal educational achievement among students can be explained through poor parenting – through either failing to exercise the new entitlement to choose effectively, or failing to engage with schools as active partners and participants. The burden of sustaining meritocratic ideology is shifted from the shoulders of government.

Fragmenting public systems of education may not only legitimate the political authority of the state and the credibility of capitalism as the most feasible mode of production, it may also be an example of the way in which the state, during periods of gross economic pressure, seek ways to cut back on public expenditure generally in order to privilege the needs of capital (e.g. through tax cuts) and thus provide the best possible conditions for sustaining productivity and maximizing profit. The reforms have not generally been followed by increased investment into education beyond initial 'pump-priming' money or cash incentives for favoured schemes. The trend for self-management of schools brings little more than 'the capacity to "manage" specific resources and centrally determined policy at the school site within the context of increasingly contracting state revenues' (Robertson 1993: 118). The rhetoric may sometimes stress community control and professional empowerment, but devolution is 'not what it purports to be – it is a budget cutting exercise masquerading under the banner of schools getting more control of their own affairs' (Smyth 1993a: 22). As we saw in Chapter 2, this certainly seems to have been the case in Victoria.

The political challenge

It should be clear from this discussion that, although the extent of any underlying social changes can easily be exaggerated by various 'post-ist' forms of analysis, both the discourse and the contexts of political struggles in and around education *have* been significantly altered by recent reforms. Not only have changes in the nature of the state influenced the reforms in education, the reforms in education are themselves beginning to change the way we think about the role of the state and what we expect of it. Green (1990) has pointed to the way in which education has not only been an important part of state activity in modern societies, but also played a significant role in the process of state formation itself in the eighteenth and nineteenth centuries. The current changes in education policy may similarly be linked to a redefinition of the nature of the state and a reworking of the relations between state and civil society.

The new policies foster the idea that responsibility for education and welfare, beyond the minimum required for public safety, is to be defined largely as a matter for individuals and families. Not only is the scope of the state narrowed, but civil society becomes increasingly defined in market terms. As many of the responsibilities adopted by the state during the post Second World War period begin to be devolved to a marketized version of civil society, consumer rights increasingly come to prevail over citizen rights. Yet while some aspects of education have been 'privatized', not so much in the strictly economic sense as in the sense of transferring them to the private sphere, others have become a matter of state mandate rather than local democratic debate. Despite the rhetoric about 'rolling back' or 'hollowing out' the state, certain aspects of state intervention have been maintained – indeed, strengthened. The strong, evaluative, state is a minimalist one in many respects, but a more powerful and even authoritarian one in others. In Britain, it is not just that policies of deregulation have allowed the government to abdicate some of its responsibilities for ensuring social justice, but in increasing a limited number of state powers (most notably through the National Curriculum and its associated system of testing) it has actually strengthened its capacity to foster particular interests while appearing to stand outside the frame.

Although some theories of globalization hold that the state is becoming less important on economic (Reich 1991), political (Held 1989) and cultural (Robertson 1991) grounds, at the present time there is little to support the postmodernist predictions of Usher and Edwards (1994) of the decline of the role of the state in education, at least in relation to the compulsory phase of provision. While this phenomenon of a strengthened state alongside policies of devolution and choice is particularly evident in Britain, similar trends can be identified in many countries (Gordon 1995; Apple 1996; Arnove 1996). Even if we concede that there has been, within our five countries, a reduction in the profile of the nation state as an international entity and a convergence of policy approaches, there is nothing to suggest that it is weakening its grip on areas of internal regulation. Despite the transferral of a number of responsibilities away from national or local bureaucracies, in none of our five countries has there been a marked reduction of the role of governments overall. Wohlstetter *et al.*'s (1995) analysis of US charter school legislation supports this view, suggesting that policy-makers appear prepared to grant increased autonomy to schools and parents at the local level, but less prepared to relinquish control from higher levels of government. This trend is reflected elsewhere, for, as we have seen, measures which devolve powers down to individual schools are often set alongside others which augment central control.

Yet these particular political responses to globalization and the situation confronting modern nation states are not inevitable. Interestingly, Green (1996) suggests that very few of the economically and educationally successfully Pacific Rim countries with which Western governments so frequently compare their performance have adopted the particular combination of policies discussed here. We should also remember that neither enhanced choice nor school autonomy is necessarily linked to a conservative agenda and that such measures have, in other circumstances, sometimes been part of a more progressive package of policies. Indeed, as we have already noted, some of the reforms originated in a different tradition, but have subsequently been incorporated and transformed by a rightist agenda. And while we should not underestimate the significance of those changes which are evoked – but inadequately characterized – by terms such as post-Fordism and postmodernity, we should not assume that the policy responses that are currently fashionable are the most appropriate ones. In some of the nations with which we are concerned here, it is arguable that the political left was rather slow in recognizing the significance of the changes and thus allowed the right to take the initiative. Yet the following chapters suggest that, however appealing the rhetoric of recent reforms may have been to groups who felt betrayed by earlier social democratic policies, the current alternatives do not appear to be delivering their promise. We agree with Henig (1994: 222) that 'the sad irony of the current education-reform movement is that, through over-identification with school-choice proposals rooted in market-based ideas, the healthy impulse to consider radical reforms to address social problems may be channeled into initiatives that further erode the potential for collective deliberation and collective response.' There is an urgent need to consider how the potentially progressive elements of current education reforms might be rearticulated with an alternative political agenda. We shall therefore return in our final chapter to consider some alternative responses, which respond to global changes and national circumstances while displaying a commitment to democratic modes of decision-making and the pursuit of social justice.

Part II

THE SCHOOL,

THE STATE

AND THE MARKET

4 SCHOOL MANAGERS, THE STATE AND THE MARKET

In education, as in other services such as housing, health and welfare, it is possible to identify the promotion of a new institutional culture which has been termed variously 'new public management', 'new managerialism', 'entrepreneurial governance' and 'corporate managerialism'. The scrutiny and reorganization of the management of public education is not a new phenomenon, but most reforms until now have typically involved shifting responsibilities horizontally across government offices or vertically between layers of administration. The more thoroughgoing reformulation of relations between the centre and the periphery currently under way has focused and individualized management responsibility in new and different ways. Where devolution has gone furthest, headteachers and principals increasingly stand at the interface between governments and local stakeholders, especially consumers. Such a position requires that they engage both with the demands of the evaluative state in terms of meeting centrally determined objectives and with the day-to-day 'business' of running their school and ensuring its survival within the education market.

The 'new' education management

One indicator of the redefinition and expansion of role of the headteacher or principal is the remarkable growth of 'education management studies' over the past decade. As Grace (1993: 353) has remarked 'education management studies has risen to a position of potential dominance. Not only do texts on various aspects of education management begin to be a significant sector of educational publishing but, more pervasively, the language, assumptions and ideology of management begin to dominate the language, consciousness, action and modes of analysis of those working within the education sector.'

Grace's observation derives from his experience of working as a university academic in schools of education in English and New Zealand universities. But his comments apply equally well to other national contexts. In many parts of the industrialized world, and certainly in each of the countries with which this book is concerned, the provision by higher education institutions of post-experience education management courses, many closely associated with the school improvement theme, is a major growth activity attracting ever increasing enrolments from among existing and prospective school managers. Although specialist training for principals is well established in some countries, such as the USA, it is now rapidly developing elsewhere. In England and Wales, a new national qualification for headteachers has recently been introduced and may eventually become compulsory. Those undertaking management responsibilities are no longer considered to be adequately prepared for their new role through conventional teacher education and classroom experience.

The international dimension of this trend is illustrated by the widespread dissemination and adoption of the ideas of key missionaries in education management. Caldwell and Spinks, for instance, have written two influential books, *The Self-managing School* (1988) and *Leading the Self-managing School* (1992), that figure prominently on almost every recommended reading list. Together or individually, they have also been extensively involved as policy consultants in at least three of the countries discussed in this book – Australia, New Zealand and England – while Caldwell is one of the visiting tutors on the international MBA programme organized by the University of Southern California for the principals of self-managing schools to which we made reference in Chapter 3.

The rise of the 'management guru' reflects what Clarke (1995) refers to as a 'naturalizing' of management which is premised on a number of assumptions about the characteristics of public and private sector organizations and the role of managers within them. More specifically, Clarke identifies two themes which underpin the new managerialism: 'universalism' and 'isomorphism'. Universalism holds that all organizations are basically the same and, irrespective of their specific functions, need to pursue efficiency. As managers embody the quest for efficiency, all organizations need to be managed. Isomorphism is the assumption that commercial organizations are the most naturally occurring form of coordination, compared with which public sector organizations are deviant. It follows that for public sector organizations, such as schools, to become more efficient they need to become more 'businesslike' – an important element of which is to incorporate the good practice of business management. Unlike bureaucrats, professionals and politicians who have controlled public sector provision in the past, the new managers are held up as innovative and dynamic, flexible and transparent, customer-centred and strategic (Clarke 1995).

There is, however, nothing that is self-evidently 'natural' about any form of management. As Bottery (1992: 2) states in his book *The Ethics of Educational Management*, 'the management of schools . . . needs to be aware of, and be ready to examine, the values, principles, and attitudes proposed for its practice. Indeed . . . there is a strong interaction between values and management, for the choice of values will have important ramifications for the kinds of management adopted, just as the kind of management chosen will affect the implementation of those values held as most suitable and desirable.' In this respect, it can be seen that the new education management signifies an increasing permeation of business values into what might hitherto have been considered a 'purely' professional domain.

Ball (1994) identifies three variants in the new educational discourse surrounding self-management: financial management, entrepreneurial management and professional management. The discourse of financial management is, claims Ball (1994), closest to the 'big business' perspective in that it highlights education as a financial enterprise and encourages management to confront the economic realities of schooling. Although similar in many ways to financial management, entrepreneurial management celebrates the economic foundation of education and emphasizes the market as the most efficient and equitable distributive mechanism. The discourse of 'professional management' is the more acceptable representation of devolution in that it provides a vocabulary which links management directly to classroom practice and articulates with a teacherly 'professional' perspective on planning and purpose. It is, he argues, 'clean' management 'insofar as it treats the school in isolation and concentrates on the business of *education* rather than education as *business*' (Ball 1994: 67, his emphases). But far from offering alternative and oppositional forms of practice, Ball argues, the new professional management merely serves to legitimate the more business-oriented versions.

School management texts, such as those by Caldwell and Spinks (1988, 1992), may draw on a professionalized vocabulary, but the exhortations to engage in goal-setting, policy-making, planning, financial budgeting, implementing and evaluating performance are more reminiscent of business than that previously associated with educational institutions. As in Chubb and Moe's (1990) analysis of 'the organisation of effective schools', which is premised on the superiority of private schools, Caldwell and Spinks place a high premium on the leadership roles which school principals must perform in order to transform the operations of schools in the direction of greater self-management. In *Leading the Self-managing School*, they identify four kinds of 'transformational leadership' which, in combination, are said to help to contribute to quality in education. These include: 'cultural leadership', 'a capacity to work with others to build a shared commitment to the cultural underpinnings of the school' (p. 89); 'strategic leadership', by which Caldwell and Spinks mean the capacity to take charge of one's own agenda, which involves principals 'keeping abreast of trends and issues, threats and opportunities in the school environment and in society at large . . . sharing their knowledge with others in the school's community . . . establishing structures and processes which enable the school to set priorities and formulate strategies which take account of likely and/or preferred futures' (p. 92); 'educational leadership', which involves the 'nurturing of a learning community' (p. 115) where the focus is upon building 'the strongest possible mutually supporting relationships among principal, teachers, parents, students, [and] other

Table 4.1   Main characteristics of the bureau-professional and new managerial regimes

Bureau-professionalism/Welfarism	New managerialism
Public service ethos	Customer-oriented ethos
Decisions given by commitment to 'professional standards' and values, e.g. equity, care and social justice	Decisions driven by efficiency, cost-effectiveness and search for competitive edge
Emphasis on collective relations with employees, through trade unions	Emphasis on individual relations, through marginalization of trade unions and new management techniques, e.g. total quality management, human resource management
Consultative	Macho
Substantive rationality	Technical rationality
Cooperation	Competition
Managers socialized within field and values of specific welfare sector, e.g. education, health, social work	Managers generally socialized, i.e. within field and values of 'management'

Source: From Gewirtz *et al.* (1995: 94)

members of the community' (p. 137); and 'responsive leadership' which addresses issues of accountability and involves leaders demonstrating the ways in which they respond to 'the needs of the student, the local community and society at large' (p. 139). Caldwell and Spinks see these professional capacities arising out of the new opportunities provided by self-management, which include the introduction of markets in education. They suggest that concerns over equity within markets will soon be dissipated, and that it is simply a matter of time before the 'market model' gains widespread acceptance. It has, they argue, 'educational integrity' (p. 195).

The contrasts between 'old' and 'new' style education management are highlighted by Grace (1995), who posits a shift from a social democratic to a market phase of school leadership. Similarly, Gewirtz and Ball (1996) have identified two 'ideal-type discourses of school headship', which they term 'welfarism' – or, after Clarke and Newman (1992), 'bureau-professionalism' (Gewirtz *et al.* 1995) – and 'new managerialism' (see Table 4.1). Welfarism denotes 'a primary ideological commitment to the material and emotional well-being of individuals and to the creation of a better and fairer society' (Gewirtz and Ball 1996: 3). New managerialism, on the other hand, is 'untainted' by the dominant welfarist values of the post-war era. It is essentially technicist in character, involving 'the smooth and efficient implementation of aims set elsewhere within constraints also set elsewhere' (Gewirtz and Ball 1996: 4).

It could be argued that Gewirtz *et al.* offer a somewhat partial interpretation of the changing principles of school management – presenting on overly romantic picture of bureau-professionalism and an unduly critical version of new managerialism. Sociological research into bureaucracies and professions suggests that they are as much to do with the consolidation of power and protection of privilege as with altruism. Indeed, welfarism itself has been exposed as fundamentally patriarchal and racially structured in its organizing principles and practices (e.g. Williams 1991). By contrast, there are alternative representations of the new managerialism which point out its progressive and liberating potential. As Knight *et al.* (1993b) comment, if 'older public service style bureaucracy could be likened to a pyramid, the current leaner, flatter, more corporate mode is more aptly compared with a clothes-hanger'. Some of the 'new times' theses discussed in Chapter 3 seem to regard this as an accurate representation of the reforms, which move schools beyond the constraints of hierarchy, secrecy and paternalism and into an era of flexible specialization in which managers in general, and women managers in particular, are given the freedom to empower themselves and others.

While Gewirtz *et al.* might provide a harshly critical perspective on the redefinition of management, through articulating new managerialism with marketization, they do draw helpful attention to the way in which many headteachers and principals are actually, as opposed to rhetorically, being repositioned by the reforms. School managers are experiencing more than a discursive shift, they are caught up with the restructuring of education along a number of fronts which appear to be reorienting their work and redistributing authority within schools in ways which bear little resemblance to the optimistic accounts of the new management advocates. Blackmore (1995: 45) argues that, despite the rhetoric, the self-managing school retains 'strong modernist tendencies for a top-down, executive mode of decision-making . . . [alongside its] "weaker" post-modern claims to decentralise and encourage diversity, community ownership, local discretion, professional autonomy and flexible decision-making'.

The changing role of the school manager

A fairly uncontroversial conclusion that can be reached through looking at the available research is that the nature of headteachers' and principals' work is changing as a result of recent education policies. This is apparent in all our countries. For instance, in the USA, Hess's (1990) evaluation of the early impact of the 1988 Chicago School Reform Act describes several major role changes being experienced by principals in the restructured system, the most prominent of which is that they are cast more in the role of chief executives than hitherto and have a strong sense of responsibility to their managing boards, the local school councils. Ford's (1992) more empirically detailed study of ten Chicago principals fills out further the implications of this change in role. In particular it notes the extent to which it entails for principals a radically increased emphasis on budgetary considerations, carrying with it the implication that they are less preoccupied than previously with leadership roles that stress teaching and learning. This is endorsed by Bennett *et al.*'s (1992) survey of principals' reactions to the same reform, which found that over one-half of respondents reported 'spending more time [than before] on school management' at the expense of providing 'instructional leadership' and engaging in related activities that 'bring them into more direct contact with students' (p. 24).

In Victoria, Australia, Blackmore *et al.*'s (1996) case studies of Schools of the Future found that both teachers and principals reported shifts in the nature of principals' work away from teaching and learning. This is confirmed even by Odden's (1995) positive evaluation of Victorian schools, where he found a move away from direct involvement in instructional leadership to other and broader leadership roles. Among these, he lists setting visions, developing strategic plans, working on budget and personnel issues, raising funds to enhance school facilities and marketing the school. He claims that the more successful principals appeared to be acting more like 'chief executive officers' than headteachers. A somewhat similar experience of educational self-management is evident in New Zealand. A series of surveys of principals, trustees and teachers in a national sample of primary and intermediate schools found that the *Tomorrow's Schools* reforms had shifted substantial administrative and financial responsibilities from the Department of Education and education boards to school staff and trustees (Wylie, 1994).

The new budgetary responsibilities which come with self-managing status, together with the imperatives of central government evaluations, appear to be increasing workloads for headteachers and principals as they undertake the administrative duties that would previously have been performed at other levels in the system. There is some evidence that this is leading to role conflict. Studies in America and England show that principals and headteachers are uneasy about some of the implications of their new management role (e.g. Bennett *et al.* 1992; Evetts 1996), in particular those aspects which isolate them from colleagues and students. In New Zealand, Wylie's surveys reveal concern that the administrative workload requirements of their new jobs 'make it difficult [for them] to be innovative or to address children's learning' (Wylie 1994: 135).

Despite these reservations, it would appear that principals and headteachers broadly welcome the reforms. Claims that headteachers themselves are enjoying the new management responsibilities are supported by Levačić (1995), who researched the impact of the local management of schools policy on eleven schools in one English local authority. She paints a mostly positive picture of the benefits of delegated decision-making on the work of headteachers. 'Local management has empowered [them], and by and large they like it' (Levačić 1995: 136). To be sure, the headteachers investigated by Levačić comment negatively on the costs of time spent on issues other than directly educational matters. But, generally, they consider local management beneficial in terms of increasing their capacity to plan strategically and concentrate resources on direct teaching and learning.

While headteachers and principals are generally supportive of the new reforms, their staff often appear less than enthusiastic, an issue which we consider more fully in the next chapter. With reference to the Chicago reforms again, Sebring *et al.* (1995) found that a relatively low proportion of teachers surveyed (only about 30 per cent) hold their principals in 'high regard', with roughly a further one-quarter having 'very low' estimates of the work they do. These teachers, the report concludes, 'do not see the principal as promoting high standards . . . nor do they see [her or him] as facilitating a broad involvement in school improvement' (p. 16).

The contrasting perceptions of the benefits of the new emphasis on management may well reflect the extent to which headteachers and their staff have been differentially privileged under the reforms. In many cases, the devolution of decision-making to the school has resulted in a concentration of power 'at the top'. In smaller schools, this power is usually concentrated in the hands of the headteacher alone. But in larger schools, the headteachers increasingly surround themselves with a cohesive 'senior management team'. Webb and Vulliamy (1996), in research funded by a teachers' association, found that, even in medium-sized primary schools in England and Wales, headteachers were building management teams to help them deal with the multiple innovations. Although the extent to which duties are delegated even within senior management teams is variable (Maychell 1994), they create further divides between management and teachers (Webb and Vulliamy 1996). Streamlined to make quick responses to the demands of the government or the market, these teams constitute 'a species of *cabinet* – a restricted form of 'headquarters staff' . . . the responsibility and function of which is more in keeping with systems of corporate management than with the principle of collegiality' (Neave 1988: 17).

This increasing divergence between the corporate priorities of the headteacher and 'senior management team' and the educational concerns of classroom teacher colleagues is leading to a growing gap between the manager and the managed, and the consolidation of vertical, rather than horizontal, management structures. Thus, paradoxically, the coupling of site-based management with market mechanisms and competence-based assessments may be leading to an exaggeration rather than a reduction in bureaucratic, top-down control. As Codd (1993: 8) argues with reference to New Zealand, the ingredients of objective setting, planning, effective management, internal monitoring and external reporting recommended by the government defined 'an organisational culture that was to be hierarchical, competitive, individualistic and highly task-oriented'.

In Australia, Blackmore *et al.* (1996) reveal that most initiatives in Victoria's Schools of the Future programme were 'principal-led'. Although there was some difference between the two primary and two secondary schools studied, inasmuch as the former were more strategic and the latter tended to 'take up every issue and "run with it" ' (p. 7), staff did not feel involved and Blackmore *et al.* report 'a deterioration in the relationship between teachers and principals' (p. 17). Odden (1995: 10), who is generally supportive of recent policies, found that, while some principals in Victoria were able to delegate, 'less successful and more stressed principals were either centralizing power and decision-making in their offices, which undercut nearly all other attempts to involve teachers in decision-making, or trying to be centrally involved in both CEO [chief executive officer] type duties and instructional leadership, which simply stretched them beyond their limits of time and energy.'

A study of resource management in a sample of eighteen English locally managed and grant-maintained schools, undertaken by Thomas and Martin (1996) at the University of Birmingham, highlights the pivotal role played by the headteacher in whole school decision-making: 'in all schools, except one, the headteacher alone is mentioned as the decision-maker in one context or another' (p. 53). Thomas and Martin, we should point out, also offer examples of classroom teachers taking proposals to the headteacher and of the positive role played by senior management teams in reaching key decisions. Even so, the impression given is one in which headteachers elect to play the most prominent role in suggesting new ideas and generating innovation, and the policy of local management both facilitates and legitimates this enhancement in their leadership status. And while Thomas and Martin found considerable evidence that headteachers took very seriously the language of participation, and were not slow to convert this into specific arrangements to facilitate greater levels of collegiality, it has to be said that any such participation was very much on their terms and often more symbolic than substantive.

Granström's (1996) research into the changing professional culture of Swedish schools found a similar pattern of lack of teacher involvement in decision-making. The recent reforms in Sweden appear to have offered teachers, as well as headteachers, greater opportunities for participation, but these are not being realized. While Granström claims that the 'low trust' culture is as much a legacy of the past as it is arising from the new policies, he identifies a number of negative consequences which result 'when decentralization is forced upon an unprepared hierarchical organization' (p. 180). He found that headteachers went through the motions of involving teachers, but tended to delegate 'impossible' or 'imaginary' tasks.

Thus it would appear that where staff are involved in decision-making, their participation is often more characteristic of 'contrived collegiality' (A. Hargreaves 1994) than genuine collaboration. Hargreaves describes contrived collegiality as 'a safe administrative simulation of collaboration' in that it is administratively regulated, compulsory, implementation-oriented, fixed in time and space and predictable. Webb and Vulliamy (1996) found that while many headteachers did seek to develop participatory structures, the growth of centrally determined demands being placed on them often militated against genuine collaboration. In all but the smallest primary schools, headteachers were caught between injunctions that they embrace collegial management styles and the 'institutionalisation of increasingly directive and controlling mechanisms' (p. 456).

There are, of course, differences in the ways in which headteachers respond to their new positioning between the state and the market. For example, Grace's (1995) research on the changing nature of English headship carried out in the period 1990–4 identifies a number of variations. Based on detailed semi-structured interviews involving over eighty headteachers (64 men, 24 women) of secondary and primary schools, Grace identifies three 'broad ideal-type' responses. First, there are the *headteacher-managers*. This group, predominantly male in composition and strongly 'managerialist' in professional orientation, celebrates its perceived empowerment resulting from local management and is 'confident about [its] new working relations with governors and the likely success of their schools in a new competitive market culture in education' (Grace 1995: 73). The *headteacher-professionals*, on the other hand, have a number of concerns about 'loss of important professional relationships and values in a management and market culture in schooling', (p. 74) in particular the degree of 'distancing' from the work of direct classroom teaching and compromising collegial relations generally. Lastly, there is a small group of what Grace describes as *headteacher-resistors*, which, as the name suggests, is made up of headteachers who are not enamoured by the changes to their role brought about by local management and who seek ways to oppose and subvert those aspects of the reform considered inimical to the educational enterprise. Members of this minority group, however, are forced to face up to and recognize an awkward dilemma, namely that the very policies to which they object are ones which, if adopted, 'could bring to their schools and their pupils considerable material and resource benefits'. It would seem likely that this last response will become increasingly difficult to sustain as the demands of the market and the state combine to drive a wedge between preferred and required management practices. Raab *et al.*'s (1997) study of schools in three local authorities in Scotland and England found that variation in headteachers' responses depended on the degree of decentralization and marketization. In those areas where schools remained relatively 'shielded' there was less conflict between professional values and new management practices. This would indicate that the strategies adopted by headteachers are to some extent determined by the local context rather than personally held values. In addition, the research by Gewirtz *et al.* (1995) suggests that, if schools are particularly 'buoyant' in the market, headteachers may be able to retain elements of 'professional' management. However, headteachers of schools with fragile market positions have little choice but to engage with the business ethics of new managerialism.

Of course, some might support such a separation between management concerns and educational issues. David Hargreaves (1994a), for instance, argues for a formal separation between non-teacher chief executives and headteachers as leading professionals, making an analogy with the health service. However, few doctors in NHS Trust hospitals in Britain or Crown Health Enterprises in New Zealand would argue that this separation has enhanced their professionality or made it easier for them to make clinical decisions independently of financial considerations. Indeed, Thomas and Martin (1996: 178) are concerned that, if headteachers become too detached from the practices of teaching and learning, their decisions on the allocation of resources to support what goes in the classroom 'may be ill-informed and, as a result, inappropriate to educational needs and priorities'. Shifts in the direction of greater educational self-management therefore raise some serious questions about its effects on the nature of the school community. While headteachers themselves often claim that local management increases the involvement of classroom teachers in decision-making, a study of its effects on industrial relations in schools by Sinclair *et al.* (1993) suggests that the very logic of the reforms is that headteachers 'are no longer partners in the process of educating pupils – they become allocators of resources within the school, managers who are driven to ensure that the activities of employees are appropriate to the needs of the business, and givers of rewards to those whose contribution to the business is most highly regarded' (p. 8).

Women and the new education management

The articulation between new managerialism and issues of gender is complex and contradictory. The new management discourse talks of flexible structures which rely on more holistic, collaborative and non-hierarchical leadership – qualities which some have identified as being characteristic of female organizational practice (see, for instance, Shakeshaft 1993). Caldwell and Spinks (1992) draw on arguments that suggest that in the future women may be better suited than men to manage schools. But, at the same time, the entrepreneurial dimension of 'going it alone' that is implicated in some forms of school-based management can be seen to emphasize traditionally masculine attributes. Indeed, as outlined in Table 4.1, Gewirtz *et al.* (1995) characterize the new managerialism as 'macho' as opposed to 'consultative'.

Of course, women headteachers may respond to the prevalent masculine discourse of managerialism differently from their male counterparts. Hall (1996) studied six women headteachers in England over a period of 18 months and argues that Grace's typology of headteacher responses mentioned above may not be equally applicable to men and women. On the basis of her research, she claims that women headteachers may develop an alternative version of the new educational entrepreneurialism 'that eschews managerialism in order to preserve the integrity of the educational enterprise' (Hall 1996: 192).

But while individual women may approach the new management in particular ways, the evidence on the extent to which women as a whole have been advantaged within the restructuring process is limited and ambiguous. With reference to Victoria, Blackmore (1996a) suggests that there has been a 'remasculinization' at the centre as regional branches of the administration, often with high concentrations of women, have been removed. But there has also been a feminization of educational work at the level of the school. In Victoria, women are still underrepresented in formal leadership, but recent years have seen a rise in the proportion of women principals from 21 to 31 per cent. In Sweden too, there has been a significant increase in the number of female assistant principals during the 1990s. Ouston (1993) reports on a slight rise of women heads in England and Wales, from 46.7 to 48.5 per cent in the primary sector and from 16.5 to 18.3 per cent in the secondary sector between 1988 and 1991.

However, we should be cautious about attributing the increasing proportion of women managers to the restructuring alone. As Blackmore (1996a) argues, the rise in the number of women principals and assistants in Australia and Sweden owes much to the centrally initiated equal opportunities programmes of the mid-1980s. Even the limited success of these programmes is likely to be diminished within devolved education systems where 'equity is being "main-streamed" and "downstreamed", becoming everyone's and no one's responsibility' (Blackmore 1996b: 1024).

While past policies and current economics may have brought about an increase in the number of women managers, there is little to suggest that self-managing schools offer contexts in which their alleged skills of collaboration and facilitation are coming to the fore. Blackmore's (1996c) research on Victorian principals reveals the many dilemmas which women managers in particular face. They not only found it distressing to have to compromise their own professional values in order to operate effectively in the market place, they also found that the increased competition between schools isolates them from other women principals – one of their few sources of support in the past.

Blackmore (1996c: 8) also argues that the dominant images of leadership within the Schools of the Future programme 'tap into an equation between good leadership and those modes of masculinity closely identified with rationality, control and authority'. We need, of course, to be careful not to overstate the power of such discursive representations or the extent to which principals reflect these values. However, our own experience of grant-maintained schools' headteachers would endorse the impression that self-managing schools can encourage and celebrate a particularly masculine form of management.

There seems little to suggest, then, that within school management 'the future is female' in any positive sense – in terms of either the kind of leadership qualities required or the proportion of women undertaking them. If the rise in the number of women principals stems from equal opportunities programmes established in the 1970s and 1980s, then we may see a decline as such programmes are dismantled. Moreover, as Waring (1992) points out, the increasing representation of lay people on governing bodies and school boards with responsibility for appointing heads may have serious implications for women. His own research on an English governing body showed that some governors held negative perceptions of women managers. While in his case study a woman head was eventually appointed, this particular governing body was largely female. Given that most trustees and governors are white, male and middle class, we are likely to see increasing bias in favour of the selection of heads and principals who are also white, male and middle class. It is possible to suggest that the recent emphasis on management, which is so strongly associated with masculine attributes, will outweigh any developments which might support more 'female' practices and women managers.

It is also probable that the increasing polarization of schools (discussed more fully in Chapter 8) will penalize women disproportionately. In a survey of primary schools in England, Hill (1994) found that women headteachers were underrepresented in the larger schools which, under the LMS funding formula, are likely to be most advantageously resourced and to pay higher salaries. Hill also draws attention to the relatively high cost of women seeking to return to the main professional grade after a career break – a cost which schools now bear directly. When women do gain senior management posts, it may be increasingly associated with their willingness to take on 'difficult' schools. Blackmore (1996a) draws attention to the widening gap between resource-rich and resource-poor schools in Victoria. Women principals are located mainly in those which are resource-poor – in localities with high ethnic and racial diversity. A complementary process might be operating in the United States, where the decline in the number of men heading elementary schools (Fullan 1991) may reflect their increasing undesirability as workplaces (Hall 1993). Interestingly, Dominelli (1996) notes a similar development within the management of social work in England. As Blackmore (1996a: 11) comments, 'The paradox therefore, is that women . . . in positions of "power" at the local level as "educational leaders" are mediating the restructuring of education in ways which devalues the work of women educators more generally.'

Managing the state and the market

As mentioned earlier, Grace's (1995) research reveals that headteachers do not respond to their new roles in a uniform way. Nevertheless, principals and headteachers of self-managing schools are placed under considerable pressure to engage positively with the new modes of management. The deployment of alternative strategies carries a high risk in a context in which the penalties of disengagement can be fatal to the future of the organization. It is difficult, therefore, to represent headteachers as the 'winners' of restructuring. It is not just the size and nature of the workload which has changed; headteachers are also being subject to new forms of accountability themselves. Their positions have become more vulnerable as they are held more personally to account. For instance, the principals' contracts in the Schools of the Future in Victoria specify that 15 per cent of their salary is dependent on school performance. The new challenges and pressures are evident in the high turnover rates. In Victoria, 70 per cent of principals in 1995 had been appointed in the preceding four years. Similarly, New Zealand has experienced a 40 per cent turnover in principals since 1989 (Wylie 1995a).

Competition between schools often leads to a reduction in cross-school collaboration, leaving headteachers and principals increasingly isolated from each other. In some cases, they are also less protected by the intermediary levels of professional support to which they could previously turn. This means that they experience the impact of the reforms on a more individual basis. This personal dimension is important. There has always been a sense in which headteachers have felt responsible for the future of their schools, but this is heightened in the education market place, where success and failure becomes a matter of how well they exercise their management and leadership roles and compete successfully for students. In our research (Halpin *et al.* 1994) on English grant-maintained schools we detected a strong bond between the headteachers' personal vision for education and the mission of the school. More recently (Fitz *et al.* 1997), we have highlighted the crucial role played by headteachers in assessing the nature of the local education market and the sort of curriculum provision they judge to be more likely to continue to attract parental interest. The headteacher seems to have a stronger sense than before of being 'in charge' and of having to guide the school towards a successful future. State regulation at a distance, along with the opportunities and responsibilities which derive from institutions expected to act like private enterprises in a competitive market, brings specific consequences. While it consolidates the head's position as the key interpreter of both the policy framework and the market – the national *and* local contexts, in other words – the disciplinary mode also *personalizes the responsibility* for 'success' and 'failure'. The 'enabling' framework, then, sits alongside another which causes judgements about individuals and institutions to be made, which in turn can and do evoke professional and market censure (Fitz *et al.* 1997).

It is important to recognize that the shift in principals' and headteachers' practices, and the redistribution of authority within the school, is not simply the result of personal preferences for particular modes of management. It is a product of the reformulation of relations between the centre and the periphery. As Ball (1993: 65) argues, 'Schools are inserted into a new paradox; they are to be given greater autonomy within the constraints and pressures of market forces; they are to be able to exercise flexibility in order to be more responsive. The relative certainties of local democracy and bureaucracy are to be replaced by the relative uncertainties of enrolment-based funding. The point about both management and the market is that they are a "no hands" form of control as far as the relationship between education and the state is concerned.' Thus, on this understanding, the devolution of ever increasing decision-making capacity to site-based managers in schools is the means whereby the central state is able simultaneously to exercise a degree of control over what they do and shift responsibility when things go wrong. Heads and principals are increasingly forced into a position in which they have to demonstrate performance along centrally prescribed criteria in a context over which they often have diminishing control.

5   CHANGING TEACHERS'
WORK

The theory of school self-management often suggests that it is those nearest the 'action' – that is, teachers – who will be most empowered by this reform. In some cases, it is seen as a long-overdue recognition of teaching as a mature profession, where its members are entrusted to make decisions unencumbered by political and bureaucratic interference. Thus, D. Hargreaves (1994a) regards recent changes as potentially enhancing the professionalism of teachers. In practice, though, recent reforms have often been characterized by the extreme 'disrespect and disregard that reformers have shown for teachers themselves' (A. Hargreaves 1994: 6). This has particularly been the case where devolution has become linked to school choice. As L. Angus (1994) argues, within the Victorian Schools of the Future programme in Australia, teachers are the 'object of policy' rather than 'professional participants' in it. In some cases, this is deliberate. Many advocates of reform in the USA argue that school-based management without parental choice merely reinforces the 'producer' interest of teachers (Domanico 1990; Moe 1994).

As a result, some commentators have taken the view that, far from enhancing the professionalism of teachers, recent reforms are part of a deprofessionalization process (Harris 1993). Yet, as Lawn and Ozga (1986) have pointed out, the concept of professionalism not only is a contested one, but has also been used both to support the occupational strategy of organized teachers and, by the state, to control them. Similarly, devolution of decision-making can be part of different political agendas and have radically different consequences in different contexts. Thus, as Kallos and Lundahl-Kallos (1994) suggest, the decentralization and flexibility favoured by teachers themselves in Sweden in the 1980s could affect them very differently in the context of neo-liberal policies of deregulation. Teachers who have lived through the 1980s and 1990s in Victoria would be likely to echo that view.

Table 5.1   Alternative conceptions of teaching

	Technocratic-reductionist	Professional-contextualist
Role model	Skilled technician	Reflexive practitioner
Criterion of good practice	Competence	Integrity
Pedagogical aim	Attainment of specific learning outcomes	Development of diverse human capabilities
Administrative context	Efficient management (hierarchical)	Professional leadership (collaborative)
Type of motivation	Extrinsic	Intrinsic
Form of accountability	Contractual compliance	Professional commitment

Source: After Codd (1995: 27)

Whether or not what we are witnessing here is a struggle between a professionalizing project and a deprofessionalizing one, it is certainly a struggle among different stakeholders over the definition of teacher professionalism and professionality for the twenty-first century. Hatcher (1994: 55) suggests that this involves an attempt on the part of the state to replace the ideology of professional autonomy with a new form of 'incorporated professionalism' based on a 'market-driven technical rationalist ideology'. This chapter considers research that explores the ways in which, in this context, recent reforms are actually affecting the professional lives of teachers and the character of the profession.

Empowerment or intensification?

Robertson (1996a) claims that talk of increased professionalism in Australia masks the fact that teachers' work has effectively been proletarianized, both ideologically through a loss of control over policy and technically through tighter specification of the content and pace of their work. Similar developments are evident in New Zealand, where, Codd (1996: 11) argues, 'there is now a dominant managerial discourse within the culture of New Zealand schools which competes with the traditional educational discourse of many teachers.' Codd has elsewhere characterized, as shown in Table 5.1, the contrasting conceptions of teaching enshrined in these competing discourses.

This echoes some of the trends we identified in Chapter 4, in particular the shift from a democratic to a market phase of school leadership (Grace 1995) or, alternatively, from 'welfarism' to 'new managerialism' (Gewirtz and Ball 1996). Such shifts may help to explain why research evidence suggests that teachers seem less enthusiastic about recent reforms than do their headteachers and school principals. In any event, much of the more positive English research on the response to school self-management is based on questionnaires to headteacher respondents; that is, those responsible for the efficient management of the delegated budget and whose authority has been significantly enhanced by the self-management reform. Although there is no evidence of a widespread desire on the part of teachers to abandon local management entirely, it is noticeable that the relatively few classroom teachers who were interviewed in the Birmingham University study were far more cautious than headteachers about its benefits (Bullock and Thomas 1994). Marren and Levačić (1994) also found classroom teachers less positive about self-management than either school governors or headteachers. In their study, headteachers generally welcomed self-management even where their school had lost resources as a result of it, while classroom teachers were far more sceptical about its benefits even in schools which had gained in resources.

Bowe *et al.*'s (1992) book *Reforming Education and Changing Schools* suggests that this may be linked to the effects of both self-management and the National Curriculum as they are working out on the ground in secondary schools. They see these reforms as contributing to a growing gulf between senior managers and teachers and a clash between managerial and educational values. Broadbent *et al.* (1993), however, report evidence from other schools that the demands of local management were (initially at any rate) absorbed by a central 'coping group' of senior managers whose efforts were able to leave the core educational values of the school relatively unscathed. But, according to other work, including some from New Zealand (Murfitt 1995), it seems to be middle managers in secondary schools who experience the greatest pressures, from both above and below.

Marren and Levačić (1994) are not sure whether their own evidence that classroom teachers are more critical of self-management than are senior managers is necessarily indicative of a cleavage in values between teachers and managers. They do, however, suggest that greater class teacher involvement in financial decision-making may be needed if self-management is to result in significant improvements in teaching and learning. While most teachers have little or sometimes no influence in making decisions about, say, the overall budget of their schools, some do exercise influence when it comes to spending money which has been delegated to them for specific purposes, such as the purchase of curriculum support materials. But the greater number of classroom teachers operate very much on the margins when it comes to financial management and, it needs to be noted, many report that they prefer it this way. As Levačić (1995: 189) comments, 'financial management . . . is largely regarded by classroom teachers as one where they have limited interest and expertise. In their view, it is the principal's proper function to resource the learning core of the school and protect it from undue disturbance . . . Most principals concur with this and do not seek teacher involvement in budgeting except in resourcing the curriculum and in keeping them informed about the general financial situation of the school.' Indeed, there is a view that financial management is a specialized task and that senior management needs to get better at it rather than to share it.

Yet divisions between managers and teachers do not merely result from personal preferences or technical efficiencies in the division of labour. Although the rhetoric of school-based decision-making holds out a promise of enhanced collegial relations under devolved systems of schooling, the reality is heavily influenced by the way in which devolution has become articulated with other discursive shifts, and changing technologies of control and accountability, which impact upon organizational identities and teachers' professional lives.

While it is difficult to separate out the effects of the various individual reforms on teachers' work, the overall picture seems clear. A survey conducted at Warwick University (Campbell and Neill 1994) on the effects of the National Curriculum on primary school teachers, funded by a teachers' union, concluded that there had been no overall improvement in standards but teachers had been driven to burnout. A 54-hour week was the norm for infant teachers, with one in ten working more than 60 hours. The teachers in the study talked of tiredness, irritability and depression, of sleeping badly, increased drinking, occasional crying in the staffroom and a sense of guilt that they were neglecting their own families. Although this has to be seen as coming from a particular pressure group, the sponsor was actually one of the least militant unions and one broadly in favour of the reforms.

Another study, at about the same time, for the School Teachers' Pay Review Body (STRB), found that primary headteachers worked on average 55.4 hours a week and classroom teachers 48.8 hours a week, but this included junior school teachers who had thus far been less affected by the demands of national testing than their infant school counterparts. The equivalent figure for secondary headteachers were 61.1 hours and for classroom teachers 48.9 hours per week (Rafferty 1994). However, more recent figures produced for the STRB in 1996 showed that, while the hours worked by headteachers and their deputies had not increased significantly since 1994, primary classroom teachers were working two additional hours a week and secondary teachers 1.4 hours. Secondary heads of department had experienced a 2.3 hour increase in the same period. Most of the extra time is apparently being spent on preparation, record-keeping, testing and assessment rather than on teaching (Rafferty 1996: 1). Thus, it is clear that teachers as well as headteachers are experiencing heavier workloads as a result of the reforms, but the latter are enjoying relatively more autonomy and authority under self-management than the former.

In New Zealand, Wylie (1994) found that 'teachers' levels of satisfaction with their work were the lowest of the three groups [heads, trustees and teachers] now responsible for schools'. Nearly half reported a negative impact from the reforms on their job satisfaction, while only 25 per cent reported a positive one. Particularly significant seems to have been the increased administrative load on teachers and its impact on the quality of teachers' lives out of school. Even though the National Curriculum loading is a less significant factor than in England, Wylie found teachers working 48 hours, while in more urban samples Bridges (1993) reported 51 hours for primary teachers and Livingstone (1994) an average of 54.5 hours for teachers and principals together. As a result, New Zealand teachers reported high levels of stress, declining job satisfaction and a desire to leave the profession, even where they felt recent reforms had brought some benefits.

Increased working hours and the intensification of teachers' labour have also been noted in Australia by Robertson and Soucek (1991). Their study of the impact of devolution on teachers in Western Australia found teachers working longer as a result of 'the need to constantly attend meetings . . . the escalation of accountability and control initiatives, the pressure to be more entrepreneurial, and an increasing scarcity of resources' (Robertson 1996a: 45). A recent study of 71 Queensland primary schools showed teachers working a 50-hour week, with their non-teaching duties spreading well beyond the time for which they could reasonably be deemed to have been paid. A diary study led the researchers to report an 'overwhelming impression' of a 'desperate search for fragments of time into which limitless activities must be fashioned'. Descriptions of teachers' 'free time' were characterized by statements about 'a dash to the toilet' and 'grabbing a cup of coffee' (Andrews *et al.* 1996: 10).

The cumulative effect of all this must raise serious concerns about the health of schools as organizations. Wylie (1994) concluded that New Zealand school communities had probably reached the limit of what they could provide to support the reforms in terms of money and time. Teachers varied considerably in their views about the influence of the reforms on relationships within the school, but Wylie herself alerts us to the fact that a significant proportion of them (20 per cent) reported some worsening in their relationship with their principal attributable to the reforms. Similarly, in the context of Victoria's Schools of the Future programme, Blackmore *et al.* (1996: 17) report 'a deterioration in the relationship between teachers and principals'.

At the very least, there is considerable ambiguity about the role and status of teachers in self-managing schools. As Blackmore *et al.* (1996: 8) point out in the case of Victoria, 'Teachers perceived that while rhetorically *Schools of the Future* drew upon postmodern assumptions about change (flexibility, professional autonomy, flat organisations and diversity) in terms of effect in practice [they] imposed modernist solutions (line management, hierarchy, standardisation and the increase in administration).' An increase in administrative work is also a factor mentioned by Swedish teachers, who claim it is actually resulting in fewer opportunities for genuine cooperation and common planning. Some developed 'highly irrational' fantasies associated with the omnipotence of the headteacher which impeded collaboration (Granström 1996), and one study found teachers claiming they were being 'forced' to cooperate with other teachers (Crump and Nytell 1996). This is consistent with A. Hargreaves's (1994) distinction between 'contrived collegiality' and 'collaborative cultures'.

Some of these tensions probably arise from a shift in what seems to matter within schools. The concentration on competence within the teaching profession has meant that some activities are privileged over others. Teachers in the Schools of the Future researched by Blackmore *et al.* (1996) felt trapped into particular responses to the changes. They may have wanted to act as 'buffers to change' and protect aspects of their professional identity that they felt were under threat, but it was also important to be seen to 'perform' in more visible ways. As one teacher commented, 'What I do in my classroom is no longer valued – the teachers who are on lots of committees, do extra-curricular activities . . . are seen to perform. Yet they do so at the detriment of what they do in the classroom. Yet they are the ones who get the top jobs in the new system' (Blackmore *et al*. 1996: 9). This concern with visible performance contrasts with the collegial relations emphasized within the school effectiveness and school improvement literature.

Although, in resource terms, devolution in the USA has not generally gone as far as it has elsewhere, much of the rhetoric of the reform movement has emphasized the importance of empowering teachers. However, even there, the research evidence suggests that this has often not come about in practice. In reviewing the failure of many American site-based management initiatives to bring about the expected improvement in school performance, Wohlstetter and Odden (1992) have pointed to a lack of employee involvement in many schemes. Rather than merely devolving budgetary, personnel and curriculum decision-making to school level, they argue for regarding site-based management as a comprehensive governance reform that will involve teachers actively in making changes to curriculum and instruction. Other studies show considerable variations in the extent to which schools have changed in practice (Cawelti 1994) and identify important differences in the meanings given to site-based management by some of the key actors involved (Gibbs 1991).

Wohlstetter and her colleagues (Wohlstetter and Odden 1992; Wohlstetter and Mohrman 1993; Mohrman *et al*. 1994; Odden and Wohlstetter 1995) have suggested that site-based management will only have positive effects if it is implemented in accordance with what, drawing upon the literature of private sector management, they term the 'high-involvement model'. This requires teacher involvement in decision-making, good information, knowledge and skills, power and rewards – and they suggest that this last condition has too rarely been met. Wohlstetter (1995) also argues that site-based management must be augmented by a range of school-, district- and state-level strategies that facilitate interactions involving various stakeholders and provide a direction for those interactions.

A survey of the views of elementary school teachers about the reforms in Chicago (Consortium on Chicago School Research undated: 3) found that, 'although a clear majority of the teachers support school reform, the overall level of endorsement is not a consensus opinion'. Less than a fifth of teachers expressed 'strong negative attitudes about school reform', and, 'on balance', teachers were pro-reform. However, the report noted that it was also 'fair to assume that in many school communities cooperation among teachers around reform has yet to develop fully'. Nearly 60 per cent of teachers felt they had influence on decisions that directly affected them, though less reported influence on specific policies such as staff development (52 per cent), the curriculum (44 per cent) and the budget (23 per cent). About a third expressed reservations about being able to express themselves freely in their school. The overall tone of the survey report is consistent with that of other 'official' reports on the Chicago reforms, which, as we shall see in Chapter 6, show no tangible impact on student performance as yet but claim that the reforms will eventually prove successful.

None of this suggests that school-based management has given teachers a strong sense of empowerment or unequivocally enabled them better to bring about improvements in student learning. Yet there is certainly evidence where devolution has gone furthest of 'management by stress' consistent with the claims of those commentators who regard the reforms as a way of diverting crises away from the centre down to individual units in a process of 'vertical disintegration' (Watkins 1993; Robertson 1995). In the next section, we consider the impact of devolution and choice on teachers' sense of identity with the broader profession and on the operation of teachers' organizations.

Effects on the teaching force and the unions

In England and Wales, the atomization of the education service has sometimes meant a loss of support for teachers and fragmentation of the profession. For example, in some areas, LEA support networks have fulfilled an important function. With the devolution of most funds to individual schools, local teachers' centres and other forms of support have often been removed or reduced in scope, even for teachers in LEA schools operating under local management. This problem can be even more acute in the case of grant-maintained schools and city technology colleges, whose staff can easily become isolated from the broader professional community. Glatter (1993: 8) argues that the quasi-market model does not preclude partnerships between autonomous schools, but that 'the environment of heightened competition is now framing all such relationships.' He also questions whether, without some kind of semi-permanent infrastructure to promote and facilitate collaboration, the start-up and maintenance costs of partnership may be too great for most schools to contemplate. Citing Fullan (1991) and Louis and Miles (1992), he suggests that the erosion of customary networks and support structures could have very serious consequences, since 'as we should know well by now, effective change in schools depends as much on providing support as it does on applying pressure' (Glatter 1993: 8).

Another concern, already hinted at above, is that support and pressure do not appear to be equitably distributed among teachers. Teachers in some contexts are likely to require more support than those in others. While the reforms enable some schools to take advantage of their new found freedom, there is little evidence that school-based initiatives alone can overcome system-wide sociological influences on schooling. In this situation, there is a danger that too much emphasis upon the power of individual school faculty to seek their own salvation will, in inner-city areas, only result in further damage to the morale of an increasingly exploited workforce.

The reforms may also exacerbate divisions within the teaching force. In one secondary school in England, Mac an Ghaill (1992) suggests, while the majority of teachers remained old-style 'professionals' or 'old collectivists', who continued to identify with the wider labour movement, a significant minority had entered into the spirit of the reforms with enthusiasm, becoming what he calls 'the new entrepreneurs'. In a primary school case study, Troman (1996: 473) distinguished between 'old professionals' who generally sought to reject new managerial constructions of professionalism and a larger number of 'new professionals' who complied with some of the new demands but resisted others. However, while rejecting the notion that the teaching force has become utterly compliant in the face of the state's imperatives, Troman suggests that the combination of Ofsted inspection and school self-management may increasingly limit the 'spaces' available for 'resistance within accommodation'. Menter *et al.*'s (1997) research in an English county town shows that, even though market forces have had less impact on the primary sector than the secondary one, the changing financial and administrative imperatives are having a serious effect on the institutional cultures of primary schools. Staff experienced a significant loss of control over teaching, as even those heads who were reluctant to do so became more managerial.

Some divisions within the profession can be seen as structural. Sinclair *et al.* (1993) suggest that, as a result of the English reforms, teachers face increased workloads, attempts to use them more flexibly to counter the effects of budget restrictions, divisive approaches to performance-related pay and the replacement of full-time, permanent, qualified and experienced staff by part-time, temporary, less qualified and less experienced and therefore less expensive alternatives. A report by the National Foundation for Educational Research confirms that many of these trends have accelerated since the introduction of local management, particularly in those schools adversely affected by the use of average staffing costs in the funding formulae (Maychell 1994). This, of course, has potential implications for both teachers' conditions of service and the quality of education.

In particular, such management practices may be accentuating the sort of 'dual labour market' that has always existed in teaching, often based on a gendered division of labour (Apple 1986; Shilling 1991). Ozga (1993) and Soucek (1996a) suggest that, in their different ways, the reforms in England and Wales and parts of Australia have served to reduce the core of established and costly teachers and enlarge the more flexible and less expensive peripheral labour force. According to Robertson (1995: 12), this 'flexible deployment of teaching staff within the self-managing school, or staffing segmentation, parallels similar post-Fordist developments within the wider economy'. She has suggested that such developments are not only a feature of restructuring in neo-liberal led states such as Victoria, but have also been seen in initiatives of the federal Labor government, such as the National Schools Project (Robertson 1995: 13, citing Chadbourne 1992).

Robertson (1995) anticipates that the casualization of labour will have differential effects on males and females. Blackmore (1996a) too suggests that, given women's position in the peripheral labour market, they are likely increasingly to be disadvantaged and exploited by restructuring reforms currently under way in Australia. Indeed, in many classrooms, parents, predominantly mothers, were being used as unpaid substitute teachers (Blackmore *et al.* 1996). At the other end of the hierarchy, Chapman (1988) provides evidence from a study in Victoria which suggests that, where there are opportunities available for teachers to be involved in school-based decision-making, men tend to take advantage of them more than women.

It has also been suggested that the reforms encourage individual rather than collective notions of teacher professionalism (Blackmore 1990). One source of support for teachers has traditionally been their trade unions. Gordon and Wilson (1992: 257) describe how in New Zealand 'the government has sought to reduce the power of teachers and their unions, to erode their conditions of work and . . . to cease to recognise teachers' unions in a formal way.' At least until recently, teachers' unions in Australia have retained considerable influence over education policy-making, though in some states more than others. However, Robertson (1995) reports pressure to break the power of the teachers' unions across Australia as unions try to resist the intensification of labour in schools. She further suggests that the attack on unions is designed 'to minimise the power of collective forms of representation while at the same time imparting the idea of "provider capture"' (Robertson 1996b: 15).

Barber (1996: 189), an advocate of reform in England, concedes that 'while individual teachers might gain from the new policies, their organisations might be weakened.' Soucek (1996b: 309), though, suggests that the simple individual/collective distinction is too simple. He regards the reforms as encouraging 'political individualism' but 'technical collectivism', where individuals in a culture of competition and performativity are held accountable for the performance of others through team working, quality circles and other forms of 'contrived collegiality' (A. Hargreaves 1994). Meanwhile, they seem to be losing their collective voice through attacks on unions and the loss of collective bargaining.

Nevertheless, Sinclair et al.'s (1993) research in England, to which we have already referred, suggests that the reforms have not yet entirely succeeded in breaking down the traditional power of teacher unions within the state education system. Subsequently, this has been demonstrated by the successful action by teachers' unions, often in partnership with parents, against the workload associated with National Curriculum assessments (Hatcher 1994). Despite the devolution of many aspects of decision-making to individual schools, LEA-wide networks are still in operation and legal confusion about who is technically the employer in LEA schools operating under self-management means there are a number of industrial relations issues that still have to be tested in the courts. However, in many grant-maintained schools and city technology colleges, where the issues are more clear-cut, unions have been trying to resist being marginalized by management. Within some city technology colleges, which operate outside both national and local agreements, in-house staff associations have been established by managements and the less militant unions have been offered 'no-strike' agreements.

In many LEA schools, unions have been seeking to strengthen their plant-level bargaining capacity. There have also been suggestions, in both the USA (Kerchner and Mitchell 1988) and England and Wales (Barber 1992), that the teaching unions need to develop a new mode of operation, sometimes termed 'third generation', 'professional' or 'strategic' unionism, in which they negotiate educational as well as industrial issues and potentially become partners with management in educational decision-making to serve the best interests of learners. This is certainly the view held by Nathan (1996), who argues that unions will have to, indeed are already beginning to, abandon their 'old style' resistance to US charter school initiatives and develop a new role. He believes

that unions should seek to join the movement through contracting out services to charter schools and through collaborating with school districts and
charter schools to introduce and revise teaching programmes for public school
teachers. Self-management is therefore both a threat to traditional styles of
trade unionism and a means of securing new forms of labour representation.
It could also be a way of giving classroom teachers a voice in management
without diverting them from their primary role as educators of children.

A key issue arising from the research on self-managing schools reported
earlier in this chapter is how far it is possible to give classroom teachers a sufficient degree of involvement in resource (and other) management decisions
without diverting them away from pupil-related activities in the same way as
had already happened to headteachers on the evidence of the Birmingham
study (Bullock and Thomas 1994). In most respects, Levačić (1995) is not able
to point to many occasions in which teachers have a strong sense of participating in managing the whole school, notwithstanding their occasional
involvement in various working parties or consultative meetings. What she
illustrates instead is a version of the Caldwell and Spinks (1988) approach to
self-management which distinguishes clearly between those who make policy
– in this case the principal and other members of a relatively small senior
management team – and those who implement policy, for which read teams
of classroom teachers led, more often than not, by a curriculum coordinator
or subject head of department. How far, then, might it be possible to overcome
this problem by partnerships between management and unions?

Barber *et al.* (1995) mounted a small research project to see how far teacher
unions in England were actually involved in school-based decision-making on
the ground. During the school year 1992/3, a union-funded survey was conducted among teacher union representatives in schools to discover the extent
to which they were involved in decision-making about budgets, curriculum
and school development planning. Only 14 per cent of respondents said they
had ever been consulted about the budget, 15 per cent about the curriculum
and 17 per cent about the school development plan. Subsequent fieldwork
suggested that even these figures exaggerated the extent of genuine consultation, let alone formal involvement of unions in school management.

This is hardly surprising given the broader political and industrial context
of deskilling, reskilling, intensification and substitution of labour in which the
British reforms have been introduced. Nor is it surprising that both unions and
management were sceptical about whether greater union involvement in
management was feasible in present circumstances. There was therefore little
evidence of the union representatives participating in issues other than those
associated with 'second generational unionism'; that is, giving advice to members, negotiating with management over grievances and campaigning on
issues related to pay and conditions of work.

Some headteachers stated that playing down their members' interests was a
prerequisite to the unions becoming more involved in school development
planning, but school representatives pointed to the danger of their unique
critical perspective thereby disappearing, to the detriment of all concerned.
With the potential breakdown of national or even LEA-level bargaining on

certain issues, leaving them to be resolved at site level, it is likely to become increasingly important for school representatives to be able to explore the relationship between resources, conditions of service and educational outcomes at institutional level. Yet both headteachers and union representatives felt that a central concern with the needs of learners might involve union representatives abandoning their more traditional concerns.

There is a fine line to be drawn between third generation trade unionism and the sort of collaboration that makes it difficult for unions to bargain for their members' interests. In some city technology colleges, trade unions were not recognized for bargaining purposes and staff associations lacked any teeth. These city technology colleges are run by trusts dominated by business sponsors, and they have sometimes been seen as the model for the future. But, while pay in these schools is usually at a higher level than in other local schools, conditions of service are also very different. It is a moot point whether free private health insurance is adequate compensation for longer working hours, fixed term contracts and performance-related pay. Flexibility and claims of enhanced professionalism can too easily become a cover for exploitation of teachers and worsening conditions of service.

Sullivan (1994) has suggested that lack of consultation with teachers over the reforms at national levels in New Zealand is in danger of creating a low-trust hierarchical system rather than a high-trust collegial one. However, Wylie (1994) shows no major change in either direction in teachers' sense of involvement in school-level decision-making between 1991 and 1993, though there had been some slippage since 1989 in the quality of the information teachers felt they were getting on matters affecting their work. Nevertheless, following a report for one of the teachers' unions in New Zealand which emphasized the considerable potential of shared decision-making for enhancing the efficiency and effectiveness of schools (Hill 1992), some interesting action research on the value of various models of shared decision-making was undertaken there (Capper 1994). As a result, Capper concluded that school self-management by itself is an insufficient condition for the achievement of collaborative decision-making. Furthermore, unless they are handled very carefully, any positive moves in this direction may be stymied by their implications for already excessive workloads discussed earlier (Livingstone 1994). Similarly, even the more participatory forms of teacher involvement in decision-making in the USA come up against this problem. In Minnesota charter schools, for example, 'as much as teachers appreciated being board members and making administrative decisions, wearing two hats required a great deal of time and effort' from which they would eventually require some relief (Urahn and Stewart 1994: 51).

In Sweden, there is no real evidence of enhanced staff participation within the newly decentralized schools. Granström (1996), for instance, found that team meetings were little more than 'make-believe' games where staff went through the motions of collaborating while hanging on to their traditional hierarchical position characteristic of schools as 'low-trust' institutions. In this account, teacher resistance was seen to stem from the hierarchical tradition, lack of professional knowledge and 'collective regression' in which lack of security results in teachers 'clinging' to irrational assumptions and fantasies. Nytell (cited in Crump and Nytell 1996) carried out interviews with over 200 teachers and found that attitudes towards change were often negative. Although he comments that younger teachers were generally less negative than their older colleagues, there was resistance to policies, at both local and national levels. Like Granström, Nytell tends to focus on institutional and professional culture as the stumbling block to greater collaboration and innovation.

However, Gitlin and Margonis (1995) argue that those teachers who take a more conventional view of their employee status may be acting entirely rationally. They suggest that it is important to take seriously the political insights of those teachers who resist attempts to engage them in management without addressing the broader meaning and consequences of the reforms. Robertson (1996a: 52) argues that teachers need to recognize and conceptualize 'the various ways in which the proletarianization of their work is the result of the penetration of the commodity form into schooling and the labour process', but sees the ideology of professionalism as inhibiting this development.

Re-forming teacher education

One explanation sometimes given for the limited educational impact of the reforms to date is that too many teachers currently in schools are ill-suited to implement them. Either they have been inducted into a system based on different priorities and different practices or they have been actively encouraged during their training to be critical of government priorities. It is therefore not surprising that some attention has been paid to the training of new generations of teachers. In particular, there has been a questioning of the undue influence of university-based teacher educators on people entering the profession. Although this theme is also present in the most recent report of the Holmes Group in the USA (Labaree and Pallas 1996), where both 'alternative routes' and state-mandated 'standards' are being developed in some states, it has been most evident in government and media criticism of teacher education in England and Wales (Lawlor 1990). In what follows, we focus on the English reforms, which are increasingly being regarded as a possible model for other countries to follow.

Official discourse in England and Wales over the past decade or more has been strongly influenced by the New Right notion that the teacher education establishment is a producer interest insufficiently responsive to market forces. The introduction of new routes into teaching and the strategy of locating more and more elements of training in schools can be understood partly in these terms. However, policy has not been entirely driven by neo-liberal policies of deregulation. Neo-conservative fears about Marxist 'enemies within' both universities and teacher unions (Hillgate Group 1987, 1989), together with vocationalist concerns about international competitiveness (Hickox 1995), meant that the Conservative government did not pursue a policy of total deregulation or a wholesale devolution of teacher training to the schools. The result has been a two-fold strategy on the part of the state. Although one element has involved an attempt to shift much of the responsibility for training from higher education into schools, the other has required a 'focus on the competences of teaching throughout the whole period of initial teacher training' (DfE 1992b). Thus, the British government has shown a concern to shape the content of teachers' professional knowledge, initially through the introduction of a common list of competences to be required of beginning teachers, regardless of the nature of the route by which they have achieved them, and more recently by the proposals for a national curriculum for primary teacher education.

D. Hargreaves (1994b) and Berrill (1994) claim that the increasing responsibility given to schools for teacher education in England is a recognition of the maturity of the teaching profession as a whole. But critics argue that basing training in particular schools can limit the development of broader perspectives on education, especially when specifying a limited range of competences may also encourage restricted rather than extended notions of professionality (Hoyle 1974). Jones and Moore (1993) suggest that an emphasis on competences will serve to undermine the dominant discourse of liberal humanism within the teaching profession and replace it with one of technical rationality, while Adams and Tulasiewicz (1995) complain that teachers are being turned into technicians rather than 'reflective professionals'. These distinctions parallel the contrasting 'technocratic-reductionist' and 'professional-contextualist' conceptions of teaching identified by Codd (1996) in the case of New Zealand and cited earlier. Maclure (1993) sees the downgrading of university involvement in teacher education as nothing less than an attempt to dismantle the traditional defences of teaching as a profession.

On this argument, the erosion of a higher education involvement in initial teacher education has not so much devolved responsibility to teachers in schools, but led to the imposition of an alternative and more restricted state-mandated one. Schools and teachers may be 'empowered' to develop their own 'local' professionalisms and compete with one another – but only within a very narrow frame. Other potential stakeholders who might foster an alternative collective definition of teacher professionalism, whether higher education institutions, LEAs, teacher unions or a General Teaching Council, have been marginalized in the process. The role of the Teacher Training Agency (TTA), established in 1994 and part of the 'quango state', is particularly significant here (Mahony and Hextall 1996). Such a blend of market forces and central control is entirely consistent with the model of devolution under the evaluative state discussed in Chapter 3. Even if some aspects of the changes in initial teacher education might be characterized as reflecting broader trends in professionalism sometimes associated with 'postmodernity' and 'globalization', there has also been a strong modernist aspect to the reforms consistent with the Thatcherite political project and priorities of the British nation state in relation to education.

In recent research in England, we have endeavoured to understand not only these attempts to redefine teacher professionalism, but also responses to them and the extent to which the reforms are actually impacting upon the professional competences and professional characteristics of beginning teachers (Whiting *et al.* 1996). We found that 'reflective practice', rather than 'technical rationality' still appeared to be the most popular discourse of legitimation within university and college (and indeed school) based courses, even though it was somewhat less dominant than it had been five years previously (Barrett *et al.* 1992). At the same time, though, the use of competences in courses had increased significantly. Yet the official list of competences has often been criticized for embodying technical rationality and neglecting more reflective and critical competences. However, our survey showed that only about 8 per cent of courses restricted themselves to using the competences specified in the government circulars, while over 75 per cent had chosen to supplement the official lists with additional competences of their own. Fieldwork indicated that there was little objection to the idea of competences among course leaders, because they felt that reflective competences could be added to the official list in order to sustain a broader definition of professionality. In other words, while not openly resisting government directives, they felt able to limit their impact.

Nevertheless, it became clear that many of the higher education staff who had taken a leading role in developing reflective competences were among those most susceptible to early retirement and casualization in an era of retrenchment. 'Core' teacher education staff in both higher education and schools were increasingly becoming those concerned with curriculum subjects and classroom management. Furthermore, practice in schools varies considerably in relation to many issues with which teacher education has been concerned. For example, a recent Equal Opportunities Commission report found 'wide variation amongst schools and LEAs . . . in the awareness and applications of gender issues' (Arnot *et al.* 1996). The shift of more educational and professional studies into schools, with their different 'local' discourses around education, means that treatment of these areas of work is already becoming highly variable, not only across different universities and colleges, but also across different partner schools of the same university, except where there are strongly collaborative forms of partnership (Furlong *et al.* 1996). In the medium term, this variability of school-based practice seems likely to narrow the core definition of teacher professionality among beginning teachers as a whole by restricting commonality largely to the officially prescribed competences. In view of this, the effectiveness of resistance on the part of teacher educators to the state's attempt to redefine teacher professionalism must be questionable. School-based initial teacher education, combined with an official list of prescribed competences, seems likely over time to produce greater consistency of preparation for a narrow set of basic teaching skills alongside increased variation and fragmentation in student experience in other areas.

Although some similar tendencies have been seen in Australia, there is evidence that teacher unions and teacher educators, at least until the 1996 federal elections, have been able to resist the more restrictive elements and even to exploit the reforms for progressive purposes. Preston and Walker

(1993) claim that a non-reductive version of competences is actually helping to enhance teacher professionalism, while Knight *et al.* (1993a) argue that what they regard as post-Fordist approaches to management can foster a flexibility, diversity and responsiveness which has been largely lacking in teacher education as it has traditionally been conducted. They acknowledge a long-standing tension between the profession's claim to particular and specialist knowledge and expertise and a degree of relative autonomy and a requirement that it be open to the needs and concerns of other groups in a democratic society. Devolution of decision-making could, they suggest, herald the emergence of what they call 'democratic professionalism', which seeks to demystify professional work and facilitate 'the participation in decision-making by students, parents and others' within the community.

However, the progressive consequences of this envisaged by Knight *et al.* (1993a) in Australia seem unlikely to be forthcoming on any significant scale in a situation like that in England, where 'local' definitions of professionalism are marginal in relation to a strong core definition of teacher professionalism based on a restricted notion of professionality, produced with the help of technologies of control that include the specification of competences, Ofsted inspection, TTA funding decisions and so on. Yet, while some other countries are beginning to follow a similar route, there is probably rather more variation in this field than in school-level reforms, reflecting the different dispositions of political forces around higher education and teacher education in different nation states.

Conclusion

The predominant picture in the countries we have looked at is that restructuring has yet to produce widespread benefits for the teaching profession, even in countries which have emphasized the professional aspects of the reforms. This is hardly surprising when, as Kallos and Lundhal-Kallos (1994) imply in the case of Sweden in the early 1990s, the professionalization project of the era of social democracy has been replaced with a neo-liberal one which emphasizes individual competitiveness rather than collective gains. Nevertheless, many individual principals and some teachers do seem to have relished certain aspects of the reforms, though often at a considerable personal cost. Others have felt a loss of control over their professional and personal lives. As in other aspects of neo-liberal strategy, the marginalization of 'venues where formerly dispossessed groups shared power' has often left the most vulnerable teachers open to a dual attack from the state and local school managements (Carl 1994: 305). Yet, as we shall see in the next two chapters, the attempt to undermine the collective 'producer interest' of the teaching profession has not yet brought about the benefits for underachieving students and disadvantaged communities that the advocates of the reforms have sometimes predicted.

6 CLASSROOMS AND THE CURRICULUM

Chapters 4 and 5 indicate that headteachers and teachers are being subjected to a range of pressures which are changing the nature and volume of their work. For advocates of the reforms, however, such changes are long overdue. As we noted in Chapter 5, the reforms appear to be as much about regulating teachers as empowering them. The education profession, according to many neo-liberals, has contributed to the alleged mediocrity of public education. The introduction of market forces is one means of making teachers more accountable, alongside the implementation of centrally determined curriculum and assessment regimes.

Some neo-liberals find the imposition of these centralizing measures contradictory and counterproductive. In relation to the National Curriculum introduced in England and Wales, Flew (1991: 43) argues that any benefits of devolution have been 'neutralized and frustrated by the intrusions of the dominant directive and centralizing drive towards a more intensive and uniform monopolistic provision'. But, as discussed in Chapter 3, the articulation of the centralizing and decentralizing measures may not be as contradictory as it appears.

First, the imposition of national and state-level curricula and assessment programmes can enhance the ability of the state to steer at a distance, as well as supposedly providing consumers with comparable data to distinguish between schools. But, second, while advocates of the market assert that it will undoubtedly lead to higher scholastic attainment than bureaucratic control, there are fears that its operation may be obstructed if the suppressive influence of the educational establishment continues to prevail. In this connection, we also need to acknowledge the neo-conservative dimension of reforms. Certainly in England and Wales, but also elsewhere, the development of centrally determined curricula can be seen as an attempt to foster and regulate particular values of self and nationhood which have allegedly been threatened by suspect and subversive elements of the teaching profession and local government. Thus 'it becomes imperative (at least in the short term) to police the curriculum to ensure the pervasive collectivist and universalistic welfare ideology of the post-war era is restrained' (Whitty 1989: 331).

Many of the reform programmes examined in this book have, therefore, subjected self-managing schools to pressures from two different directions. The content of what they teach and how they assess is regulated by the government, and their performance is evaluated and rewarded or penalized through parents' choices. This chapter draws on a variety of empirical analyses to consider whether, and in what ways, this new disciplinary framework might be refocusing and redefining student learning. The first section considers the question of levels of attainment. In addition to the overall question of self-managing status and student performance, it explores whether the often-claimed characteristics of organizational autonomy – market accountability, effective use of resources and teacher empowerment – are evident in self-managing schools.

The second section focuses on how the various tensions between the centralizing dimensions of assessment-led curricula and the decentralizing mechanisms of marketization might be impacting on the classroom. Among the huge outpouring of research on recent developments, there is remarkably little that explores what goes on inside the classroom. However, perhaps this omission reflects the absence of attention given to student rights and experience within the recent reforms. In the discourse of the evaluative state, education is increasingly assessed and regulated in terms of organizational outputs rather than intervening processes. The limited amount of research in this area, and its often impressionistic nature, mean that we need to be careful not to overstate any apparent shifts or overdraw their significance. Nevertheless, it would appear that the tensions between the strong state and market forces are increasingly manifest within the classroom and may well be subjecting students to new 'lessons' in regulation and competition.

Self-managing schools as 'beacons of excellence'?

A key element of many of the reforms is the development of standardized indicators of performance which are to be used not only as a means by which governments can monitor 'outputs', but also as a way of providing 'consumer information' to parents. In England and Wales, New Zealand and several states in the USA and Australia, schools are required to publish student attainments to enhance market accountability. These are then often compiled as league tables – ranking schools within localities and even nationally. Success and failure become transparent, so that governments can monitor the relative success of schools and parents can make informed choices.

It is perhaps hardly surprising that politicians and the media, particularly those with right-wing persuasions, have been quick to use these league tables to support their conviction that self-managing schools outperform others. In England and Wales, for instance, the tables have been used by politicians to show that grant-maintained schools 'achieve better results than LEA schools' (DfEE 1996: 21). This impression is endorsed by media. A report published by a national newspaper, the *Sunday Times* (4 August 1996), offers parents a guide to the country's 'best' maintained schools. On the basis of examination results at Advanced Level (which students usually take at 18), the paper lists 90 of the 'best' schools in England – 58 of which are grant-maintained.

It is clear that some grant-maintained (GM) schools *do* obtain better exam results than many LEA-maintained schools. But the GM sector has a number of characteristics, other than institutional autonomy, which would make it somewhat surprising if they did *not* do better. First, the GM sector contains a disproportionate number of grammar schools operating selective admissions policies, as well as an increasing number of comprehensive schools that are taking advantage of the newer provisions that enable them to select a large part of their intake without formally changing their character. Of the 58 GM schools cited by the *Sunday Times* report, 48 are wholly selective, while at least two others select a percentage of their pupils (in one case, 50 per cent) according to ability. The selective nature of these schools means that their intakes are also socially advantaged. A crude but useful indicator of the socio-economic profile of a school is the proportion of the pupil population needing free school meals. While, in publicly funded schools as a whole, nearly one-fifth of pupils were known to be eligible for free school meals, this was the case for only two out of every hundred GM school pupils (MacLeod 1995). In addition, there is little doubt that GM schools, at least in the first few years of the policy, were advantageously resourced. Although, as discussed later, the link between the level of school resources and student attainment is not easily established, schools that are advantageously equipped are likely to be more attractive to parents. As further discussed in Chapter 8, popular schools are increasingly able to be selective in their choice of pupils. Many grant-maintained schools may thus be maximizing their advantages, not so much through improving the quality of provision, but through increasing the proportion of advantaged students in attendance.

Similar issues arise with the many case studies of individual schools, or neighbourhoods, that have been 'turned around' after being given increased autonomy. Within the United States, there have been celebrated instances whereby schools, and whole districts, have turned failure into miraculous success (see Chubb and Moe 1990). But, again, as with the success of grant-maintained schools, we need to treat such claims with scepticism. Henig (1994: 142), for instance, argues that the much vaunted East Harlem 'miracle' (Bolick 1990; Fliegel 1990) has 'escaped any serious effort at controlled analysis'. Not only have the apparently impressive gains in achievement now levelled off, or even been reversed, it is impossible to be sure that the earlier figures were not merely the effect of schools being able to choose students from higher socio-economic groups from outside the area. This doubt surrounds many of the individual instances of success provided by advocates of institutional autonomy (e.g. Nathan 1996) and single school evaluations. A report by the Chicago Panel on School Policy (1995) outlines the example of William Bishop Owen Scholastic Academy, a magnet school modelled on the 'back-to-basics' philosophy, which shows 'clear and sustained' gains in mathematics and reading, together with high parent involvement. Its popularity is such that the school is oversubscribed. But, even though it selects partly by lottery, the student body is more white and more affluent than its neighbourhood would suggest: 37 per cent of Owen students are classified as 'low income', compared to 81 per cent for the district's elementary school population. It is, therefore, impossible to determine whether these results reflect changes in the mode of school governance or the composition of the student population.

Cross-sectional comparisons between different types of school or longitudinal studies of school performance before and after becoming self-managing which do not take into account the 'input' characteristics of students are not just meaningless but misleading. In this connection, we need to question the effectiveness of the accountability mechanisms which are to be derived from reporting raw test scores. In England and Wales, the Conservative government argued that these provide the only meaningful information for parents. But if parents are to be able to make considered judgements about the extent to which individual schools 'make a difference', it is likely that they need some sort of 'value-added' measure that seeks to determine how well a school has performed compared with what might be expected in the light of the nature of its clientele, in terms of their prior test scores or socio-economic status, or a combination of such indices. Parents using 'output' data alone to distinguish between schools may well be selecting institutions that are relatively ineffective but attract more academically able students and dismissing others that are making significant improvements in students with lower prior attainment scores.

Despite the claims of policy-makers, there is very little reliable research which shows that self-managing status raises student performance. Even in the USA, where the tradition of quantitative and longitudinal comparison is strong, few programmes have been evaluated in terms of performance and few of these evaluations have shown clear achievement gains (Hanushek 1994). For example, the Chicago reforms, which have been regularly monitored, do not appear to be leading to higher academic attainment thus far, leading Steffy and English (1995) to predict that it is unlikely that they will have any positive effect on student learning in the future. Indeed, the goal of bringing student achievement in Chicago up to national norms within five years seems to have been abandoned as the reform has increasingly come 'to stand for process rather than outcome' (Lewis and Nakagawa 1995). In general, Mohrman et al. (1994) claim, the overall impact of reform on learning outcomes has so far been disappointing, indicating a lack of relationship between school-based management and improved school performance (Ogawa and White 1994).

Part of the problem lies in collecting the amount and type of data which would need to be gathered over sustained periods of time for meaningful comparisons to be made (Gray et al. 1995). As Goldstein et al. (1996) argue, the confidence intervals on most school performance data, particularly when analysed in relation to intake achievement, pupil gender and school type, are so wide that only a few schools located at either extreme can be separated with any degree of reliability.

The difficulty of establishing a connection between self-managing status and student performance is not only a problem for policy evaluators, but also raises even more doubts about the relationship between market accountability and school improvement. If Goldstein *et al.* (1996) are correct in asserting that even the more sophisticated indices of school effectiveness are of little use in distinguishing schools, it is hard to see how school performance can be linked to, and levered up by, consumer choice.

Of course, it could be argued that the devolution of decision-making will in *itself* make schools more efficient and effective. If school managers are given control over their budgets they will be able to direct more money where it matters. Similarly, if teaching staff are no longer subject to bureaucratic and political interference they will be empowered to make a difference. There is little, however, to support either argument – and even if such connections could be empirically established, they need to be set against the impact of the strengthened role of government in target-setting and evaluation.

Self-managing schools and the question of resources

The relationship between school performance and school resourcing is, in general, difficult to determine. The particular relationship between self-managing status and the more effective use of resources is even more obscure. Given the complexities of undertaking econometric analyses of this sort, it is not surprising that many research studies rely on professional accounts. But these raise a number of issues. Some staff are likely to be more favourably disposed towards the reforms than others. As Chapters 4 and 5 reveal, they have certainly been differentially privileged, with principals and headteachers gaining significantly increased powers. As we noted in Chapter 5, in England and Wales, the Birmingham University research (Bullock and Thomas 1994) and the study by Marren and Levačić (1994) found that classroom teachers were more sceptical about the impact of the reforms on teaching and learning than their headteachers. Doubts over principals' ability to act as 'expert witnesses' on questions of attainment are also raised by a report from school inspectors in England and Wales which claimed that 70 per cent of primary headteachers were failing to monitor how well their pupils were being taught. It said that 'the monitoring and evaluation of curriculum coverage was more frequently undertaken than that of standards or quality' (Ofsted 1994: 6). One has to be somewhat cautious about the value of claims by these same headteachers that self-management has improved pupil learning.

The Birmingham research team's initial survey (Arnott *et al.* 1992) showed that 84.4 per cent of head teachers either agreed or strongly agreed with the statement that 'local management allows schools to make more effective use of its resources', while only 7 per cent disagreed. However, 61 per cent agreed (and only 18 per cent disagreed) that, as a result of local management, meetings were being taken up by administrative issues, which lessened their attention to students' learning. When it came to the statement that 'children's learning is benefiting from local management', the 34.5 per cent who agreed or strongly agreed were balanced by 34.6 per cent who neither agreed nor disagreed and 30.9 per cent who disagreed or strongly disagreed. Thus, it was rather unclear what their concept of greater effectiveness actually related to. In the final report (Bullock and Thomas 1994), the proportion of headteachers making a positive assessment concerning improvements in pupil learning had increased somewhat over the previous three years, but significantly this assessment came mainly from those schools which had experienced an increase in funding as a result of self-management.

While the Birmingham team concluded that self-management was broadly a successful reform, they conceded that, before a more definitive conclusion could be drawn, more evidence was needed, particularly on the relationship between resourcing levels and learning outcomes. It would seem likely that the relationship between funding and school effectiveness will depend on a number of variables. Work carried out by Robertson *et al.* (1995) in the USA found that high levels of additional resources were not necessary to implement what they termed 'meaningful reform' among teachers, and that when they were available they did not necessarily bring about such reform. However, the research does concede that such resources are beneficial – especially when they are directly related to reform objectives. Research undertaken by Cooper (1994), also in the USA, goes further and suggests that as more money is passed down to the instructional context, including paying for better qualified or experienced teachers, there are tangible benefits for pupil performance. In some cases, though, the new funding mechanisms may make it more difficult for funds to filter into the classroom. Bulk funding of teachers' salaries in England and Wales is done on the basis of average rather than actual salaries and schools whose budgets have been squeezed by the effect of this can therefore expect negative consequences. And Cooper's research would also suggest that if the funding that *is* passed down to schools does not reach the instructional context – that is, teachers and classrooms – then its benefits will be more questionable. While some schools may now have increased purchasing power after paying salaries and maintenance costs, other elements of the reforms can bring about reductions in the amount of resources finding their way into the classroom. Certainly, in England and Wales, the close linking of self-management with parental choice has sometimes meant that resources are diverted into marketing rather than instruction, and successful marketing becomes essential to protect future years' budgets. Gewirtz *et al.* (1995) show how schools are increasingly 'investing' money in such marketing strategies. Although such investment may make financial sense for schools if it secures higher enrolment, the cumulative cost of such marketing can be substantial. Gewirtz *et al.* (1995) calculate that if every school spent £1000 on marketing each year – a conservative figure – the total annual marketing bill for the UK as a whole would be £28 million.

If the link between resourcing at classroom level and attainment is a close one, as Cooper suggests, then it also argues against the current English funding formula, which can reward or punish a school with sharp year-on-year changes in resourcing as a result of changes in school rolls. Indeed, it almost argues for a retreat from an extreme form of pupil-based funding either to funding based on average rolls over a number of years (as the Birmingham research team suggest) or to curriculum-led staffing – or even to some form of positive discrimination. This is particularly important in that the schools most affected by budgetary difficulties, and therefore least likely to report a positive impact on pupils' learning, were often those with pupils from disadvantaged communities. Wylie's (1994) study of the fifth year of self-managing schools in New Zealand identified schools in low-income areas and schools with high Maori enrolments as experiencing greater resource problems than others. However, she did not find this correlated with perceptions of the success of the reforms or with evaluations of the influence of the reforms on pupil learning, and she admits to being puzzled by this. However, apart from in a few pilot schools, New Zealand did not then have bulk funding of teacher salaries and there remained more opportunities to apply for equity funding, so it may be that the funding differences there were less severe in their impact.

In short, there is little to suggest that self-managing schools use their resources more effectively to raise student achievement. While they have greater budgetary control, this does not necessarily mean that more money finds its way into the classroom. Money, and time, can be diverted into the increased amount of administration required by government and marketing strategies. Moreover, per capita funding can create financial uncertainty and penalize schools where resources are most needed. Chapter 8 discusses the equity implications of this more fully.

Just as it is hard to demonstrate that self-managing schools make more effective use of financial resources, there is not much to support the claim that self-management releases what management theorists term 'human resources' to effect changes in the classroom. Marks and Louis (1995) attempted to relate teacher empowerment, identified as an outcome of school-based management, with students' academic performance through an analysis of 24 'restructuring' elementary, middle and high schools in the USA. They found that teacher empowerment was an important, but far from sufficient, condition for effecting changes in the classroom. While teacher empowerment may have had strong indirect effects on teachers' practice, they claimed there were no *direct* effects of teacher empowerment on pedagogy or performance. This argument would be supported by evaluations of the Chicago reforms, where the few initiatives that have appeared tend to be 'add-ons' which, Hess (1992: 277) argues, 'are likely to have little effect on the regular instructional program experienced by most students' and are 'unlikely to significantly improve student achievement levels'. He concludes, 'teachers . . . have taken increasingly involved roles in planning for school improvement, but do not see reform requiring much change in their basic classroom practices' (p. 283).

While it may be difficult to establish a direct relationship between staff involvement and student achievement, there is evidence to suggest that some conditions are more favourable for effective schooling than others. For instance, Wohlstetter *et al.*'s (1994) study of 'struggling' and 'actively restructuring' schools in North America reveals that certain aspects of school-based management can contribute to putting in place the conditions for change, in particular the organizational mechanisms needed to generate interactions for school-level actors around curriculum issues. However, they argue that decision-making power on its own is not sufficient. School staff also need increased professional development, access to information and reward systems for the model to work.

It is hard to see how these criteria can be met in the current wave of restructuring, as teachers increasingly come under the pressures of the market and the evaluative state. Chapter 5 certainly provided no evidence that the majority of teachers found their new working conditions empowering. Murphy (1994) concludes that one of the reasons why few US studies have shown clear gains in student achievement is that the effect of school-based management (as in England, Wales and New Zealand) has too often merely been to place additional administrative burdens on teachers. Furthermore, the required professional supports are often threatened when resources are moved from the centre – whether at national, state or district level – to the periphery. As Marks and Louis (1995) indicate, staff development (an essential component of Wohlstetter *et al.*'s 'high involvement' model) is one of the easiest areas to cut at a time when education services are subject to shrinking funds.

Leaving staff development and rewards in the hands of individual institutions must also raise issues of sustaining teaching performance and commitment in the long term. Research published by the Minnesota House of Representatives (Urahn and Stewart 1994) reports that, while reduced administration costs may be a factor in helping to maintain favourable staff:student ratios in charter schools, these schools were also often paying experienced, but highly committed, teachers relatively low salaries. There must be doubts whether the short-term gains that arise from a change of governance and commitment to a new sense of 'mission' can be sustained over time. As Pauly (1991) argues, motivation is likely to slip once the initial excitement fades away.

There is, then, little evidence to show that student performance improves as a result of self-managing status. While it might be premature to expect significant gains at this stage, it is equally hard to see how the particular combination of decentralizing and recentralizing measures is likely to enhance student achievement in the longer term. Parents do not have access to data with which to make the kind of informed decisions that would encourage schools to be more effective in their practices, rather than more selective in their intake. While schools may have greater budgetary control, and their staff may appear to be less constrained by local bureaucracy, the new demands of the market and the state would appear to militate against any potential benefits. On the other hand, this does not mean that classrooms have been unaffected by the imposition of national curricular standards and assessment regimes and the fostering of market forces.

Redefining the curriculum

Broadfoot (1996), in her account of the relationship between education, assessment and society, argues that we are now witnessing a new culture of assessment. She identifies an international trend away from using assessment as a means of 'competition' towards using assessment to determine 'competence'. Although in England and Wales and in New Zealand these moves are being resisted in the more advanced traditional academic courses, she argues that they are well established elsewhere. In the compulsory phase of schooling in particular, Broadfoot (1996: 50) claims that we are seeing 'a greater homogeneity or rationalization of curriculum provision within a detailed framework of sequential targets rather than the provision of curriculum guidelines in terms simply of courses of study or subjects to be covered'. In England and Wales, as in New Zealand, progress within the National Curriculum is monitored through sequential standard assessment tasks within each subject at different levels. An Australian national curriculum is still under discussion (see Macpherson 1991), but 'key competences' are being built into curriculum frameworks (Curtain and Hayton 1995). In the United States, where testing has a long tradition, the 'Standards Project' has involved 18 states in developing assessment-led curriculum programmes. Broadfoot (1996) argues that these developments provide the mechanisms to regulate competition, attest for competence, determine content and provide for individual control. But they are also linked to increasing regulation and evaluation of the school system as a whole. The publication of performance indicators represents an important dimension of market accountability and the consolidation of central control – the rise of Neave's (1988) evaluative state.

As we have seen in Chapters 4 and 5, the rise of this evaluative state has brought about changes at an institutional level. Structures of authority are reordered as managers and staff seek to maximize organizational performance. Relations between staff and students are also likely to become more goal-oriented as the educational enterprise becomes defined in terms of output rather than process. Some commentators have expressed concern that the emphasis on assessment and accountability is diminishing the quality of teaching. For instance, Toch (1991) claims that new curriculum developments require adequate administration – the lack of which leads to 'superficiality' within academic courses. Relatedly, Gillman and Reynolds (1991) argue that accountability programmes render teaching more standardized and superficial and warn of the dangers of 'teaching to the test'. In general, there are already indications that recent curriculum reforms in the context of devolved systems of schooling are leading to a culture of 'performativity' rather than an enrichment of learning opportunities. More specifically, there is some evidence that the emphasis on student attainment rather than learning process is leading to an increasing fragmentation and unitization of the curriculum, the marginalization of non-assessed fields of enquiry and a more rigid compartmentalization of students.

Within England and Wales, the specification and design of the original National Curriculum and its assessment in terms of separate academic subjects has, in many cases, led to a narrowing of the school curriculum. The emphasis on the 'core' subjects, together with the requirement that schools publish test results as the main indicator of educational success, is leading to pressure on non-core subjects, such as music and art (Pollard *et al.* 1994). Non-assessed learning appears particularly vulnerable to marginalization. For example, although the National Curriculum Council advised schools to teach five non-mandatory 'cross curricular themes' – namely health education, citizenship, careers education and guidance, economic awareness and environmental education – our own research found that the fact that these did not have the force of law meant that hard-pressed teachers gave them little priority (Whitty *et al.* 1994). Even where cross-curricular work was taken seriously, its precarious existence alongside the dominant school subjects has been further jeopardized by the low priority assigned to it by official curriculum and inspection agencies after 1990. Troyna (1992) argues that LMS has 'buckled' existing developments in anti-racist education. As discussed more fully in Chapter 8, the devolution of budgets to individual schools has diminished local capacity to address such issues. Moreover, Troyna draws on research that indicates that areas such as equal opportunities and multicultural education are not seen as priorities by school governing bodies (Webb 1991).

There are also suggestions that the unitization of the curriculum changes the mode of learning and relationships between students and staff. Robertson and Soucek's (1991) research in a Western Australian secondary school found that the new 'Unit Curriculum' turned out to be less student-centred than it first appeared. In parallel with criticisms of the English curriculum, they claimed that 'it was at the same time both highly tailored and modularized into consumerable packages and excessively assessed. These features worked to compartmentalize school learning and teaching, as well as to develop an intense sense of alienation between the student and the teachers . . . exaggerating the reductive, technocratic and fragmented nature of much school knowledge' (reported in Robertson 1993: 130).

We should not of course forget that teachers carry their own professional values – values which may be at odds with those inscribed in policy. Bowe *et al.*'s (1992) research in four London schools found that the ways in which the National Curriculum was implemented varied widely as teachers reinterpreted it to reflect their own priorities. However, we need to be careful not to exaggerate the leeway teachers have to redefine programmes. In addition, the narrowing modes of professionalism found within teacher education programmes, as reported in Chapter 6, must lead one to be concerned about the intellectual source of future curriculum developments. Curriculum change may stagnate, not just because of centrally imposed regulations and performance indicators, but because of increasingly restricted opportunities for initial and continuing professional development within devolved systems of schooling. With reference to England and Wales, the implications of decentralization for pre-service and in-service teacher professional development and the knock-on effects within the classroom are highlighted by Bennett and Carré (1995). Reporting on the result of two national surveys of primary school teachers, they found that many did not feel competent to teach key areas of the National Curriculum. Lack of adequate training opportunities and the move towards competency-led school-based teacher education will be detrimental as 'The focus in schools is more likely to be on providing tips for teaching based on limited understanding of subject content' (Bennett and Carré 1995: 195).

In addition to 'rationalizing' curriculum content, the associated assessment regimes seem to be altering the way in which subjects are taught and to whom. For instance, a major longitudinal project based on interviews in 48 schools in England and Wales found that primary teachers claimed it had reduced their professional autonomy (Pollard *et al.* 1994). In line with the changes in teachers' work reported in Chapter 5, a majority of teachers claimed that the National Curriculum had increased administration, nearly one-half spoke of more time spent on planning and over one-third claimed it had increased stress and anxiety. Hughes (1997), also drawing on the work of Pollard, argues that teachers now spend less time on 'topic work' and are abandoning the 'integrated day' previously associated with progressive primary school teaching in England. This has also been a feature of the Victorian reforms. Blackmore *et al.* (1996) report how teachers in their case study felt under pressure to move away from their preferred ways of teaching, which tended to be more open-ended, explorative and integrative, to more structured task and outcome orientations.

The gradual trend away from progressive pedagogies reflects a more general shift towards traditional education. As we discussed in Chapter 3, many of the New Right reforms reflect a curious combination of neo-liberalism and neo-conservativism. Most obviously in England and Wales, but also in other countries, states and governments are using strategic evaluation mechanisms as a way not just of regulating performance, but of controlling what is learnt. Although government-defined curricula nearly always recognize the increasing importance of technology, they also tend to embody a narrow and sometimes nationalistic selection of culture. But the revival of traditionalism in education represents more than government preference. It provides a clear illustration of the way in which government control and market forces can work together to shape institutional responses.

There is little doubt that the past few years have seen increasing emphasis placed on 'old-fashioned' education. Again, most evidence of this comes from England, but anecdotal accounts from other countries suggests that it is occurring elsewhere. Although we recognize that schools promote themselves through 'double-coded signals' whereby 'aspects of progressivism feature alongside re-invigorated traditionalism' (Gewirtz *et al.* 1995: 137), modernization is usually a poor relation compared to the drive for traditionalism. The attempt to promote old-fashioned values is apparent even in those supposedly progressive high-tech institutions, the city technology colleges (Whitty *et al.* 1993). Our own research has revealed that grant-maintained schools, far from being the centres of innovation which some had hoped, appear to have 'opted into the past' (Halpin *et al.* 1997a), with any measures that have been adopted to give the curriculum a technological flavour being heavily qualified by a proliferation of traditional values and symbols. This rediscovery of tradition is not unique to the opted out schools, though. Although the flexibility and extra resources of GM status enable these schools to indulge themselves further than others, many LEA-maintained schools are busy brushing up their uniforms and outlining rules that emphasize their new traditionalism and play down their past progressivism. This trend is endorsed by other research. Woods (1992) also comments on the way in which the schools paid attention to uniform. The issue of uniform crops up again and again in Gewirtz *et al.*'s

(1995) account of the effects of the introduction of the education market place.

As we have argued elsewhere (Power *et al.* 1996), this traditionalism cannot be adequately accounted for by central government directives alone. Neo-conservatives have tapped into a popular discontent, whether real or manipulated, with progressive education. In this instance, politicians and parents become powerful allies in steering schools away from potentially radical modes of teaching and learning. As Broadfoot (1996: 60) argues, 'in co-opting parents and pupils – who are . . . some of the more conservative participants in the education system – into the accountability process, the mechanisms of control over the education system, and teachers in particular, are in fact strengthened.' In substantive terms, the market itself thus seems to reinforce traditional norms rather than fostering the diversity claimed by its advocates.

The gradual trend away from mixed ability teaching and the resurgence of various forms of tracking and streaming, including selective schooling, provides another example of allegiance between neo-conservatives and parents – or, more precisely, particular groups of parents. In England, this is a noticeable occurrence in virtually all the case study schools researched by Gewirtz *et al.* (1995). In the USA too, Wells and Oakes (1997) observe how the increased influence of some parents, particularly affluent white parents, is preventing schools from implementing detracking programmes: 'To the extent that . . . activated and involved parents do not see detracking reform as in their best interest, they will prevent it from moving forward. Deregulated schools, responding to the demands of their most powerful, efficacious and vocal consumers, will be obligated to comply.'

In both England and Wales and the USA there is an increased emphasis on the needs of 'gifted' children. Many self-managing schools are introducing 'fast-track' classes which provide 'enriched' opportunities. As Gewirtz *et al.* (1995: 168–9) argue, 'Whilst there are good grounds for schools developing and improving provision for "able" children, the main driving force appears to be *commercial* rather than *educational*.' At the same time, less academically able students, in particular those with learning difficulties, tend to receive fewer resources. 'Special needs' teachers are redeployed to other areas and are often the first to be made redundant when the school has to balance its budget. Perhaps the most extreme form of segregation is the alarming rate of students being excluded from schools in England (see, for instance, Williams 1994; Parsons 1996).

The hidden curriculum of reform

These trends indicate that students' experiences and opportunities within market-oriented schools are likely to be highly differentiated. But they also suggest that a new 'hidden curriculum' of marketization may be developing. Ball (1994: 146) claims that 'insofar as students are influenced and affected by their institutional environment, then the system of morality "taught" by schools is increasingly well accommodated to the values complex of the enterprise culture.' Old values of community, cooperation, individual need and equal worth, which, Ball claims, underlay public systems of comprehensive education, are being replaced by values that celebrate individualism, competition, performativity and differentiation. These values and dispositions are not made visible and explicit, but emanate from the changing social context and permeate the education system in myriad ways.

The reinvigorated traditionalism taking place in many schools provides an example of how the messages of the market and the preferences of governments may complement each other. In other instances, market forces may contradict, even undermine, the 'old-fashioned' values and sense of nationhood that governments ostensibly seek to foster. This contradiction may reflect more than the ideological distance between neo-conservatism and neo-liberalism. It could represent the tension of attempting to maintain a stable and strategic centre in an increasingly fragmented and atomized context. The market, as Marquand (1995) reminds us, is subversive: it 'uproots communities, disrupts families, mocks faiths and erodes the ties of place and history'.

To some extent the potential subversion of the market is contained through strong regulatory measures and the delimiting of parental involvement. But neo-conservative agendas may be increasingly compromised by the growing presence of corporate interests in the classroom. Whereas the school curriculum has traditionally transcended – indeed actively distanced itself from – the world of commerce, the growth of self-managing schools and the promotion of market forces within education are forging a new intimacy between these two domains. Commercial penetration of the curriculum is evident in all our countries. In the USA, for instance, the commercial satellite network Channel One offers schools free monitors on condition that 90 per cent of students watch its news and adverts almost every day. Molnar (1996) cites a wide range of examples where corporate businesses entice schools to promote their products. In many countries, there are schemes whereby equipment can be purchased with vouchers from supermarket chains, the take-up of which is enhanced as a result of budget constraints and the removal of public control (Roberts 1994). In Australia, the NSW Teachers Federation tried to seek a ban on a promotional scheme in which Mars confectionery wrappers were exchanged for school equipment. They were informed by the Department of School Education that 'We are a devolved system and it is a promotional activity, and the person ultimately responsible is the principal' (Lewis, *Sydney Morning Herald*, 20 April 1994). Harris's (1996) report on the Australian Coles programme reveals not only the vast amount of time teachers can spend counting dockets, but also the promotional space occupied by visible tallies and scoreboards as well as the advertising on the computer equipment eventually acquired. Such promotions are particularly attractive to schools in need of extra resources. In England, schools have been given clearance to sell space for advertising – a large school with 100 poster sites might earn £10,000 (Durham 1996). The proliferation of commercially sponsored curriculum materials and promotions has been such that an independent organization designed to protect consumer interests has published a good practice guide for teachers, governors, LEAs and parents (National Consumer Council 1996).

Advertising in schools is likely to provoke a number of anxieties. Those on the left will be concerned that curriculum materials portray a partial, and inaccurate, account of business interests. In this connection, Molnar (1996) quotes a study guide on banking which defines 'free enterprise' as the symbol of 'a nation which is healthy and treats its citizens fairly'. Harty's international survey of corporate products in the classroom found that 'the biggest polluters of the environment – the chemical, steel, and paper industries – were the biggest producers of environmental education material' (Harty 1994: 97). Neo-conservatives, on the other hand, may be critical of the cultural threat of what is sometimes called 'McDonaldization'. There are fears that schools will develop 'an anti-intellectual emphasis' and 'a consumptionist drive to purchase status goods'. Indeed, Harty (1994: 98–9) alleges that the permeation of multinationals 'contributes to a standardised global culture of material gratification . . . [which will] impinge on the cultural integrity of whole nations'. In this scenario, far from encouraging students to appreciate the particularities of their regional or national inheritance, schooling becomes implicated in the training of desires, rendering subjects open to the seduction of ever changing consumption patterns and the politics of lifestyling.

It might be argued that the tension between the neo-conservatives and market forces is evident, but also accommodated, within the contrasting messages of the overt and the hidden curriculum. While, at the level of direct transmissions, students are to be taught the values of the cultural restorationists (Ball 1990), the context in which they are taught may undermine their canons. The content of the lessons emphasizes heritage and tradition, but the form of their transmission is becoming increasingly commodified within the new education market place.

This tension is discussed in a recent paper by Bernstein (1996). He argues that the increasing deregulation of the economic field and the increasing regulation of what he terms the symbolic field are generating new forms of pedagogic identity, in contrast to both the 'retrospective' identity of old conservatism and the 'therapeutic' identity associated with the child-centred progressivism of the 1960s and 1970s. An emergent 'decentred market' identity embodies the principles of neo-liberalism. It has no intrinsic properties, and its form is dependent only upon the exchange value determined by the market. It is therefore contingent upon local conditions and is highly unstable. A 'prospective' pedagogic identity, on the other hand, attempts to 'recentre' through selectively incorporating elements of old conservatism. It engages with contemporary change, but draws on the stabilizing tradition of the past as a counterbalance to the instability of the market. While the decentred market pedagogy can be seen to foster 'new' global subjects, the 'prospective' pedagogy seeks to reconstruct 'old' national subjects, albeit selectively in response to the pressures of a new economic and social climate.

Thus, while the reforms seem not yet to have led to major improvements in pupil achievement, it can be argued that schools are 'teaching new subjects' in terms not so much of the content of the overt curriculum as of the subjectivities they foster. In the curriculum, there may be an emphasis on 'imagined communities' that are often exclusive rather than inclusive, but at the same time collectivities are being atomized in a culture of individual and institutional competition. The impact of these developments on coming generations can only be a matter of conjecture at this stage. But, as we shall see in the next chapter, they are already making the rhetoric of community empowerment seem rather at odds with the realities of the reforms, particularly for many disadvantaged communities.

7 THE SELF-MANAGING
SCHOOL AND THE
COMMUNITY

At the heart of Chubb and Moe's critique of the 'one best system' of schooling is the claim that democratic control of education selectively advantaged the interests of some groups at the expense of others:

> The winners were elements of business, the middle class and educational professionals, especially the latter, for they would be running the new bureaucratic system. The losers included . . . a sizeable portion of the less powerful segments of the American population: the lower classes, ethnic and religious minorities, and citizens of rural communities. Their traditional control over local schools was now largely transferred to the new system's political and administrative authorities – who, according to what soon became official doctrines, knew best what kind of education people needed and how it could be provided most effectively.
>
> (Chubb and Moe 1990: 4)

In the name of public service and under the mandate of democracy, Chubb and Moe claim, politicians, bureaucrats and educationists have progressively furthered their own ends under the guise of professional expertise and impartiality. Devolution not only reduces the inefficiencies of the monopolistic and bureaucratic control, it also serves imperatives of social justice. Placing decision-making in the 'hands of the people', so the argument often goes, enables local communities to develop forms of education which reflect their interests and preferences rather than those imposed from above.

The precise way in which decision-making is placed in the 'hands of the people' varies, and often appears contradictory. To some extent, notions of 'community' are antithetical to many of the educational reforms examined in this book. Articulating devolution with choice privileges the individual's right to choose and plays down collective responsibility, even 'society' itself.

Indeed, the marketization of educational provision fosters a form of possessive individualism that is somewhat at odds with discourses that emphasize the 'stakeholder society' or the 'rebuilding of the social order', variants of which proliferate in the public pronouncements of politicians and opinion leaders of diverse ideological persuasions.

This apparent contradiction, however, has not prevented many supporters of quasi-markets from invoking concepts of community to strengthen their appeal, in reference to some mythical but warmly remembered past. They appeal to the common values and aspirations of groups that have been under-represented within existing democratically controlled systems and sidelined by alternative reforms, which have tended to focus on issues of class and social mobility rather than cultural diversity. It is important to note that in this sense the notion of community, or more precisely community of interest, extends beyond the geographical boundaries of the neighbourhood school, and certainly moves far away from the idea of neighbourhoods devised by politicians in their attempts to balance and regulate school intakes.

The elasticity of the discourse of 'community' within political justifications of devolution and choice helps us to understand why these policies are so attractive to such a diverse range of constituencies. Thus, for instance, advocates of charter schools include 'rural white fundamentalist Christians running from what they perceive to be the too liberal curriculum in the public schools, urban blacks or Latinos who feel the public system has short-changed their children and want community-based schools to reflect their cultural heritage, progressive teachers who feel stifled by public school regulations and top-down management systems, and entrepreneurs seeking to invest in the educational "industry" and prove that businessmen run better schools than educational bureaucrats' (Wells *et al*. 1996: 3).

The ways in which these differing communities are to be brought back into education decision-making vary widely both across and within specific reform programmes. At one end of the scale there are policies which offer the potential for groups to act collectively and seek public funds to set up their own schools. At the other end are the individualized entitlements of parental choice. Between these two extremes, there are a range of mechanisms which are designed, at least rhetorically, to enhance community representation in governing existing public schools and to promote partnerships between schools and parents.

The diverse and conflicting notions of 'community involvement' embodied in the various reforms makes it difficult to draw clear conclusions about how these new 'entitlements' are being experienced. The role of community and parental representation in governing schools has been narrowed to focus largely on administrative and financial issues. This has meant that some trustees and governors are likely to be considered more useful than others. It would seem that some communities of parents are also more desirable as 'partners' in the educational process. Both the market and the need to meet government objectives are potentially leading to a commodification of parents – with some being far more valuable for the professional expertise, finance and voluntary help they can bring to the school.

'New' schools in the community

Given the critiques developed by the New Right concerning the 'dull uniformity' of bureaucratically controlled systems, one might have expected to see a more widespread emergence of policies enabling communities to develop their own alternatives. As we have seen, the earlier forms of 'community schools', in particular the Catholic and Protestant schools to be found in the private sectors in Australia and the USA, are often held up by those on the right as embodying the kind of characteristics they would like to see in the public sector. Recently created community-led schools are, however, few and far between. In several of our countries we are seeing the introduction of new specialized schools, but it is important to note that these tend to result from government intervention rather than any clear popular demand. In England, the CTC experiment provides one example of such a 'top-down' approach. So too do the specialist schools introduced by the state of New South Wales in Australia. Moreover, while the charter school movement allows sponsors and parents to start new schools, these tend to account for a minority of the sector. In California, for instance, which has one of the largest and most diverse charter school sectors, only just over one-third of the institutions that make it up are brand new. But even here many of the new schools have been created as a result of state-directed measures or professional initiatives. Raywid's (1994b) classification of 'alternative schools' distinguishes between *popular innovations*, which include 'schools of choice' and reflect organizational and administrative departures from traditional institutions, and *last chance* and *remedial focus* schools, both of which seek to provide an education for students who have been 'failed' by or proved 'uneducable' in conventional schools. Much of the diversity within the charter school movement arises from the latter two kinds of initiatives. In Minnesota, for instance, the PEASE Academy caters for students with drug or chemical abuse problems, while those who are not in school or who have weapons violations may attend the City Academy (Urahn and Stewart 1994). Clearly these schools do offer particular students an alternative form of school experience, but they have often developed from professional initiatives rather than representation from their client communities.

In England and Wales, the possibility of various communities seeking public funds to start their own schools is a relatively new phenomenon, even within the recent wave of restructuring. As a result of heavy campaigning, particularly by small groups representing private Muslim and evangelical Christian schools (Walford 1995), the 1993 Education Act allowed independent sponsors or governors of existing private schools to apply to the government to establish sponsored grant-maintained schools. Although applicants have to fulfil a number of commitments, such as finding at least 15 per cent of capital funding and ensuring that the National Curriculum is taught, there are no overt restrictions on underlying religious or philosophical beliefs, teaching methods or specialist orientation. As Walford (1997) points out, 'this particular policy change might be seen as a prime example of a growth in the diversity of different types of school as a result of parental pressure.' However, the number of 'new' additions joining the grant-maintained sector down this route has been tiny – currently only three, all of which are long-established independent Roman Catholic schools, although a dozen other institutions, mostly secondary schools, have published proposals which are presently under consideration. Interestingly, not one of the groups initially involved in lobbying for this policy change has, at the time of writing, been successful in receiving government approval.

This does not mean that there have been no significant moves of this sort elsewhere. In the USA there are some examples of community-initiated, rather than professionally-directed, applications for charter school status (for details, see Nathan 1996). In New Zealand, there are indications that the new opportunities are being taken up by groups who had been disadvantaged by the 'old' system. *Kura Kaupapa Maori*, for example, have in some cases been able to take on board the financial autonomy that comes with the 'bulk funding' initiative (Wylie 1995b). In general, though, the development of new community-led schools is likely to be emblematic rather than marking a substantial shift in the nature of provision.

Government reluctance to encourage communities to start their own schools is less paradoxical than initially appears. As has been evident in the preceding chapters, the discourse of restructuring may emphasize local agency, but the welter of centralizing measures means that any such movements will be tightly constrained. On a purely fiscal basis, it is clear that the emergence of a multitude of small publicly funded schools will not coincide with an agenda of restraining public spending. Indeed, if one of the objectives of recent policies is to encourage privatization, then it might be important not only to reduce funding in the public sector, but also to ensure that the private sector retains its market niche as the main supplier of specialty education. But we should bear in mind that much government policy, at state or national level, is about overseeing performance and consolidating cultural preferences. A proliferation of alternative schools will not only be more difficult to monitor, but may also foster modes of teaching and learning that produce 'inappropriate' outcomes.

It is not perhaps surprising that most measures allowing some form of collective involvement concentrate on converting the governance of existing schools. Both the charter school initiative and the grant-maintained schools policy make it possible for groups of parents, or other community or school representatives, to 'take control' of existing institutions. Nathan (1996: xiii) is enthusiastic about the equity implications of this development in the USA, claiming that it 'is part of a two-hundred-year effort in the country to expand opportunity, especially for those who are not wealthy and powerful'.

Our own research in this area leads us to be more sceptical about claims such as these. With reference to the grant-maintained schools policy, we found little evidence to indicate that parents experienced greater participation in the governance or general life of their school (Power *et al.* 1994). Parents usually took part in the voting process if they had children at the school, and most of them that we interviewed had voted in favour of 'opting out'. Yet we gained little impression that their support was based on any desire to participate more fully in the future direction of the school. Indeed, for many parents their backing was more a reflection of loyalty to the headteacher than the result of deliberation on issues surrounding opting out. In schools where the headteacher was heavily involved in promoting grant-maintained status, our data supported Rogers's (1992) argument that parents often constitute little more than 'ballot-fodder'. Our interviews with parent users of both grant-maintained and LEA schools indicated that the different degree of autonomy experienced by each type of school had no significant bearing on levels of parental involvement. In fact, more parents from LEA self-managing schools (over 50 per cent) claimed to be involved with their child's school than those using ones that had opted out (44 per cent). In other words, there seemed to be no relationship between the status of the school and the extent to which it involved parents, thus raising doubts about the claim that the more powers are devolved to the level of the school, the more likely it is for that school to involve parents in increasingly imaginative ways.

In contrast to Nathan's (1996) confident predictions, we did not find that the grant-maintained schools policy was providing new opportunities for communities that have been poorly provided for in the past. In England, our own survey of the early grant-maintained schools reveals that the majority were situated in leafy suburbs rather than inner-city areas (Fitz et al. 1993). Similarly, one of the most striking features of the charter schools movement in California is the degree to which it tends to attract to it parents and teachers who respectively live and work in relatively privileged communities. As Grutzik et al. (1995: 18) show on the basis of demographic information derived from census data, 'the communities surrounding charter schools [in California] are primarily white and have income levels at or above the city and county averages.' It would appear that any new opportunities are being colonized by the already advantaged, rather than the 'losers' identified by Chubb and Moe.

Lay representation in self-managing schools

Within many of the reforms, community involvement has been conceived in terms of enhancing local representation in the management of existing institutions. As we stated in Chapter 2, in England and Wales the 1986 and 1988 Education Acts brought about changes to the composition and responsibilities of the governing bodies of primary and secondary schools. Schools operating under local management are now legally required to have a governing body consisting of representatives from parents of the school's students, teachers at the school and people appointed by the LEA. Parent governors are elected by parents of registered students at the school and serve for a period of four years. This core membership is encouraged to co-opt on to the governing body additional people drawn from the local community who might be thought of as having something useful to contribute, in particular individuals with 'business' interests.

School governing bodies must meet at least once in every term, which, in practice, means at least three times in any one school year. They are required to undertake a multitude of duties, of which the following are arguably the most important: they are responsible for the general conduct of the school; they must ensure that the curriculum of the school meets the requirements of the National Curriculum; they have delegated responsibility for managing the school budget; they must take part in procedures for selecting and appointing staff; and they must make information about the curriculum of the school and students' achievements available to parents. The aim is to devolve as many decisions as possible to schools by shifting resources from central administration to school budgets managed by governors and head teachers.

Governing bodies of grant-maintained schools share many of the same responsibilities and features as those operating within the LEA sector. For example, they too include teacher and parental representatives as well as people from the local community, although some of the latter are required to have experience of 'business' and the number of serving parents is greater. Similarly, like their counterparts in LEA schools, the governors of grant-maintained schools are expected to draw up and monitor the curriculum and manage the budget. Unlike LEA school governors, grant-maintained governors are required to exercise full responsibility for the school budget. The school receives a maintenance grant which is based on the total amount of funding it would have enjoyed had it remained under LEA control. Grant-maintained school governors are accountable for the effective management of all this money, which they use to pay the teachers and other staff for whom they act as employer, buy books, equipment and so on, fund the upkeep of the premises and provide essential services such as school meals for students and advisory support for teachers.

Outlining these responsibilities reveals the limited nature of community participation. As Johnson (1989: 115) argues, although recent policies have afforded new opportunities, these are narrow in scope: 'the ambition appears to be to abolish the local politics of education, by reducing it to an economics'. The form of participation which the new self-managing schools require is primarily financial rather than genuinely democratic. Of the approximately 75,000 parents currently serving as governors of locally maintained schools in England and Wales, it is estimated that roughly 20 per cent come from a business background. The proportion of businessmen and women who are co-opted or who serve on grant-maintained schools' governing bodies is likely to be substantially higher. Not only has the delegation of budgets increased the financial responsibilities of governors, but the imposition of the National Curriculum has taken out of their hands many of the issues connected to teaching and learning which they may have previously debated.

Just as increasing target-setting and evaluation by the state has reoriented the work of the headteacher and principal along the lines of chief executive officers, there has been some pressure for boards of governors to act like boards of directors. In a few cases this has led to open conflict between boards and headteachers, most notably in Stratford in east London (Anon 1992). Elsewhere, there is rather more evidence of the marginalization of some governors, in particular those who bring no financial expertise. There has always been a serious power differential between professionals and lay participants, but this is being underscored by the new responsibilities. Unless governors contribute to the managing and marketing of the school, it would appear that they are seen to have little to offer. Of course, as we saw in Chapter 4, there are variations in the ways in which headteachers respond to the demands placed on them and their schools. For example, Grace (1995: 89) identified a group of headteachers of LEA-maintained schools who were 'prepared to share their powers of leadership with newly constituted governing bodies and welcomed this possibility as a necessary development in the culture of English schooling'. For such headteachers, 'the more active involvement of school governors in leadership and management enriched and strengthened the cultural, personal and material resources available for educational developments within the school' (ibid.). But these headteacher-democrats are exceptional. Most, it seems, prefer to adopt a 'strong, patriarchal authority' stance towards the lay membership of the governing body and eschew radical redistributions of power in its direction.

Grace's conclusion here is echoed in the research of Deem *et al.* (1995). They investigated longitudinally the working patterns and organization of a cross-section of governing bodies of ten self-managing primary and secondary schools drawn from two contrasting LEAs in England. Their conclusion is unequivocal: 'governing schools has become an important arena for the exercise of citizenship. It is however an imperfect one because, while there has been a numerical redistribution in tipping the balance from the "bureau professionals" to the lay governors, the latter have not gained power over schooling in any real sense, let alone helped the communities that they are supposed to represent to gain power' (Deem *et al.* 1995: 62). This finding is endorsed by other researchers, notably Levačić (1995) and Thomas and Martin (1996), all of whom stress the degree to which governing bodies under self-management are more or less at the mercy of edicts originating with the headteacher and other senior school managers. Even when lay governors have opinions they wish to express, it seems that they face great difficulty in making their 'voice' heard, let alone in having their views taken seriously. A part of the problem here is the knowledge that most lay governors draw upon in the deliberations of the governing body. As Deem *et al.* (1995: 85) stress, when it bears on educational institutions and processes, it tends to be 'incomplete, fragmented and, on occasion, inaccurate'. Consequently, the more expert and informed perspectives of the headteacher and the teacher governors tend to hold centre stage and carry more weight. This factor, combined with evidence that indicates that women and ethnic minority lay governors are sometimes discriminated against in terms of how much they are drawn into discussion and their views positively sought, or that they have insufficient confidence to assert them uninvited, ensures that the professional, or perhaps more accurately, managerialist, interests dominate in most circumstances.

But this is hardly surprising if one considers that educational self-management allocates increased managerial powers to headteachers who, by virtue of their new roles, become the main conduit for all significant information coming into and going out of the school. This capacity enables them to manage and out-manoeuvre lay governors should they wish to do so. To that extent the reforms have increased rather than reduced some forms of professional control and thus contributed little to empowering other communities of interest. As Deem *et al.* (1995: 155) conclude: 'merely enabling new groups to become governors does not necessarily empower them. The persistence of engendered and ethnicized organizational forms and practices, and the difficulties of dislodging patterns of . . . teacher and headteacher dominance over the administration of schools, have provided a formidable set of obstacles.'

In New Zealand, too, the experience of educational self-management has involved passing new responsibilities to lay people, who are much more involved than hitherto in the administration of local schools. As we indicated in Chapter 2, the key element of these reforms has been the creation of boards of trustees to govern schools, which mostly comprise elected parent representatives, who outnumber a minority professional interest made up of the school principal and a staff representative. There is also provision in the case of secondary schools for student representation. Boards of trustees share some of the responsibilities of their governing body counterparts in England and Wales. Again these are often dominated by managerial and financial concerns. For example, they are expected to manage a delegated budget and to appoint the principal and staff. But, as we pointed out above, there is a crucial operational difference. Unlike those in England and Wales, self-managing schools in New Zealand each have a 'charter', which is drawn up and agreed between the trustees and central government. The charter, which includes educational aims and objectives and targets, is a form of contract that reads and looks like a mission statement. The trustees are made accountable by central government for setting and overseeing the policies that will meet the educational aims they have set for themselves in their charter.

At one level, the New Zealand reforms might seem to offer more hope for the inclusion of hitherto underrepresented communities. As we noted in Chapter 2, the policy context for their introduction was very different to that which gave rise to the implementation of LMS and grant-maintained status in England and Wales. First, unlike the English experience, the reforms in New Zealand, from the outset, put great stress on equity and on improving the educational provision and life chances of children who historically had not been as well served by the school system as others. Second, a guiding principle in the initial implementation of school self-management in New Zealand was the desire to foster a close working partnership between lay members of the community, for which read chiefly parents of children at the school, and the professionals at the school level. Despite these considerations, the impact of the reforms on community involvement in the running of schools in New Zealand shows many similarities with what has happened in England and Wales in the wake of its school restructuring initiatives. There is little evidence, for example, that the membership of boards of trustees is sufficiently representative of the local school population. According to Wylie (1994), the shift to self-management in New Zealand has not led to an increase in the involvement of people from low-income groups in the running of particular schools.

Gordon's (1995) study of ten schools operating under the reforms similarly concludes that insufficient attention is being paid to adequate community representation on boards of trustees. Board members, she says, are 'mostly male and overwhelmingly ... European' (p. 65), and dominated, even in working-class communities, by middle-class representation. She also comments negatively on the manner in which the desire to include trustees with business experience is compromising claims for representation by minority, in particular Maori and Pacific Island or, groups.

On the other hand, Wylie (1994), mirroring Grace (1995), is able to report the existence of mainly good working relations between professional teaching staff and voluntary trustees, though how this impacts on the nature of school decision-making is less clear. In the course of our work on grant-maintained schools in England, for instance, we found that 'good' relations were those in which governors supported rather than challenged professional judgements. Golby and Brigley (1989) found similar process at work in the governing bodies of LEA schools. The results of Wylie's (1994) survey do not indicate either way the extent to which principals actually share power with lay trustees or seek ways of subverting their majority influence. However, she is more certain about the patterns of school involvement by parents who are not trustees. This shows little significant change over the period of the reforms, 'indicating that something more than a shift to school self-management alone is needed to bring [them] into schools' (Wylie 1994: 86). Moreover, although the reforms were intended to increase educational opportunity for disadvantaged groups, it is the schools in low-income areas which appear 'to be unable to benefit from [their] emphasis on parental support' (ibid.). Relatedly, parental contribution in general to policy formation 'remains limited', although boards of trustees seem to be increasingly responsive through 'holding public meetings, setting up working groups, or taking issues to others beyond the school itself' (Wylie 1994: 112).

This last finding, on the other hand, needs to be set alongside the outcomes of a recently finished single-site case study of a New Zealand high school which concludes that, while parent-elected boards of trustees and policies of school choice give parents in principle the right to influence aspects of school policy and practice, there is a considerable gap between this formal mandate and the emergence of attitudes and skills required on the part of school personnel to make this a practical reality (see Robinson and Timperley 1996).

The size and complexity of educational systems and their administration in the USA mean that it is not possible to give any comprehensive coverage of comparable developments in that country. Charter schools are required to outline how their governance structures will ensure parental involvement, but there is little research on the outcomes of the various arrangements. For an American example it may be more instructive to look towards Chicago, where schools councils have been established as part of that city's attempt to foster systemic school improvement. Indeed, the Chicago reforms are sometimes upheld as a strong expression of 'community control' (Ogawa and White 1994).

In 1988, the Chicago public schools embarked on a course of reform that gave each of the system's 530 schools increased responsibility for managing its own affairs. A central feature of this reform was parental empowerment, the main vehicle for which is the local schools council (LSC). Each school is governed by one. It is a mostly elected body consisting of six parents, two community representatives, one student (two in high schools), two teachers and the principal. The Chicago reform therefore has a strong democratic thrust to it. Indeed, Elmore (1991: vii) argues that, while it has 'elements of both regulatory and professional control, it is mainly based on a theory of democratic control'. Certainly it seems to move beyond the notion of school and system improvement through professional empowerment to a model that puts far more emphasis on parental and community empowerment in achieving this end.

The LSCs in Chicago are probably the nearest equivalent in the USA to governing bodies in England and Wales or boards of trustees in New Zealand. Like the latter, they have a majority of parents and have hitherto had responsibility for a much smaller proportion of the school budget than English and Welsh governing bodies. After initial suggestions that LSCs might hire and fire principals at will, they have generally concentrated on buildings and health and safety issues, though they have also sometimes taken a key role in relation to equal opportunities. Lewis and Nakagawa (1995) suggest, however, that most parents have assumed supportive 'enablement' roles rather than being genuinely empowered by involvement with the LSCs. And, ironically, the few parents on the LSCs who seemed to adopt an 'empowerment' stance were white, middle-class males.

A report by Sebring et al. (1995) suggests that the reforms have brought better ties to the community in a number of Chicago schools, without threatening principal and teacher responsibility for professional matters. Forty-three per cent of teachers felt that the reforms had had a positive impact on relations with the community, and this seems to have been the single most significant outcome. Only about a third of teachers reported other changes in practice that might be expected to bring eventual benefits in learning outcomes, and these were concentrated in about a third of elementary schools, while the impact of the reforms on high schools has remained hard to discern at all. As with other forms of site-based management, the Chicago version seems so far to have changed the form of governance without having that widespread impact on outcomes predicted by its advocates. Even more pessimistic is the conclusion of Lewis and Nakagawa (1995: 168) who argue that 'even if reformers alter the indicia of success to equal simply community participation, the Chicago school reform falls short – because participation alone has not led to empowerment in any real terms'. They regard it as having had more to do with the politics of racial inclusion and the defusing of conflict, and argue that, whatever the intention, 'the very participation of the parents legitimizes the professionals' grip on policy making and school operations' (p. 149).

Since 1984, most state education systems in Australia have moved towards the introduction of devolved management, entailing a significant delegation of decision-making responsibility to the level of individual schools. This move towards schools as more autonomous units of decision-making is seen by its supporters as both more democratic and more equitable in terms of serving parents more directly and being able to prioritize according to local community needs. One plank in this development has been the emergence of attempts to foster greater community and parental participation in the running of local schools. This has taken a variety of forms. States such as South Australia and Queensland, for example, have long experience of using school boards or councils as key sites for the deliberation of curriculum policy, although their efforts in this direction have been seriously compromised by centralizing tendencies which involve increased state-wide monitoring of student achievement, teacher evaluation and prescriptive policy directives. Much of the localized power, in any event, appears to lie with the principal rather than teachers and parents. Moreover, the actual structural relationship between schools and parent bodies within devolved systems of educational management in Australia varies considerably, with some states – New South Wales for example – having made few if any moves to establish school councils of any description.

Victoria provides an example of the various ways in which representation can be defined, controlled and eventually removed according to shifting political contexts. Initially, as we indicated in Chapter 2, there were two representative committees in schools, the local administrative committee (LAC) and the curriculum committee (CC). Formalized through industrial agreements negotiated between the state authorities and the teacher unions in Victoria, which previously had thrown their collective weight behind the successful election of a Labor administration, these committees were introduced as a means of providing increased opportunities for teachers and parents to deliberate on issues of mutual concern. They were subsequently, and speedily, dispensed with by the incoming Liberal–National government, less inclined than its Labor predecessor to forge close working links with the teacher unions – particularly when it was embarking on extensive cuts in funding.

Watkins and Blackmore's (1993) closely observed case study of representative committees in one Victorian secondary high school does not lend much support to those who might want to look nostalgically at the work of LACs as a significant embodiment of the democratic control of schools. For a start, most of the issues deliberated appear to be ones close to the hearts of teachers; parental concerns were rarely discussed, as was the case with issues to do with equality of opportunity. On the other hand, despite these weaknesses they provided at least one arena in which issues of policy could be discussed by both professionals and lay members. Indeed, their continued informal survival is testimony to the need for such a forum to exist.

The demise of the representative committees in Victoria also illustrates the extent to which governments will intervene to remove interference from the smooth running of the restructured system, especially when they perpetuate old-style union and welfare ideologies. Although these bodies can hardly be characterized as subversive or obstructive, inasmuch as they lacked executive 'teeth', neither were they seen as contributing in any useful way to the restructuring.

Although Victoria provides an extreme example of the rhetorical rather than real promotion of community involvement, many of the measures examined in this book are based on the need to enhance individual rather than collective involvement. That is to say, while parents may be represented within policies as part of a broad community of interest, on occasions wielded in opposition to the power of the education profession, it is their entitlement as champions of their own children's education which is increasingly the more dominant theme.

Parents as 'partners' with schools

As discussed above, within each of our countries there is a shift towards competence- or outcome-based assessment as a means of accountability to both the government and parents. In line with transforming the parental role to one of consumer, some policies have provisions which seek to increase parental entitlements to be informed of, and involved in, their own children's education. In England and Wales, for instance, the government has developed *The Parent's Charter* (DfE 1994), which outlines parents' rights to reports on their children's progress and regular independent inspections. Pronouncements concerning the need for parents to be involved in their children's education are nothing new. Recent education policy, however, signals a further reformulation of the role of parents from one which concerns their duties to one which emphasizes their rights. Whereas, in the past, discussions surrounding parents and schools focused on how parents should fulfil their responsibilities as co-educators, the discourse which underlies much current thinking increasingly outlines the obligation of schools to fulfil their responsibilities towards parents. Yet, although these measures are usually presented as a mechanism by which market forces make schools more accountable to parents, in some cases the notion of partnership is used to make parents more accountable to schools. It is possible that we are seeing not just the commodification of students (Gewirtz *et al.* 1995) but also the commodification of parents.

As mentioned in Chapter 6 and more fully explored in Chapter 8, the development of quasi-markets in education is leading to a situation in which 'successful' schools are consolidating their market position through 'cream-skimming'. The rise of 'contracts' between schools and parents provides one mechanism to assist schools in this process. MacLeod (1996) comments that, despite the talk of 'partnership', home–school contracts are as much about ensuring that parents have the 'right' dispositions towards school policies such as discipline and homework. He cites the leader of a headteachers' association who sees such agreements 'as a very useful additional support for schools where parents are failing to encourage their children or acknowledge the school's disciplinary policy. No parent has anything to fear from signing it – only parents who want to be difficult' (MacLeod 1996: 2). Where signing this contract forms part of the enrolment procedure, it not only ensures that schools can make particular demands from parents in the future, but also provides a means of excluding those who are not seen as assets.

In the USA, the potential for weeding out 'difficult' parents is also a feature of the contracts between parents and charter schools. These can involve parents promising to invest substantial amounts of time and money. The main admissions requirement in many of California's charter schools is that parents be committed to supporting their children and the school, but the nature of this support can take different forms. In some proposals they have to attend orientation meetings at the beginning of the school year and subsequently to sign an agreement or contract in which they commit themselves to a minimum of from two to three hours of school service per month (Dianda and Corwin 1994). Becker et al.'s (1995) study of Californian charter schools confirms they have better records than most other publicly funded schools in getting parents to engage in fund-raising, attend meetings and take on leadership roles. The role of parents as financiers is evident in a number of charter school prospectuses. For instance, the Palisades School in Los Angeles has implemented a 'booster' programme in which parents are graded according to the amount they donate. Levels of membership are ranked 'supporter' ($5–99), 'contributor', 'sponsor', 'benefactor' and 'patron', and ultimately 'dolphin circle' status for the price of $1000 plus.

It is probably too early to assess the extent to which charter schools will become increasingly socially selective. While Medler and Nathan (1995) suggest that charter schools recruit a high proportion of 'at-risk' students, both Becker et al. (1995) and Grutzik et al. (1995) argue that some of their features, such as the emphasis on parental involvement, may have the effect of excluding students from certain disadvantaged groups. As Grutzik et al. (1995: 20) comment, 'we worry that for some families these kinds of requirements are heavy burdens given the nature of their economic situations, their cultural perspectives on schooling, and their family obligations. Certain families, for example those in low-income brackets who work long hours, have fewer transportation options, or speak limited English, may never be part of charter school communities. Does charter school legislation allow schools to say that they only want children from families that hold the same values and priorities that they do?' Becker et al. (1995: 18) make this argument equally sharply: 'what we perceive to be occurring . . . is that [charter] schools are being organized to exclude students based on a new criterion of undesirability . . . The criterion being chosen is not the private school's criterion of "ability to pay", nor is it based on academic ability, test score performance or record of behavior, nor on racial or ethnic membership . . . Instead, it is the criterion of having supportive and educationally involved parents.' If charter schools do become increasingly selective, this would certainly be consistent with our research on city technology colleges in England. Even though these schools are expected to have a pupil composition which reflects that of the surrounding neighbourhood, they appear to adopt definitions of 'merit' that benefit members of some minority ethnic groups rather than others. In particular, there have been claims that they favour Asian pupils at the expense of Afro-Caribbean ones (Whitty et al. 1993).

Conclusion

Developments around community and parental involvement in systems of schools of choice are highly complex. Neo-liberals might argue that none of the measures discussed above has been sufficiently robust to tackle the dominance of the education profession – which continues to protect its own vested interests at the expense of others. However, as we saw in Chapter 5, this paints too simple a picture, for teachers are also struggling to find some sort of voice within the current wave of reforms. It seems more likely that, as schools become increasingly driven by central government demands and market forces, the relationship between communities and schools becomes redefined. Both pressures lead to conditions in which the kind of deliberation that many progressive educators and community groups fought for in the 1970s and 1980s is just no longer viable. The economic imperatives of the state militate against the establishment of alternative schools, while the evaluative needs of target-setting, together with the cultural preferences of the neo-conservatives, limit the input of lay members to helping managers to manage. Although professionals have often devalued the contributions of underrepresented communities, the current climate endorses the perception that the only 'outsiders' who can make a useful input to schools are those with professional expertise – more often than not, white, male and middle class. It also emphasizes the value of individual rather than collective community contributions.

Although little research has looked at the ways in which the composition of school governing bodies is being increasingly differentiated, it would seem likely that the most socially advantaged schools will also be able to draw on more expertise from their communities. Thus, it is unlikely that community involvement as currently conceived will effect a radical repositioning of Chubb and Moe's 'winners' and 'losers'. As Gordon (1993) has demonstrated in the case of New Zealand, community empowerment has severe limitations in this respect, since communities are far from equally endowed with the material and cultural resources for self-management of their schools. Lewis and Nakagawa (1995: 172) conclude from their Chicago research that 'the exogenous factors that lead to the failure of the minority poor in schools . . . would seem to require more than a change in school governance can deliver.'

The differential ability of some groups to pursue their own interests at the expense of others, even if only at the local level, has led some to suggest that the way forward is to remove forms of collective representation altogether. For instance, Raywid (1994a) advocates 'focus' schools, built around specific educational or ethical principles, partly because they *do not* generally seek to engage parents and the community in school governance. Parental entitlements come from the right to choose rather than the right to participate. However, as we discuss in the next chapter, there is a substantive body of research that indicates that unequal cultural and material resources feature as much in the process of choosing a school and being offered a place as they do in processes of governance and participation.

Part III

PROBLEMS AND

PROSPECTS IN THE

POLITICS OF

EDUCATION

8 EFFECTIVENESS, EFFICIENCY AND EQUITY

This chapter draws together findings about the consequences of devolution and choice for effectiveness, efficiency and equity in the school system. It begins with a critical review of the relationship said to exist between devolving decision-making to schools and the promotion of institutional effectiveness. It then examines evidence that indicates that self-managing schools may be better able to promote efficiency in resource use, before looking at their more questionable role in fostering greater equality of opportunity. The chapter proceeds to relate changes under way within schools to those between schools in deregulated systems of provision, where self-management becomes articulated with parental choice to create quasi-markets in education services. In particular, it looks at the likely impact of such developments on the range of school provision in terms of increasing diversity and hierarchy. We consider these issues from two directions: changes in the student composition of schools and changes in the nature of provision on offer.

Self-managing status and school effectiveness

In Chapter 6 we reviewed the evidence presently available on the impact of recent restructuring on student performance. The general conclusion was that there were insufficient grounds to claim that self-managing schools are currently enhancing student attainment. So, while it is clear that self-management results in changes to certain school processes, there is considerable ambiguity about how or whether these have positive consequences for student outcomes. Levačić (1995: 105) concludes that 'There is very little evidence . . . of local management [of schools] stimulating any significant changes in the way schools operate with respect to their core technology of teaching and learning.' Thomas and Martin (1996: 28) concur, remarking that 'delegation is no guarantee of improvement'. Nor, it appears, is it a sufficient or even neces-sary condition for innovation generally. On the contrary, the English experi-ence of educational self-management indicates that the devolution of financial and other decisions to schools is as likely to encourage attempts to conserve or reinvent the past (see Halpin *et al.* 1997a on this theme), particu-larly in the areas of curriculum policy and delivery. On this basis, we are more inclined, then, to the view expressed by Knight (1993: 136) that, 'although financial delegation appears to give schools greater freedom for major inno-vation, there is little evidence yet that this is occurring.'

These findings question the claim that a good case for educational self-management can be 'argued on the basis of findings from studies of school effectiveness' (Caldwell and Spinks 1988: 8). A recent review (Sammons *et al.* 1995: 8) of school effectiveness research identifies 'eleven factors for effective schools'. These include:

- the professional leadership role played by senior managers, but the princi-pal in particular;
- the existence of consensus on the aims and values of the school;
- a concentration on the quality and quantity of teaching and learning;
- purposeful teaching;
- supportive relations and cooperation between home and schools;
- an ethos which fosters continuous professional development.

There is little to suggest that these characteristics are found in self-managing schools more frequently than in those still under local democratic control. Indeed, two school effectiveness studies in England, both of which predate the introduction of local management, one based on secondary schools (Rutter *et al.* 1979), the other on primary schools (Mortimore *et al.* 1988), indicate that schools can operate very successfully in the absence of auton-omous status. Of course, it could be argued that the more successful schools in these studies might have achieved even higher standards if they had been managed as autonomous institutions. But there is no way of knowing that.

In relation to the specific attributes cited above, the role of leadership has certainly become more significant in self-managing schools. However, as we discussed in Chapter 4, it is often managerialist in orientation rather than the participative approach identified as a key feature of effective schools. Chapter 5 revealed little evidence of consensus within self-managing schools – indeed, there seems to be a growing gap between management and staff. Oppor-tunities for professional development for teachers appear to be threatened rather than enhanced by the delegation of budgets to schools. There is cer-tainly a concentration on the *quantity* of teaching and learning within many of the schools that have been researched, but this tends to be in response to centrally determined curricula. The demands of these programmes, and the extra administration entailed, may be damaging the *quality* of teaching and learning. As Chapter 6 indicated, there is a narrowing of the scope of the cur-riculum and a concentration on assessment. Nor is there much, even in the Chicago experience, which emphasizes this aspect of reform, to suggest that relations between schools and their communities are transformed through self-managing status (Chapter 7).

Supporters of self-managing status might argue that it is the combined imposition of government imperatives and market forces that undermines the capacity of schools to be the kind of institutions outlined within the effective schools literature. However, it is also worth questioning the principles and premises that underpin school effectiveness research itself. All the attributes outlined above seem self-evidently positive, but they may constitute the *consequences* rather than the *basis* of 'successful' educational practice. As Gray and Wilcox (1995: 221) conclude, following their exhaustive review of the field, 'often what has been identified [as making a difference] are literally correlates rather than causes of school effectiveness . . . the so-called "key" factors may only explain part of the variance between schools (rather than all of it) and consequently represent, at best, partial causes'. Indeed, for all its apparent statistical sophistication, the best that Chubb and Moe's (1990) strident defence of autonomous schooling is able to demonstrate is that their data on particular 'organizational factors' explain only about 5 per cent of the variation in student outcome scores.

External characteristics of schools account for far more variation in school performance than organizational features. By concentrating on the internal processes, the work on school effectiveness and school improvement fails 'to explore the relationship of specific practices to wider social and cultural constructions and political and economic interests' (L. Angus 1993b: 335). This lack of contextualization can lead to a false optimism, exaggerating the extent to which local agency can challenge structural inequalities. As Angus argues, the lack of engagement with sociological theory can mean that the discourse of school effectiveness is trapped in 'a logic of common sense which allows it . . . to be appropriated into the Right's hegemonic project' (L. Angus 1993b: 343). Thus, while those working in the areas of school improvement and school effectiveness would probably distance themselves from the values of neo-liberalism, there is more common ground than appears at first sight. Both the New Right and the school effectiveness lobby take the discursive repositioning of schools as autonomous self-improving agencies at face value, rather than recognizing that, in practice, the atomization of schooling too often merely allows advantaged schools to maximize their advantages. For those schools ill-placed to capitalize on their market position, the devolution of responsibility can lead to the devolution of blame.

Efficiency, equity and educational self-management

Whether increased funding leads to increased performance is a highly contentious and politically loaded issue – as is evident in the fierce debate between Greenwald *et al.* (1996a, b) and Hanushek (1996). Greenwald *et al.*'s (1996a) re-examination of existing US research into the effect of school resources on student achievement leads them to suggest that money *does* make a difference, and that lack of clear gains in student performance within public education arises from worsening social conditions rather than unproductive schools. However, Hanushek (1996) disputes their findings, and argues that there is no straightforward relationship between school resources and student performance: that the issue is one of more effective use rather than amount of funding. Scornful of a continuation of what he terms 'pure resource policies', Hanushek suggests that schools need to be subjected to more decentralized performance incentives.

Part of the problem, as Hanushek himself argues, is that there are currently few conclusive data about the economics of school resourcing. As Thomas and Martin (1996: 23) observe, because 'we do not know . . . precisely how pupils learn and the appropriate mix of resources [needed] to support that learning', it is at the present time impossible to determine technically if schools are being more cost-effective in ways that would satisfy an economist. As with student performance, it is certainly too simplistic to relate any improvements in attainment to a more expeditious use of resources. It is often difficult to disentangle the mode of funding from the scale of funding. Take, for instance, the grant-maintained schools policy in England and Wales. In the policy's earlier days, grant-maintained schools were to be funded on a 'level playing field' with LEA schools in order to establish the benefits which accrue from self-managing status. However, as the number of schools opting out failed to match political objectives, significant cash incentives were made available. While the rapid increase in the number of grant-maintained schools served political purposes, the differential level of funding between the grant-maintained and LEA sector obscured the issue of institutional efficiency and effectiveness. Thus, even if we concede that grant-maintained schools are doing better (and as indicated in Chapter 6 we need to be cautious of any such claims), we cannot tell whether this stems as much from their advantageous funding as from their autonomy.

As we observed above, there are many claims that educational self-management is good for resource management. Thomas and Martin (1996), for example, conclude that in all the LEA and grant-maintained schools they studied, although in some more than in others, there were in place procedures designed to ensure that resource decisions were consistent with overall strategy. Moreover, in at least three cases they concluded that senior managers were 'using their responsibilities over resources . . . in ways that [were] educationally successful' (p. 179). Much the same can be gleaned from Levačić's (1995) study of local management. She reports that headteachers 'could on the whole justify their budget decisions in relation to their aims for the school' and 'provide examples of measures taken to improve cost-efficiency' through 'economizing and instituting better value-for-money purchasing procedures' and making 'changes in the mix in which resources are used' (p. 191). She also notes developments in the increased employment of teaching support staff and the better targeting of specific resources to support particular curriculum developments. Levačić (1995: 162–3) concludes that 'local management has improved efficiency on the *input* side . . . [and] is more successful than LEA administrative allocation in concentrating the resources available on direct teaching and learning.' While this finding articulates well with the claims made by advocates on behalf of school self-management, she also notes 'a lack of strong theoretical argument and empirical evidence' that it actually improves the quality of teaching and learning (p. xi). Nor does it take account of the extra costs that the new reforms have entailed. As is evident from the preceding chapters, new curriculum regulations and marketization can involve substantial investments of time and money by individual schools. Even more importantly, Levačić's study tells us little of the equity consequences of schools' resource allocation decisions. Her investigation, like that of the Birmingham University research team, is mostly silent on this issue, chiefly because it did not strongly feature in her research design.

Levačić (1995) did not find in any of the schools she studied 'any bias towards a less equitable distribution of resources for students with special needs' (p. 195), reporting that headteachers 'expressed concern for the welfare of pupils with special needs and seemed genuine in their desire to fund additional teaching and pastoral time for servicing these needs, once basic mainstream provision had been resourced' (p. 160). Whether the concern was translated into extra provision is difficult to determine. If it was, her findings certainly do not reflect those of Gewirtz *et al.* (1995), who, as we noted in Chapter 6, argue that within their case study schools there was a distribution of resources *away* from pupils with special needs. They also found that self-managing schools were 'increasingly oriented towards meeting the perceived demands of middle-class parents' (p. 189). They claim that, far from an increase in support for less advantaged students, there was an evident trend towards 'the commodification of schooling', in which the emphasis is increasingly not on what schools can do for students, but on what students can do for the school.

So, while we are able to concur that delegating resource management to the level of school may offer the potential to encourage headteachers to allocate proportionally more resources to the socially and educationally disadvantaged, and therefore fulfil the requirements of a needs-based notion of equity (Levin, 1990), this is not an inevitable outcome. On the contrary, many of the early indications from research on how individual self-managing schools operate within market settings suggest quite the opposite.

The equity effects of quasi-markets

Although school autonomy and parental choice are not necessarily linked, we have seen that many current policies seek to bring the two together to create quasi-markets in educational services. We also noted that some commentators claim that these policies provide the best hope of educational advancement for the urban poor, who have been ill-served by social democratic approaches to the provision of education (Moe 1994; Pollard 1995).

In England and Wales, there has been a considerable amount of research looking at both the 'marketization' of public services in general and the impact of policies designed to enhance parental choice in education in particular. These studies have focused on the effects of open enrolment and the provision of opportunities for parents to choose from a greater variety of types of schools, particularly at secondary level, including schools outside LEA control. While some studies have examined the impact of the choice agenda as a whole (Bowe *et al.* 1992; Gewirtz *et al.* 1995; Glatter *et al.* 1997), others, such as those on the Assisted Places Scheme (Edwards *et al.* 1989), city technology colleges (Whitty *et al.* 1993) or grant-maintained schools (Fitz *et al.* 1993), have concentrated on the impact of the new choices that have been made available.

In a substantial study of quasi-markets in British social policy, Le Grand and Bartlett (1993) argue that the reforms in education and housing have been rather more successful than those in health and social care. In a local case study of education, Bartlett (1993) found, like the research reported in Chapters 4 and 5, that the reforms had been welcomed by many headteachers but less so by other teachers. However, he points out that, although parental choice has been increased by open enrolment 'the door is firmly closed once a school [is full]. And by encouraging an increasingly selective admissions policy in [over-subscribed] schools open enrolment may be having the effect of bringing about increased opportunity for cream-skimming and hence inequality' (p. 150). Furthermore, he found that 'those schools which faced financial losses under the formula funding system tended to be schools which drew the greatest proportion of pupils from the most disadvantaged section of the community' (p. 149). Thus, whatever gains may have emerged from the reforms in terms of efficiency and responsiveness to some clients, there were serious concerns about their implications for equity.

Le Grand and Bartlett (1993) take the view that 'cream-skimming' poses the biggest threat to equity in the sorts of 'quasi-markets' created by the Thatcher and Major governments. This danger is clearly demonstrated in the important series of studies by researchers at King's College London on the operation of quasi-markets in the capital. In an early study, Bowe *et al.* (1992) concluded that schools were competing to attract greater cultural capital and thus higher yielding returns. Subsequently, Gewirtz and Ball (1995) and Gewirtz *et al.* (1995) have shown schools seeking students who are 'able', 'gifted', 'motivated and committed' and middle class, with girls and children with South Asian backgrounds being seen as particular assets in terms of their potential to enhance test scores. The growth of the 'girl-friendliness' of coeducational schools was one of the unanticipated findings of this research. The least desirable clientele include those who are 'less able' or have special educational needs, especially emotional and behavioural difficulties, as well as children from working-class backgrounds and boys, unless they also have some of the more desirable attributes.

In these circumstances, popular schools are tempted to become increasingly selective, both academically and socially, through both overt and covert methods of selection. Where there is no chance of expanding, it appears that they try to capitalize upon and enhance the scarcity value of their product. It is noticeable that the most successful and elite private schools in England did not choose to expand during the 1980s, despite the demand for their product by the *nouveaux riches* of the Thatcherite era. Similarly, although the government provided the possibility of expansion for successful and popular public schools, some indicated that they were not interested in this option as it would threaten the ethos they have developed.

Most studies of education markets confirm that 'cream-skimming' is a major issue, though the composition of the 'cream' takes a particular form in English education. Bartlett and Le Grand (1993) suggest that cream-skimming involves favouring those clients who will bring the greatest return for the least investment, thus leading to discrimination by providers against the more expensive users. It might seem that in education this would involve going for the middle of the market, as the gifted and those defined as having special educational needs will cost more to process. As we indicated in Chapter 6, there *is* some evidence of discrimination against children with special educational needs. Bartlett (1993) argues that only if the market price varies with the needs of the client will such discrimination not take place. In other words, funding formulae need to be weighted to give schools an incentive to take more expensive children. The current premium paid for children with special educational needs may not be sufficient if it makes the school less popular with clients who, although bringing in less money, bring in other desirable attributes. Bowe *et al.* (1992) and Vincent *et al.* (1995) give examples of schools making just this sort of calculation.

However, the academically able do seem to be the 'cream' that most schools seek to attract. Such students stay in the system longer and thus bring in more money, as well as making the school appear successful in terms of its test scores and hence attractive to other desirable clients. Glennerster (1991) suggests that, given the opportunity, most schools will want to become more selective, because taking children who will bring scores down will affect their overall market position. As discussed in Chapter 6, this is especially so when there is imperfect information about school effectiveness, and particularly when only 'raw' test scores are made available, as they currently are in England and Wales.

Le Grand and Bartlett (1993) found lack of information a major limitation within quasi-markets as they currently operate in England. Although scores on National Curriculum tests are only just becoming available, and their publication has been the subject of a dispute with the teacher unions, schools in receipt of public funds were required by the 1980 Education Act to make public the results of school leaving examinations at 16 plus and 18 plus. In recent years, these results for all schools have been published in the national press. However, schools with the highest scores appear best even if other schools enhance achievement more. It remains to be seen whether the introduction of 'value added' measures will change that situation. As we noted in Chapter 6, even these more sophisticated indicators are insufficiently sensitive to distinguish between the vast majority of schools. They are unlikely to reduce the tendency of schools to favour pupils from advantaged backgrounds.

Either way, as long as schools tend to be judged on a unidimensional scale of academic excellence, many commentators have predicted that, rather than choice leading to more diverse and responsive forms of provision, as claimed by many of its advocates, it will reinforce the existing hierarchy of schools based on academic test results and social class. Walford and Miller (1991) suggest that this will run from elite private schools through city technology colleges, grant-maintained schools, voluntary aided (church) schools and a rump of LEA schools providing mainly for children with special educational needs – the ultimate residualized or safety net provision.

Within English culture, schools judged to be good, and hence oversubscribed, are most likely to be academically selective schools or formerly selective schools with a persisting academic reputation. They are also likely to have socially advantaged intakes. Although parents may choose new types of schools because they are different from the standard local comprehensive school, that does not seem to lead in England and Wales to a truly diversified system. Even if the failure of the reforms to promote more genuine diversity has been exacerbated by a restrictive National Curriculum embodying a particularly narrow and nationalistic notion of British culture (Whitty 1992), as we noted earlier, much of the evidence suggests that the operation of choice in a highly stratified society compounds the situation. Those parents who are in a position to choose seem to be choosing schools that are closest to the traditional academic model of education that used to be associated with selective grammar schools. Even new types of school tend to be judged in these terms. Our own research showed many parents choosing city technology colleges, not so much for their high-tech image, but because they were perceived as the next best thing to grammar schools or even elite private schools (Whitty *et al.* 1993).

In this situation, those schools that are in a position to choose often seek to identify their success with an emphasis on traditional academic virtues and thus attract those students most likely to display them. As indicated above, many of the first schools to opt out and become grant-maintained were selective (Fitz *et al.* 1993). A disproportionate number were also single sex with traditional sixth forms – a combination of characteristics which gave the sector an aura of elite status. These features of the sector contribute to an image that it offers a 'better' education than found in LEA-maintained institutions. To that extent, less academically successful GM secondary comprehensive schools have been able vicariously to enhance their reputations, and therefore their middle-class appeal, via the 'success' of the minority of selective schools that make up the sector as a whole. The Grant Maintained Schools Centre has claimed that the sector's test results demonstrate its academic superiority, even though, as we pointed out above, those results are almost certainly determined by the nature of the intakes of the early grant-maintained schools. Some grant-maintained comprehensive schools have reverted to being overtly academically selective, and only those that have clearly failed on traditional academic criteria are likely to risk deviating significantly from the dominant definition of excellence in their curriculum offer. We found no indications of any changes relating to the curriculum or pedagogy (Power *et al.* 1994). Furthermore, Bush *et al.* (1993) suggested that 30 per cent of the grant-maintained 'comprehensive' schools they studied were using covert selection, which is also likely to increase their appearance of academic superiority. In addition, grant-maintained schools have been identified as among those with the highest rates of exclusion of their existing pupils and among the least willing to cater for pupils with special educational needs (Feintuck 1994).

Gewirtz *et al.* (1995: 174) suggest that one effect of the development of an education market in England has been a narrowing of the 'scope' of education by placing 'almost exclusive emphasis on instrumental, academic and cognitive goals'. According to Walford and Miller (1991), even some of those intended beacons of an entirely new form of excellence, the city technology colleges, may be abandoning that distinctiveness in favour of traditional academic excellence. More generally, in a major empirical study of school parental choice and school response, Glatter *et al.* (1997) conclude that there is no evidence so far of choice producing greater diversity in the school system and some evidence of a tendency towards greater uniformity, except where there has been additional government funding to foster the development of specialist technology schools. In other words, it is government intervention rather than parental choice that has brought innovation on the supply side. With regard to hierarchy, Glatter *et al.* find no dramatic movement to date, but certainly no evidence that it has been reduced by the reforms.

Thus, in England, the entrenched prestige of traditionally academic education has produced a persistent devaluing of alternatives. If different versions of schooling have very different exchange values in competition for entry to higher education and to privileged occupations, then the high value placed on traditional academic success makes access to it a positional good and therefore in short supply. Schools seeming to offer the best chance of academic success are likely to be considerably oversubscribed. Where they are, it is the producer who is empowered and it is the consumer who has to establish fitness for the school's purposes, unless there are effective constraints on schools' right to choose.

Furthermore, as long as the notion of fitness remains a narrow one, it is unlikely that those groups that have traditionally performed poorly within the education system will benefit. Behind the superficially appealing rhetoric of choice and diversity, the reforms are resulting in a reduction in choice for many parents rather than the comprehensive empowerment of consumers which markets are supposed by their advocates to produce. While they may be enhancing the educational performance of some children, and certainly that of those schools in which the more advantaged children are concentrated, they seem to be further disadvantaging many of those very groups who were disadvantaged by the previous system. Especially where there are a limited number of schools of choice with a strong market appeal, advantaged parents and advantaged schools tend to search each other out in a progressive segmentation of the market (Ranson 1993).

Walford (1992b: 137) argues that, while choice will lead to better quality schooling for some children, the evidence so far suggests that it will 'discriminate in particular against working class children and children of Afro-Caribbean descent'. Smith and Noble (1995) also conclude from the available evidence that English choice policies are further disadvantaging already disadvantaged groups. Although schools have always been socially and racially segregated, to the extent that residential segregation exists, Gewirtz *et al.* (1995) suggest that choice may well exacerbate this segregation by extending it into previously integrated schools serving mixed localities. Their research indicates that working-class children, and particularly children with special educational needs, are likely to be increasingly 'ghetto-ized' in poorly resourced schools.

This is particularly evident in inner London, where admissions policies have been relaxed. The former Inner London Education Authority used to operate a 'banding' system which sought to ensure that all schools had a reasonable balance of levels of academic ability among their intakes. A recent study (Pennell and West 1995) has suggested that, in the light of the abandonment of this system in many parts of London and an increasing number of autonomous schools operating their own admissions policies, there is a danger of growing polarization between schools. Pennell and West (1995: 14) argue that the new system is serving to reinforce the privilege of 'those parents who are able and prepared to negotiate the complexities [of the system] compared with those who are less willing or less able to do so'.

Such trends are not, however, confined to England. A recent Australian review of such evidence has suggested that 'paradoxically, the market exacerbates differences between schools on the basis of class, race and ethnicity, but does not encourage diversity in image, clientele, organisation, curriculum or pedagogy' (Blackmore 1995: 53). Regardless of the rhetoric of restructuring, which stresses diversity, 'market status is maintained by conforming to the dominant image of a good school as being well uniformed, well-disciplined and academically successful' (Blackmore 1995: 48). And while in Australia a return to selective education in public schools may be less in evidence in some states than in others, schools are certainly being restratified along these lines. The Smithfield Project, a major study of the impact of choice policies in New Zealand, suggests that much the same sort of academic and social polarization is taking place there (Lauder et al. 1994; Waslander and Thrupp 1995). In another New Zealand study (Fowler 1993), schools located in low socio-economic areas were found to be judged negatively because of factors over which they had no influence, such as type of intake, location and problems perceived by parents as linked to these. Wylie (1994) too has noted that schools in low-income areas are more likely to be losing students to other schools. If we could be sure that their poor reputation was deserved, this might be taken as evidence that the market was working well, with effective schools reaping their just rewards. But, as in England, judgements of schools tend to be made on social grounds or narrow academic criteria and with little reference to their overall performance or even their academic effectiveness on value-added measures. Gordon (1994b) points out that 'schools with a mainly middle class and Pakeha (or, increasingly, Asian) population tend to achieve better on national examinations because of the high level of "readiness" and motivation of the pupils, and relatively low levels of social problems that impinge on educational processes' (p. 19). Furthermore, advantaged schools are able to introduce enrolment schemes that 'have a tendency to reinforce their social exclusivity' (p. 18). Yet schools perceived to be poor are not actually closing but are remaining open with reduced rolls, declining funding and low morale, thus producing a self-fulfilling prophecy.

The current funding regime in New Zealand, like that in England, makes it difficult for schools in disadvantaged areas to break out of the cycle of decline. Yet the research studies suggest that many of the differences between schools result from factors largely beyond the control of parents and schools, except the power of advantaged parents and advantaged schools to enhance further their advantage and thus to increase educational inequalities and social polarization. Lauder *et al.* (1995: 53) show that, where schools can choose the students they admit, socio-economic status and ethnic factors 'appear to influence school selection, even when prior achievement has been taken into account'. This is not necessarily an argument against choice, but it is clear that procedures for selection to oversubscribed schools need reconsideration. Significantly, the Smithfield Project also found that, only in one year, where allocations to oversubscribed schools were based on 'balloting' (or drawing lots), did social polarization between popular and unpopular schools decrease.

Wylie (1994, 1995a) reports that the combination of choice and accountability measures has led to schools paying more attention to the attractiveness of physical plant and public image than to changes to teaching and learning, other than the spread of computers. It has also led to increased attention to the information about school programmes and children's progress which reaches parents, changes which 'are clearly not without value in themselves' (1995a: 163). But she also notes that 'they do not seem able to counter or outweigh factors affecting school rolls which lie beyond school power, such as local demographics affected by employment, ethnicity, and class' (Wylie 1995a: 163, citing Gordon 1994a; Waslander and Thrupp 1995).

In the USA, the early association of public school choice with racial desegregation may have ensured that equity considerations continue to play a greater part in education reform than in England and Wales or even New Zealand. Nevertheless, there are considerable concerns about the equity effects of more recent attempts to enhance choice, especially as there is no clear evidence to date of a positive impact on student achievement. The claim by Witte (1990) that there were few, if any, acceptable studies of the effects of choice on student achievement remains largely true today, notwithstanding his own pioneering work in Milwaukee.

What evidence there is about the effects of choice policies on student achievement and equity continues to be at best inconclusive (Plank *et al.* 1993), despite claims by choice advocates that 'the best available evidence' shows that parental choice improves the education of all children, especially low-income and minority students (Domanico 1990). Even some of the more positive evidence from controlled choice districts, such as Cambridge (Rossell and Glenn 1988; Tan 1990) and Montclair (Clewell and Joy 1990), which seemed to show gradual overall achievement gains, is now regarded by Henig (1994) as methodologically flawed, making it difficult to attribute improvements to choice *per se*. Furthermore, although choice has not always led to resegregation as its critics feared, improvements in the racial balance of Montclair and Cambridge schools were most noticeable during periods of strong government intervention. As mentioned in Chapter 6, the East Harlem 'miracle' has not been subjected to adequate scrutiny, even though it has had a special role 'in countering charges that the benefits of choice programs will not accrue to minorities and the poor' (Henig 1994: 142). Overall, Henig (1994), Wells (1993a) and Fuller *et al.* (1996) conclude from exhaustive reviews that the stronger claims of choice advocates cannot be upheld and choice needs to be carefully regulated if it is not to have damaging equity effects.

Private school choice

The evidence with regard to publicly financed private school choice is also contentious, but relevant to our concerns in view of current demands in many countries for an extension of the use of public funds to permit students to attend private schools. In England and Wales, despite a rhetoric of legitimation that emphasized its role in helping children from the inner city, the Assisted Places Scheme has disproportionately attracted children from 'submerged' middle-class families. The evidence from our own evaluation of the scheme (Edwards *et al.* 1989) suggests that, rather than working-class pupils from inner-city comprehensive schools, the majority of its early beneficiaries were children from middle-class homes, many of whom would anyway have attended private schools, selective grammar schools or academically successful comprehensives in suburban areas. Furthermore, the scheme was found to have relatively few minority ethnic pupils in it and least of all from African-Caribbean backgrounds. Even surveys subsequently undertaken to promote the scheme indicate that its existence had yet to penetrate the consciousness of large sections of the population to which it was ostensibly targeted (Marks 1992).

In Sweden, there are serious concerns about the equity effects of enhanced private school choice. Miron (1993) suggests that government funding of private schools is encouraging increased social segregation in urban areas because such schools are able to control the nature of their intakes far more than are municipal schools. In Australia, it is only the presence of the Catholic parochial schools that shields the private sector as a whole from such charges. Even though the funding regime has a significant equity component, there being a large subsidy for Catholic schools and a smaller one for most of the rest, public subsidies to elite private schools are considerably higher than the indirect subsidies that exist in England and Wales. The effect is that public financial assistance has encouraged the growth and legitimation of a sector that caters for a privileged minority, at the expense of competing public schools. Yet, as in England and Wales, the apparent academic superiority of many non-parochial private schools is still largely a product of their privileged intakes (Anderson 1993).

In the United States much of the controversy surrounding the alleged benefits of private schooling centres on the various interpretations of the data from Coleman's high school studies (Coleman *et al.* 1982) and, in particular, the work of Chubb and Moe (1990). As they themselves note, Coleman *et al.*'s (1982) study endorsing the superior performance of America's private schools has been 'pummeled from all angles' (Chubb and Moe 1988: 1086). However, even if it is conceded that that analysis remains intact, there are still significant doubts concerning Chubb and Moe's argument that private schools are better largely as a result of organizational characteristics, 'without recognizing that their findings are contingent on the special character and advantages of private schools in the current system' (Riley 1990: 549). While the data show a consistent but relatively small performance advantage for private schools once background variables have been controlled for, some argue that it is a product of their methodology and that any advantage would disappear with the use of more subtle measures of the cultural differences between low-income families using private and public schools (Henig 1994: 144). Lee and Bryk (1993) accuse Chubb and Moe of a circularity in their argument in support of school choice, and suggest that their conclusions concerning the power of choice and school autonomy are not supported by the evidence as presented. Nevertheless, Bryk *et al.* (1995) claim on the basis of their own work that Catholic schools do impact positively on the performance of low-income families, but they attribute this at least as much to an ethos of strong community values antithetical to the market place as to the espousal of market forces. In any event, critics argue that the socio-economic status of the clientele of Catholic schools is generally above the average and that the figures are affected by leakage into the public sector in the higher grades (Smith and Meier 1995; Witte *et al.* 1995a).

Witte's evaluation of the controversial Milwaukee private school choice experiment, which enables children from poor families to attend private schools at public expense, concludes in its fourth year report that 'in terms of achievement scores . . . students perform approximately the same as MPS [Milwaukee public school] students.' However, attendance of choice children is slightly better and parental satisfaction has been high. For the schools, 'the program has generally been positive, has allowed several to survive, several to expand, and contributed to the building of a new school' (Witte *et al.* 1994). The fifth year report (Witte *et al.* 1995b) reaffirms these conclusions. Although this work has been severely criticized for undermining choice policies (Greene and Peterson 1996), its main conclusion – that the stronger claims made both for and against this type of programme cannot be sustained by this evidence – seems unexceptionable. The scheme is a small and narrowly targeted one and certainly not a basis upon which to judge the likely effects of a more thoroughgoing voucher initiative.

Enhancing equity in choice systems

So far, there is little in these analyses to counter the conclusions of Carnoy (1993) in an overview of historical data about choice in the USA. Even if opportunities are opened up to some families, he argues that policy measures that place an undue emphasis on parental choice will benefit the performance only of high-demand, low-middle-income families and that a large fraction of students, particularly those from low-demand families, are likely to be worse off. This will merely increase the variance in student achievement, with some students decidedly worse off, rather than bringing about the overall improvement envisaged by the exponents of choice.

Wells (1993b) points out that the economic metaphor that schools will improve once they behave more like private, profit-driven corporations and respond to the demands of consumers 'ignores critical sociological issues that make the school consumption process extremely complex'. Some of those issues are explored further in an important contribution to the sociology of school choice by Wells and Crain (1992). That paper and Wells's own research suggest that many choice plans are based on false assumptions about how families behave in the educational market place. This means that competition will certainly not lead to school improvement 'in those schools where students end up because they did not choose to attend a "better" school'. Escape from poor schools will not necessarily emerge from choice plans because 'the lack of power that some families experience is embedded in their social and economic lives' (Wells 1993b: 48). Similarly, Gewirtz *et al.* (1992) suggest that the new arrangements for school choice discriminate against those who have more pressing immediate concerns than being an education 'consumer'. There is no convincing evidence to date that the provision of notional choices of other schools provides a realistic alternative solution for such families. In an unequal society, it seems highly improbable that the sort of market accountability favoured by Chubb and Moe (1992: 13) can replace the need for political action if equity is to be an important consideration.

Walford (1992b: 137) argues that 'the main purpose of the recent moves toward greater choice is not to build a more fair and generous educational system but to put an end to egalitarianism, and rebuild a differentiated educational system that will more closely aid social reproduction.' Furthermore, he suggests that the ideology of choice, which implies that anyone can benefit, acts partially to mask and thus legitimate this process. Whatever the intention, it does seem that this is likely to be the effect of the policies currently being adopted in many countries. Our interim conclusion from the evidence so far available is, like that of Adler who has studied choice policies in Scotland (Adler *et al.* 1989), that there is an urgent need to find a 'better balance between the rights of parents to choose schools for their children and the duties of [public] authorities to promote the education of all children' (Adler 1993: 3). In other words, we need to pay more attention to equity issues through a reassertion of citizen rights alongside consumer rights in education (Whitty 1997a), a theme we address in our final chapter.

Adler (1993) has suggested some revisions to current British policies which would take choice seriously but avoid the most unacceptable consequences of recent legislation. His particular proposals include: retaining local education authorities with a responsibility for formulating admissions policies for all local schools; encouraging schools to develop distinctive characteristics; requiring positive choices on behalf of all children and not only the children of 'active choosers'; involving teachers and older pupils in making decisions which are not necessarily tied to parental preferences; and giving priority in oversubscribed schools to the applicants who are most strongly supported. However, Walford (1992a) advocates that entry to oversubscribed schools should be based on random selection, an approach which is still used in some schools in New Zealand. In the USA, Wells (1990) argues that equitable choice schemes require clear goal statements, outreach work, information and counselling for parents, a 'fair, unrestrictive, non-competitive, and equitable admissions procedure' and provision of adequate transportation for students.

Similar safeguards are recommended in an international study of choice policies in England and Wales, Australia, the Netherlands, New Zealand, Sweden and the United States (OECD 1994). This concluded that, where there is a dominant model of schooling, choice is as likely to reinforce hierarchies as to improve educational opportunities and the overall quality of schooling. It is also argued that demand pressures are rarely enough to produce real diversity of provision, so that positive supply side initiatives are necessary to create real choice. To avoid reinforcing tendencies towards academic and social selection, popular schools may need positive incentives to expand and disadvantaged groups may need better information, better transport and perhaps even privileged access to certain schools. However, Lauder *et al.* (1995) point out that the enhanced information and travel funds alone may have little effect on the deep-rooted tendency of families of low socio-economic status to 'cool' themselves out of high status schools. In our final chapter, we explore more substantial changes in education policy and the nature of educational governance that might be required to help ensure increased democratic involvement in the running of school services, leading to greater collective responsibility for what they provide and for whom.

9 BEYOND
DEVOLUTION AND
CHOICE

The dismantling of bureaucratic control of education provision currently taking place to varying degrees in our five countries represents a significant and far-reaching strategy to reformulate the relationship between governments, schools and parents. The consequences of this restructuring can be explored along a number of fronts. In this book we have been particularly concerned with investigating the ways in which devolution and choice might be redistributing educational opportunities. The evidence we have put forward suggests that recent education policies are doing little to alleviate existing inequalities in access and participation and, in many cases, may be exacerbating them.

Sometimes the picture has been one of continuity rather than change. In terms of community participation, for instance, educational self-management has, in general, and irrespective of national context, failed radically to alter the balance of power between lay and professional stakeholders. Similarly, the devolution of decision-making to the school level has shown no necessary consequences for enhancing teacher autonomy and professionalism and appears to be making little difference to the outcomes of student learning. On the other hand, there do appear to be significant changes in the nature of teachers' work. The changing role of principals and headteachers contributes to a widening gap between managers and the managed. The concentration on performance indicators recasts the curriculum in terms of product rather than process – narrowing the scope of provision and purpose. Perhaps most worrying of all is the welter of evidence on the system-wide effects of articulating self-management with choice-driven funding mechanisms and the marketization of education generally. There seems to be little doubt that such a combination of policies is enhancing the advantages of the already advantaged at the expense of the least well off.

In making this claim, we are, of course, generalizing from the evidence available. We would not wish to deny that there are instances where self-managing status has made a positive difference to the educational experiences of students and teachers. The *Kura Kaupapa Maori* in New Zealand and some of the 'alternative' US charter schools provide examples where self-determination by communities and professionals has brought about innovative and potentially empowering educational environments. However, there are doubts as to the sustainability of such programmes and about the extent to which they can be attributed to the 'new', rather than the 'old', modes of governance. Moreover, these innovative instances need to be set alongside a prevailing pattern of educational conservatism and consolidated hierarchies both within and between schools. In short, the evidence thus far certainly suggests that the recent wave of educational restructuring has failed to facilitate more community involvement, diversify provision, enhance professionalism, increase school effectiveness or widen opportunities on a significant scale. Even where there has been a marginal redistribution of opportunities, bringing gains to specific groups, there is no evidence that current policies are bringing benefits to disadvantaged communities as a whole.

From marketization to privatization?

The Audit Commission (1996) has suggested that the current system in England and Wales may fall between two stools, by being insufficiently planned to permit effective intervention and insufficiently marketized to bring about the benefits claimed by market advocates. Commentators from the radical right see the answer as moving still further towards marketized and even privatized forms of education provision. Indeed, some advocates of market forces have argued that the indifferent performance of the reforms so far is merely evidence that they have not gone far enough. For example, a government minister responsible for the introduction of the Assisted Places Scheme in England used our own research (Edwards *et al.* 1989) showing that it had failed to attract many working-class students as a basis for arguing in favour of a fully fledged voucher scheme (Boyson 1990). Similarly, Moe's (1994: 27) only major criticism of the British reforms was that the government had 'created an open enrolment system in which there is very little to choose from, because the supply of schools is controlled by the LEAs'. In order to free up the supply side, Moe suggests, all schools should become autonomous. Tooley (1996a) favours an even more deregulated system and the abandonment of a centrally prescribed curriculum. In his vision of 'education without the state', he argues that parents and students should be free to determine the kind of schooling they feel suits them best. He envisages lowering the school leaving age and providing all students with a 'lifelong individual fund for education' which they would then be able to spend when and where they saw fit.

Much of the support for moving further towards devolved education provision derives from the alleged benefits of existing private provision. However, as we discussed in Chapter 8, the American evidence with regard to private school choice is contentious. And even if we accept that some children might

benefit from private education, there is little to suggest that extending opportunities to attend private schools more widely would benefit all groups
equally. Witte *et al.* (1995a) have undertaken an analysis of the current social
composition of private and public schools in Wisconsin and conclude that 'an
open-ended voucher scheme would clearly benefit households that are more
affluent than the average household in Wisconsin.' They go on to say that,
although some might believe that making vouchers available to everyone
would open up private schools to the poor, the opposite argument seems
equally plausible. With more money available, private schools that cannot
currently afford to select, such as some of the inner-city private schools in the
Milwaukee choice experiment mentioned in Chapter 8, could become more
selective. The already highly selective schools could then maintain their
advantage by demanding add-on payments in addition to vouchers.

The current Milwaukee programme has generally been undersubscribed and
the schools involved have not been in a position to exercise choice. But elsewhere the combination of oversubscription and self-selection in private schools
suggests that cream-skimming is as much an issue in the USA as in England and
Wales and New Zealand. Smith and Meier (1995: 61) use existing data to test the
school choice hypothesis and conclude that 'competition between public and
private schools appears to result in a cream skimming effect.' Incidentally, they
also argue that there is no reason to expect that such effects will disappear with
greater competition among public schools, especially as some schools would
begin with competitive advantages, an issue they regard as seriously under-
played by Chubb and Moe and other advocates of choice. They predict that
choice could lead to a 'two tier system' similar to that which is developing
among public sector schools in England and Wales and New Zealand.

Some on the right argue that these processes are inevitable in a system
which is only partly privatized. Tooley (1996b) argues that we need a 'one tier
private system' and claims that the potential of markets in education cannot
be properly assessed by looking at the effects of quasi-markets, or what he
prefers to term 'so-called' markets (Tooley 1995). He is right to remind us of
the equity failings of democratic systems. And, of course, empirical research
on current systems does not, indeed in principle could not, show that total
deregulation would not have beneficial effects. Yet the best available evidence
does seem to suggest that going further in the direction of marketization
would be unlikely to yield overall improvements in the quality of education
and might well have damaging equity effects. In their own recent review of the
US evidence, Fuller *et al.* (1996: 200) conclude that 'the idea that choice will
produce better results with less public authority or bureaucracy is highly problematic.' In England, the Audit Commission (1996) has argued that local agencies need to be given the capacity to play a greater role in managing the local
market for education. Even Chubb and Moe (1990), who argue that equality is
better 'protected' by markets than any political institutions, concede that
choice of school in a democracy cannot be unlimited or entirely unregulated.
So, despite the rhetoric that suggests that devolution and choice takes educational decision-making out of politics, key decisions about goals and frameworks will still need to be made in the broader political arena.

Reforming educational politics?

Atomized decision-making in a highly stratified society may appear to give everyone equal opportunities, but transferring responsibility for decision-making from the public to the private sphere reduces the possibility of collective action to improve the quality of education for all. Whatever gains are to be had from handing decision-making to parents and teachers (and they seem to be far fewer than the advocates claim), it seems that more rather than less regulation will be required if equity is to remain an important consideration in education policy. If neither market accountability nor the evaluative state is ensuring that happens, we need to consider how the interests of all citizens might better be safeguarded.

The need to provide a better balance between consumer rights and citizen rights in education, while recognizing the desirability of some facets of choice and devolution, has led in England and Wales to proposals to put a greater degree of democratic control back in the picture. In particular, there has been recent discussion around how to revive democratic involvement and accountability at local level as a counter-balance to the market and the strong central state. For example, Pryke (1996: 21) remarks that, 'despite the experiments to let schools do their own thing' – and he believes this has gone further in England and Wales than anywhere else in the world – 'the great majority of them, and parents, have recognised the need for a body to act for them as a community of schools.' Similarly, Brighouse (1996: 11), Birmingham's senior education officer, who argues that an atomized market will create chaos and 'put further distance between the educational and social haves and the educational and social have-nots', says that 'there needs to be a local agency aware of school differences, sensitively working with each school, securing equity and setting a climate for a drive towards ever higher standards.' Responding to the question as to why such bodies should be democratically accountable, he suggests that in matters of education provision 'there is a need to balance various and sometimes conflicting needs and priorities [including] the needs of very different communities within, for example, a modern city', and that difference and equity can best be seen to be held in balance in an openly democratic forum (Brighouse 1996: 14). It is not clear, though, how Brighouse's proposed local education councils (which are intended to supersede LEAs) would be constituted and how they would avoid the pitfalls of existing majoritarian forms of representative democracy whereby significant sections of the population feel unrepresented.

Similar doubts arise in relation to the recommendations proposed by Cordingley and Harrington (AMA 1996). They claim that, in England, community needs have been obscured by the current pressures on schools and school systems. They argue that greater definition and dialogue over the nature of these needs will bring a stronger sense of local identification. They then suggest these various needs be balanced beyond the individual school, with the support of a 'locally situated, locally accountable operational agency' (p. 134). Unlike Brighouse, Cordingley and Harrington see existing LEAs performing this role, although they argue that a number of steps need to be taken to avoid previous perceived weaknesses. For instance, they propose that 'elected bodies must demonstrate their ability to take long-term strategic decisions, to attract high calibre candidates, to appoint effective chairs and to make decisions on the basis of resolving the task in hand, rather than party dogma' (pp. 135–6). Again, though, they provide little indication of how such intentions can be realized and the limits of existing modes of democratic control overcome.

In the search for alternatives to existing mechanisms for democratic control, there may be some lessons from the past. Paradoxically, current forms of democracy in England and Wales may be less appropriate to diverse communities than those associated with directly elected school boards in the nineteenth century, which used 'an advanced form of proportional representation [which] ensured that all the major political and religious groupings could be represented' (Simon 1994: 12). However, although it is important to consider how such bodies might be constituted and how they might effectively address the failure of current initiatives, we have to recognize that local democratic control, whether at the level of the school or the locality, is likely to have limited impact as a free-standing reform. Many of the studies reported in this book point up the severe limitations of localized governance reforms as a means of enhancing both achievement and equality within highly stratified societies. If these limitations are to be addressed, it is important that we move beyond educational politics and address the politics of education (Dale 1992). This involves focusing on the political, economic and historical context in which schools and the various bodies that govern them are located.

Self-managing schools in context

The concentration on organizational characteristics that underlies the current fashion for self-managing schools can militate against the realization of more equitable educational outcomes – even where these policies are *not* articulated with marketization measures. As already discussed, Chubb and Moe's advocacy of markets is based upon the premise that the conditions under which private schools operate enable them to develop more effective and responsive management structures. But the identification of organizational characteristics is also a feature of the more liberal, rather than neo-liberal, school improvement and school effectiveness lobby. The central thrust of their arguments is that improving, and even equalizing, educational outcomes is dependent upon transposing the characteristics of successful schools on to unsuccessful schools. However, all the evidence suggests that institutional success or failure depends more on external rather than internal characteristics of schools. As we noted in Chapter 8, those organizational factors identified by Chubb and Moe (1990) as making the difference between public and private schooling explain only about 5 per cent of the variation in student outcome scores. The disarticulation between individual school improvement and structural inequalities is illustrated in the fact that one conclusion to be drawn from a reading of the pioneering *Fifteen Thousand Hours* research (Rutter *et al.* 1979) is that, if all schools performed as well as the best schools, the stratification of achievement by social class would be even more stark than it is now (Whitty 1997b).

Concentrating on the exogenous rather than the endogenous aspects of school achievement leads one to quite different understandings and policy implications. Instead of transposing organizational characteristics, one might think about transposing some of the socio-economic features of 'successful' schools. At the crudest level, the most effective policies are likely to be those that seek to bring greater parity of wealth and welfare to schools' constituent client groups. Anyon (1995: 89) concludes from a study of the difficulty of reform in an urban ghetto school that 'the only solution to educational resignation and failure in the inner city is the ultimate elimination of poverty and racial degradation.' When we look at the exogenous aspects of education, it becomes clear that strategies for reducing the disparities in provision and opportunity need to be connected to the broader policy arena. For instance, the current consolidation of socio-economic differences within devolved systems of schooling is as much a product of housing policy as education policy. Certainly in England and Wales, but also to some extent in other countries, the growth of the segregated suburbs after the Second World War, and particularly the establishment of extensive social housing developments, effectively obstructed the development of integrative schooling programmes (Lowe 1988).

If equity issues alone are considered, it might be more appropriate to develop policies which break, rather than strengthen, the relationship between schools and their communities. This was the rationale which underlay the controversial busing policies of American urban districts. Recognition that equal educational opportunities could not be achieved within a racially segregated education system led to the nationwide implementation of schemes which compelled black students to be transported to schools in white neighbourhoods, and vice versa. It was the enforced transportation of white students to predominantly black schools in the inner city which provoked the fiercest opposition. The determination of white parents to protect their children from what they perceived to be detrimental environments ultimately led to the abandonment of most schemes, even though nearly all the research evidence shows that integration improves black children's educational performance without lowering that of white children (Pride and Woodard 1985). The recasting of the notion of communities into 'communities of interest' may take us beyond geographically bounded criteria of inclusion – but it cannot evade the socio-economic determinants of who 'belongs' where. Notwithstanding the importance of identity politics, self-managing schools which consolidate processes of identification are as likely to favour the exclusivist tendencies of the white middle class as they are to provide opportunities for the educational re-enfranchisement of marginalized groups.

The paradox of the state

However, the injunction that we need to plan across and between welfare areas and develop interventionist strategies to regulate economic and social practices runs against the grain of current developments in politics and social theory. Indeed, as we have seen, many have argued that the current fashion for devolution arises from the failure of central planning. Leaving things to the market reflects a disillusionment with the national modernization programmes of the post-war period as much as the abrogation of individual rights emphasized by libertarians.

Concern over the negative consequences of a deregulated education system may make the state-centred options seem more attractive than they did in the past, but a straightforward return to the old ways of administering education would be neither feasible nor desirable. In decrying the effects of the market-oriented policies, it is important not to overlook neo-Marxist (and neo-liberal) critiques of the state (e.g. Offe 1975, 1984). While these suggest that the functions of the state cannot be reduced to those of the economy, neither should the state be seen as a neutral arbiter of competing claims or a benign allocator of resources. As we discussed in Chapter 3, the current phase of devolution might best be understood as a response by the state to a range of social and economic crises.

While we would not want to overemphasize the degree of social transformation taking place, even in advanced industrial societies, there is little doubt that the welfare state in general, and more specifically the education system, has lost legitimacy on a number of fronts. And it is hard to see how this can be recovered through the return of centrally imposed programmes. Not only has it been shown that middle-class families tend to gain welfare provision disproportionate to their needs (Le Grand 1987), the premises of the welfare state itself have been exposed as patriarchal (Yeatman 1994), created by male professionals in 'treacherous alliance' with middle-class mothers (Donzelot 1975). Williams (1991: 320) uses the term 'welfare capitalism' to describe the ways in which the welfare state operates to 'maintain the financial dependence of women in the home, their subordination to male authority in the home and at work, and to define, limit and constrain women's sexuality, their mothering, their reproductive powers and their access to an independent income'. The mass systems of schooling of the post-war period were developed upon the foundations of traditional class and, particularly in the USA, racial divisions. As in other areas of welfare, provision was built around the normalization of the white middle class. Expert intervention was based on the identification of 'others': working-class students, black students, students with learning disabilities. These groups were not only pathologized but homogenized. For instance, the busing schemes alluded to above were often based on a one-dimensional notion of race and served to gloss over significant differences within such notional 'communities'.

Even if such interventionist programmes were to be considered desirable again, the conditions for resurrecting them may no longer be in place. Green (1996: 41), who believes we are seeing 'partial internationalization' rather than rampant globalization, claims

it is undoubtedly true that many of the advanced western states find it increasingly difficult to maintain social cohesion and solidarity. Growing individualism and life-style diversity, secularization, social mobility and the decline of stable communities have all played a part in this . . . In some countries, where markets and individualism have gone furthest in dissolving social ties, there is reason to wonder whether national solidarism has not vanished beyond recovery.

Although Green acknowledges that states still retain strong control over the regulation of education systems through strategic performance-based funding, he argues that there has been a narrowing in the scope of educational ends where 'broader national educational objectives in terms of social cohesion and citizenship formation have become increasingly confused and neglected, in part because few western governments have a clear notion of what nationhood and citizenship mean in complex and pluralistic modern democracies' (Green 1996: 58).

Inasmuch as the current wave of reforms marks a response by nation states to the fundamental, and increasingly apparent, social and economic crises by which they are beleaguered – from both within and without – devolution can provide only a temporary solution. As Weiss (1993) argues, the conflicts and disparities within the education system are too deep-seated to be resolved by simply shifting the blame down the line. As the processes of social stratification become sharper and the failure of local initiatives more transparent, the structural limitations of the new educational policies will be re-exposed. Indeed, Green (1996: 59) argues that the refusal or inability of governments to redefine and reassert their responsibility for public education may have more far-reaching consequences 'as the social atomization induced by global market penetration becomes increasingly dysfunctional. With the decline of socially integrating institutions and the consequent atrophy of collective social ties, education may soon again be called upon to stitch together the fraying social fabric.' While the demise of some forms of national solidarity may be long overdue, the general atrophy of collective ties and consequent loss of notions of citizenship which Green predicts must surely be cause for concern. The issue then becomes one of establishing how education might best help to reconstruct the social fabric and who shall influence its design.

For, although processes of globalization may be diminishing the capacity of individual nations in some domains, the spread is uneven, and the response of the nation states, variable. This indicates that, within national contexts, it may be possible to mobilize support for more equitable strategies than those evident in most of the countries and regions we have considered.

Part of the challenge must be to move away from atomized decision-making to the reassertion of collective responsibility without recreating the very bureaucratic systems whose shortcomings have helped to legitimate the current tendency to treat education as a private good rather than a public responsibility. While choice policies are part of a social text that helps to create new subject positions which undermine traditional forms of collectivism, those forms of collectivism themselves failed to empower many members of society, including women and minority ethnic groups. We need to ask how we can use the positive aspects of choice and autonomy to facilitate the development of new forms of community empowerment rather than exacerbating social differentiation. Social democratic approaches which favoured a particular vision of the common school have lost legitimacy and we do need to find ways of respond- ing to increasing specialization and social diversity. However, the left has so far done little to develop a concept of public education which looks significantly different from the education that some of us spent our earlier academic careers critiquing for its role in reproducing and legitimating social inequalities (Young and Whitty 1977). Even if the social democratic era looks better in retrospect, and in comparison with current policies, than it did at the time, that does not remove the need to rethink what might be progressive policies for the next cen- tury. As Hatcher (1996: 55) argues, 'it would be profoundly mistaken to respond to the Right's agenda, based on differentiation through the market to widen social inequalities, by clinging to a social-democratic statist model which serves fatally to depoliticise and demobilise those popular energies which alone are capable of effectively challenging the reproduction of social class inequality in education.' But we shall have to return to the question of the state after con- sidering the possibilities inherent in a revitalized civil society.

Changing civil society

In thinking about new directions for the politics of education, it is important that we reflect critically on our own political presuppositions. Interviewed six months before his death in 1988, Raymond Williams urged left intellectuals to rethink their socialist commitment in the light of contemporary develop- ments. Although he remained convinced that the socialist analysis was the correct one, 'the perspectives which had sustained the main Left organisations were simply not adequate to the society they were seeking to change' (Williams 1989: 315). Accordingly, he insisted that a whole new intellectual beginning was required that eschewed a nostalgic backward look to the heroes of the 1960s and, as a consequence, avoided becoming trapped within the rhetoric of exhausted traditions.

In a reference to the Thatcherite era, but of relevance to all the countries we have considered here, Marquand (1989: 375) is surely right to suggest that 'if the last fifteen years of British history have any single lesson, it is that even bad solu- tions will prevail against an intellectual vacuum.' Our own view is that neither the state nor the market is likely to restore legitimacy to educational decision- making. Instead, this will require a revitalization of civil society and the development of new forms of democracy more suited to contemporary societies. Foucault (1988) pointed out that what he called new forms of collec- tive association, such as trade unions and political parties, emerged in the nine- teenth century as a counterbalance to the prerogative of the state. These formed a seedbed for the development of new ideas on governance. We now need to experiment with and evaluate new forms of association in the public sphere within which citizen rights in education policy – and indeed other areas of public policy – can be reasserted against current trends towards both a restricted and authoritarian version of the state and a marketized civil society.

So, rather than accepting what now exists as the inevitable shape of things to come, apart from some tinkering at the edges, it may be time to develop what Wright (1995) terms 'real utopias'. Wright takes the view, which we share, that 'what is pragmatically possible is not fixed independently of our imaginations, but itself shaped by our visions.' His own *Real Utopias Project* works through 'utopian ideals that are grounded in the real potentials of humanity', but also with 'utopian destinations that have accessible waystations' and 'utopian designs of institutions which can inform our practical tasks of muddling through in a world of imperfect conditions for social change' (Wright 1995: ix). These designs are not utopian in the sense that they seek to construct an 'imaginary world, free from the difficulties that beset us in reality' (Levitas 1990: 1). Nor are they monocultural and monorational. As Held (1995: 239) argues, drawing on Nozick (1975), 'we must get away from the idea that utopia represents *a* single conception of the best of all social and political arrangements' (his emphasis). Instead, Held claims that 'A society in which utopian *experimentation* can be tried should be thought of as a utopia. Utopia is a framework for utopias' (ibid., his emphasis).

Thus, if we are to avoid the atomization of educational decision-making, and associated tendencies towards fragmentation and polarization between schools and within schools, we need to create new collective and experimental contexts within civil society for determining institutional arrangements that are genuinely inclusive. In England and Wales there is currently a great deal of discussion about ways of democratizing the state and civil society short of major constitutional changes. Geddes (1996), following Held (1987), contrasts legal democracy (modern neo-liberal democracy in a free market system), competitive elitist democracy (the conventional representational party system), pluralism, neo-pluralism (quasi-corporatism) and participatory democracy. Like many people working in this field, he sees the future in terms of attempts to combine the virtues of different approaches. In particular, he seems to favour combining representative and participatory democracy, by such devices as decentralizing the policy process and establishing community councils, citizens' juries and opinion panels. However, in view of the lack of a firm constitutional basis for most such innovations, they tend to create ambiguity about whether they constitute democratic involvement in decision-making or mere consultation.

There are also moves in the USA to encourage new 'forms of group representation that stand less sharply in tension with the norms of democratic governance' (Cohen and Rogers 1995: 9) than the sorts of unaccountable 'factions' that are currently able to take advantage of both the market and existing state forms. Cohen and Rogers take the view that such innovations can improve the practical approximation even of market societies to egalitarian democratic norms. They argue that, by altering the status of 'secondary associations' within civil society, associative democracy can 'improve economic performance and government efficiency and advance egalitarian-democratic norms of popular sovereignty, political equality, distributive equity and civic consciousness' (p. 9).

In thinking about how the revitalization of civil society might be encouraged, it is important that attention be given not merely to the mechanisms of regulation themselves, but also to the most appropriate ways of deciding upon them. Such a project will involve re-examining the basis of what it means to be a citizen. As Yeatman (1994: 86) argues, 'dominant discourses of citizenship are predicated on systematic exclusions of those who are othered by these discourses.' She illustrates how modern liberal and republican conceptions of citizenship are based on the idea that a civic community is homogenous and monocultural where particularity and difference are bracketed out. The welfare discourse of citizenship is similarly exclusive inasmuch as it divides the 'independent' freely contracting individuals from those who are deemed in a state of dependency – thereby hiding our mutual interdependency and creating a category of 'needy' citizens who are denied contractual status. It is clear that any reworking of civil society must move beyond these traditional notions of citizenship.

Yeatman (1994) argues for a conception of citizenship that recognizes the contested nature of public purposes and enables different voices to re-present their cultural identities and material class and gender interests. Similarly, Nixon *et al.* (1997) argue that it should involve both a 'politics of presence' (see Phillips 1993, 1995) and a 'politics of recognition' (Taylor 1994), in which all representations are recognized as both different and equal. As they observe, 'such a citizen is to be distinguished from those who, although recognised as equal and different, have no "presence"; for example, members of a group that, although valued and celebrated, have no representation in the main forums of the polity' (Nixon *et al.* 1997: 21).

In common with other theorizations of how to re-enfranchise 'lost' citizens, these visions focus on the transformative capacity of voluntary association. Hirst (1993, 1994), for instance, seeks to show how civil society can be democratized and empowered through the principles of 'associative democracy'. Opposed to both state collectivism and pure free-market individualism, associationalism claims that liberty and human welfare are best served when as many of the activities of society as possible are organized by voluntary and democratically run 'associations'. Hirst argues that associationalist relationships can be built by citizens' initiatives freely formed by committed individuals. Giddens (1994: 15) talks of the importance of 'generative politics', which 'seeks to allow individuals and groups to *make things happen,* rather than have things happen to them' (his emphasis). This, he argues, can contribute to a 'dialogic democracy' based on the development of trust between people, facilitated through the activities of self-help groups and social movements.

These theorists suggest that such scenarios are more than idle imaginings. To varying degrees, they argue that we are currently entering a social phase in which these new politics of representation are more likely to develop. Those same social and economic crises which underlie the restructuring of public education examined in this book are seen to provide the conditions in which a new citizenry will emerge. Giddens (1991) identifies what he terms 'high modernity' as contributing to heightened social reflexivity, which will provide the necessary discretionary space in which to foster increased levels of participation in the political sphere. In fact, he sees the huge growth and proliferation of self-help groups in recent years as testimony to such participation.

Yeatman (1994: 86) claims that 'an alternative vision of citizenship, one that works with and accepts difference, is sufficiently emerged as to be named.' Like Giddens, she sees the emergence of social movements as 'a rich source of system innovation and development' (ibid.: 115). In relation to welfare, she argues for the creation of 'little polities' – spaces for negotiation between service deliverers and users with mechanisms for a more participatory approach to decision-making. Moreover, she provides examples of welfare services where approaches such as these are already under way.

While these developments must surely represent steps in the right direction, we need to be careful not to overstress their significance, or the extent of the changes taking place. As we discussed in Chapter 3, it might be too easy to interpret relatively superficial social translations as indicative of deep-rooted structural transformations. Moreover, while the restructuring of relations between the centre and the periphery may leave greater spaces for the emergence of social movements and voluntary associations, there is nothing to indicate that the strength of the state has been substantially reduced. Global developments may be weakening the sovereignty of the nation state in the transnational economic and political arena, but its willingness and capacity for internal regulation would appear to have remained, thus far, undiminished. This means that any alternative politics of education needs to engage with the big polity as well as little polities.

The state and civil society

Although some of the 'new times' theorists provide well developed accounts of how little polities might develop at the local level, they are less strong on how these would relate to the state. Giddens (1994: 15) is surely right to criticize any simplistic notion that civil society lies 'between the individual and the state'. However this does not mean that issues at the macro-level can be dissolved into the new social fluidity – even when, as Giddens claims, this will lead to new forms of dialogic community. Yeatman (1994: 89) acknowledges the importance of 'macro-polity', but argues that this is best conceived as 'a series of interconnected polities, some local, some regional, some interregional'. Cohen and Rogers (1995) do suggest that new democratic forms of secondary association themselves may be constructed by the state through a process of 'artifactuality', but Hirst (1995: 113) argues that they are better constructed by citizens 'from below'.

Perhaps it is not surprising that so much emphasis is given to 'bottom-up' developments. It reflects a well-founded disillusionment with 'top-down' formulations that have only served to disadvantage and exclude. However, in focusing on the radical potential of localized agency, we also need to address the issue of how the sanctioned authority of the state can be redirected. In relation to education, Hatcher (1996: 54) argues for a 'bottom up version of the "pressure plus support" model' of educational improvement, based on 'stimulating self-activity with a national policy framework of common entitlements which would prevent the exploitation of diversity to sustain inequality'. He suggests that this would require 'state guarantees', but it is not clear what sort of state he has in mind. As we have argued in this book, the reduction of bureaucratic and democratic control within education has actually enabled the contemporary state to consolidate its strategic position and steer institutions more effectively, but there is little evidence that guarantees of equity are high on its agenda, except possibly in the case of present-day Sweden.

Offe (1996: 113) has suggested that a multiplicity of associative groups within civil society, presumably of the type favoured by new times theorists, 'is at the very least unfavourable to the emergence and maintenance of an ambitious theory and practice of state intervention and regulation'. Yet, while it is important to resist an over-ambitious programme of state intervention and regulation, at the same time as encouraging grass-roots activity at local level, there is surely a need to bring together popular movements to put pressure on the state to pursue policies that ensure differences between groups do not become inequalities. As we argued in Chapter 3, policies of devolution and choice are partly a response to tangible social and economic changes, but we need to seek alternative political responses that do not have the consequences we have described in this book.

Calls for associative democracy can be seen as part of the struggle for recognition of diverse groups who were marginalized within the class-based politics of the past. However, winning the struggle for recognition may not be enough. As Fraser (1997: 12) argues, contemporary justice 'requires both redistribution and recognition'. Fraser identifies two types of injustice: cultural and economic. Although they can rarely be separated with any precision, she argues that each type of injustice needs to be addressed through particular forms of remedy.

Many of the programmes of devolution and choice outlined within this book have been based upon the premise that the problems within the system stem largely from inadequate representation and communication, and that they can thus be addressed through the politics of recognition. However, our review of current research reveals the limits of this kind of strategy. Lack of recognition within the education system has been systematically intertwined with socio-economic injustices that require strategies based on redistribution.

Future policies need both to recognize and redistribute, although pursuing both paths simultaneously is not straightforward. For instance, as Fraser (1997) argues, the politics of recognition tend to involve the highlighting and valuing of group differences, while the politics of redistribution look to erode the basis of social difference. In order to resolve the tension, she outlines the importance of developing policies based on transformation rather than affirmation. Only transformative strategies, in the realms of both recognition and redistribution, can move beyond superficial remedies and address the underlying structural sources of inequality.

In confronting the question of what role the state might play in this, it is clearly not desirable to revert to the kind of 'exhausted traditions' of socialism to which Williams referred. But neither need it entail abandoning the idea of a political project somewhat broader than that indicated by some of the 'new times' theorists. As Hall and Jacques argued in 1989, as old political polarities are disintegrating, so new ones are in the process of being fashioned. They claimed that, while there is as yet no adequate vocabulary to describe these polarities, new points of commonality and difference will 'turn on the line between progressive and regressive politics, modernisers and traditionalists' (p. 453). Seven years on, there must be significant doubts as to whether these particular polarities can be defined and defended. They will certainly have different inflections within different national contexts. But, despite these reservations, if changes are to be effected in the macro-polity, Hall and Jacques (1989) are surely right to argue that we need to develop and sustain political strategies that highlight points of commonality as much as difference.

Sustaining commonality and difference in education

The cultural character of education means that, even though we need to put in place redistributive measures, the politics of recognition must be addressed not just in terms of representation but also in terms of the nature of educational transmissions. In discussing the various ways in which we might seek to democratize the governance of education, it is important not to lose sight of the nature of what is being governed. In Chapters 6 and 8, we were critical of claims that decentralizing decision-making would inevitably lead to the enhancement of teaching and learning. Our review found no compelling evidence that there was any relationship between self-managing status and student achievement. In fact, some research suggested that school autonomy, particularly when articulated with marketization, was reducing the scope and purpose of education. Meanwhile, however, behaviour in 'sink schools' created by the market (for example, the Ridings School in Yorkshire) has generated a 'moral panic' about lack of social cohesion, to the extent that one of the British government's quangos, the School Curriculum and Assessment Authority (SCAA), has spawned a 'National Forum for Values in Education and the Community' (SCAA 1996). Thus, there can be 'top-down', as well as 'bottom-up', pressure to create new ways of managing education, as the realization dawns that a marketized civil society itself creates contradictions that need to be managed. In New Zealand too, a neo-liberal government has shown itself prepared to employ quasi-corporatist forms of governance to sustain its legitimacy in a period of crisis (Pearce 1996). All this helps to re-create contexts within which struggles over education can take place, though some will be more open to hegemonic incorporation than others. But, if progressive forces fail to contest such 'spaces', it will hardly be surprising if they are colonized by the right.

We have seen in England and Wales in recent years the imposition by central government of a narrow and nationalistic National Curriculum, which serves to exclude minority ethnic and disadvantaged groups. But, although that particular response was inappropriate to the needs of contemporary society, the National Curriculum remains for the time being the one symbol of a common educational system and an identifiable entitlement that people can struggle to alter, rather than leaving all provision to emerge from the individual exercise of choice (or non-choice) in the market place. It is probably not merely coincidental that it was the struggle over the National Curriculum, and more particularly the workload associated with the testing arrangements, that provoked the Major government's greatest reverse in education policy when a coalition of teachers, school governors and parents boycotted national testing in most schools and forced the government into an urgent and humiliating review of the National Curriculum (Dearing 1993). In most other aspects of current education policy, schools, teachers and parents are pitted against each other as competitors in the market place and there are few remaining arenas in which they can explore common interests and pursue collective actions.

Determining the content of any National Curriculum guidelines will inevitably involve conflict, but difficult public issues need to be confronted publicly rather than being decided by private individuals or unaccountable trusts. Moreover, the articulation of differences could be a constitutive element of the curriculum itself. For example, clearly, the idea of a 'national' curriculum is in itself problematic, especially within the current global context and, indeed, in the European one in the case of Britain and Sweden. But debates on the essentially contested nature of nationhood, and its continuing relevance (or lack of it), might themselves contribute to the education of a revitalized citizenry (Green 1996). Another strategy that has been suggested is to incorporate an element of citizenship education into the formal curriculum. D. Hargreaves (1994a), who is generally supportive of policies to encourage choice and diversity, believes that in England we should reassert a sense of social cohesion by insisting on core programmes of civic education in all schools. This also seems to be the thinking behind the SCAA proposals on the teaching of values. However, we find such suggestions less than convincing. Certainly, within the present policy context, it is unclear how far adding a component to the timetable will provide an effective counterbalance to the permeating values of the market place and the assessment prerogatives of the evaluative state. But even in less competitive conditions, we would need to look at the curriculum as a whole. As our own research (Whitty et al. 1994; Power 1996) and that of others suggests, simply supplementing existing provision is unlikely to make much difference. Indeed, the introduction of isolated elements of social education alongside conventional school subjects can serve to endorse the superiority of the traditional academic curriculum.

Attention also needs to be given to aspects of what has often been labelled the 'hidden curriculum'. These are probably the most intractable elements, as they are embedded deep in educational practices. In addition to anticipating the messages transmitted from different modes of assessment, concentrating on the hidden curriculum requires us to look at the social relations of schools. It seems likely to require the development of new sets of relations within schools as well as beyond them. More specifically, if we want students to learn democratic citizenship, we need to put in place structures of learning which embody those principles.

Concluding remarks

We have identified a number of developments that might help to provide a context in which to reconstruct a truly public education system. Bearing in mind the negative effects of the reforms we have described in this book, we believe that a genuinely revitalized civil society has some potential to counterbalance the state and prevent it dominating and atomizing the rest of society. This could provide the conditions for what Mouffe (1989) argues strong democracy requires, an articulation between the particular and the universal, a forum, if you like, for creating unity without denying specificity.

In suggesting that it might be possible to democratize both the state and civil society, it is easy to overstress the positive aspects of recent social developments and thereby exaggerate the possibilities of significant change. However, it is also easy to dismiss these alternatives to present arrangements as unrealizable. There are some who will argue, with some justification, that however cleverly democracy is reinvented, in the educational context or elsewhere, it will remain a minority pursuit of the relatively well educated and prosperous who will do their usual best to advance their own interests at the expense of the majority. This is a familiar and well grounded objection. But, again, it is based on a status quo version of reality which takes for granted the impossibility of changing the familiar; it also overlooks the fact that the familiar may well be part of the problem. As Williams once remarked in the course of defending his own views from this sort of criticism:

> I have ... been told, repeatedly, that people are just not interested enough – even, behind the hand, not intelligent enough – to make these new [democratic] institutions and processes work. The usual evidence offered is the cynicism and apathy surrounding existing electoral and democratic forms. None of us can ignore this, yet equally none of us can know how much of it is the predictable consequence of merely apparent involvement in decision-making. Too many familiar current processes frustrate or default on actual decisions, or somehow lose them in the carefully protected intricacies of reference elsewhere, that anyone can feel discouraged. But it would be absurd to reject new principles and practices on the evidence of the very faults of those older principles and practices which now make changes necessary. In truth nobody can know how any of it would work, until some of it has been tried. And it has certainly not, in any general way, been tried.
>
> (Williams 1983: 104)

But if we are seriously to engage in the kind of arguments being proposed here, we must confront the possibility that, as privileged professionals, we may not like all the outcomes. The distribution of educational goods is linked to material conditions and has material implications. Markets may produce winners and losers in a more transparent way than the social democratic policies they superseded, but it is hard to envisage any education policies that will produce only winners. If the position of the educationally dispossessed is to be improved, there are likely to be fewer opportunities for the currently favoured.

Hatcher (1996: 55) points out that 'the danger that the opening up of schools to local democratic activity will release reactionary as well as progressive dynamics is a real one'. But, whatever the risks, he argues, 'it's where a democratic politics of education starts' and he reminds us that the outcome is not inevitably unfavourable. However, on the basis of our analysis in this book, we would add that the outcome is only likely to be favourable in the longer term if progressive educators recognize as clearly as their opponents that, important as these are, local and institutional struggles over education can only be part of the picture. If they are to contribute to a broader assault on educational and social inequality, they cannot be divorced from struggles over the nature of the sort of society that *all* children should grow up in. So, while some forms of devolution and choice may warrant further exploration as part of a wider response to the unfulfilled aspirations of disadvantaged groups in modern societies, they must not be seen as an *alternative* to broader struggles for social justice.

REFERENCES

Adams, A. and Tulasiewicz, W. (1995) *The Crisis in Teacher Education: a European Concern?* London: Falmer Press.

Adler, M. (1993) *An Alternative Approach to Parental Choice.* National Commission on Education Briefing Paper 13. London: National Commission on Education.

Adler, M., Petch, A. and Tweedie, J. (1989) *Parental Choice and Educational Policy.* Edinburgh: Edinburgh University Press.

Allen, J. (1992) Post-industrialism and post-Fordism. In S. Hall and T. McGrew (eds) *Modernity and Its Futures.* Cambridge: Polity Press.

AMA (1996) *Communities, Schools and LEAs: Learning to Meet Needs.* London: Association of Metropolitan Authorities.

Anderson, D. S. (1993) Public schools in decline: implications of the privatization of schools in Australia. In H. Beare and W. L. Boyd (eds) *Restructuring Schools: an International Perspective on the Movement to Transform the Control and Performance of Schools.* London: Falmer Press.

Andrews, C., Chant, D. and Smith, R. (1996) Teachers' work: dealing with changing contexts. Mimeo, Griffith University Gold Coast, Queensland, Australia.

Angus, L. (1993a) Democratic participation or efficient site management: the social and political location of the self-managing school. In J. Smyth (ed.) *A Socially Critical View of the Self-managing School.* London: Falmer Press.

Angus, L. (1993b) The sociology of school effectiveness, *British Journal of Sociology of Education*, 14(3), 333–45.

Angus, L. (1994) Teacher: object of policy or professional participant in Sharing Education? In Deakin Centre for Education and Change, *School What Future? Balancing the Education Agenda.* Geelong, Australia: Deakin University.

Angus, M. (1995) Devolution of school governance in an Australian state school system: third time lucky? In D. S. G. Carter and M. H. O'Neill (eds) *Case Studies in Educational Change: an International Perspective.* London: Falmer Press.

Anon (1992) Preventing school fiefdoms, *Independent*, 22 February.

Anyon, J. (1995) Race, social class and educational reform in an inner-city school, *Teachers College Record*, 97(1), 69–94.

Apple, M. W. (1986) *Teachers and Texts: a Political Economy of Class and Gender Relations in Education.* New York: Routledge and Kegan Paul.
Apple, M. W. (1996) *Cultural Politics and Education.* New York: Teachers College Press.
Arnot, M., David, M. and Weiner, G. (1996) *Educational Reform and Gender Equality in Schools.* Manchester: Equal Opportunities Commission.
Arnott, M., Bullock, A. and Thomas, H. (1992) Consequences of local management: an assessment by headteachers. Paper presented to the Education Reform Act Research Network, University of Warwick, 12 February.
Arnove, R. (1996) Neo-liberal education policies in Latin America: arguments in favor and against. Paper presented at the Comparative and International Education Society Conference, Williamsburg, VA, 6–10 March.
Audit Commission (1996) *Trading Places: the Supply and Allocation of School Places.* Abingdon: Audit Commission.
Ball, S. J. (1990) *Politics and Policy-making in Education: Explorations in Policy Sociology.* London: Routledge.
Ball, S. J. (1993) Culture, cost and control: self-management and entrepreneurial schooling in England and Wales. In J. Smyth (ed.) *A Socially Critical View of the Self-managing School.* London: Falmer Press.
Ball, S. J. (1994) *Education Reform: a Critical and Post-structural Approach.* Buckingham: Open University Press.
Barber, M. (1992) *Education and the Teacher Unions.* London: Cassell.
Barber, M. (1996) Education reform, management approaches and teacher unions. In K. Leithwood, J. Chapman, D. Corson, P. Hallinger and A. Hart (eds) *International Handbook of Educational Leadership and Administration. Part 2.* Dordrecht: Kluwer Academic Publishers.
Barber, M., Rowe, G. and Whitty, G. (1995) School development planning: towards a new role for teacher unions. Mimeo, London, Institute of Education, University of London.
Barrett, E., Barton, L., Furlong. J., Galvin, C., Miles, S. and Whitty, G. (1992) *Initial Teacher Education in England and Wales.* London: Goldsmiths College, University of London.
Bartlett, W. (1993) Quasi-markets and educational reforms. In J. Le Grand and W. Bartlett (eds) *Quasi-markets and Social Policy.* London: Macmillan.
Becker, H. J., Nakagawa, K. and Corwin, R. G. (1995) The Charter School movement: preliminary findings from the first three states. Paper presented to the Annual Meeting of the American Educational Research Association, New Orleans, 18–22 April.
Bennett, A. L., Bryk, A. S., Easton, J. Q., Kerbow, D., Luppescu, S. and Sebring, P. A. (1992) *Charting Reform: the Principals' Perspective. A Report on a Survey of Chicago Public School Principals.* Chicago: Consortium on Chicago School Research.
Bennett, N. and Carré, C. (1995) Teachers' early experiences of the implementation of the British National Curriculum. In D.S.G. Carter and M.H. O'Neill (eds) *Case Studies in Educational Change: an International Perspective.* London: Falmer Press.
Berliner, D. C. and Biddle, B. J. (1995) *The Manufactured Crisis: Myths, Fraud and the Attack on America's Public Schools.* Reading, MA: Addison-Wesley.
Bernstein, B. (1996) Educational reform and pedagogic identities. Paper presented at the University of Bristol, 18 November.
Berrill, M. (1994) A view from the crossroads, *Cambridge Journal of Education,* 24(1), 113–16.
Blackmore, J. (1990) School-based decision-making and trade unions: the appropriation of a discourse. In J. Chapman (ed.) *School-based Decision-making and Management.* London: Falmer Press.
Blackmore, J. (1995) Breaking out of a masculinist politics of education. In B. Limerick

and B. Lingard (eds) *Gender and Changing Education Management*. Rydalmere, NSW: Hodder.

Blackmore, J. (1996a) The re-gendering and restructuring of educational work. Paper presented to the Ninth World Congress of Comparative Education Societies, University of Sydney, 1–6 July.

Blackmore, J. (1996b) Breaking the silence: feminist contributions to educational administration and policy. In K. Leithwood, J. Chapman, D. Corson, P. Hallinger and A. Hart (eds) *International Handbook of Educational Leadership and Administration. Part 2*. Dordrecht: Kluwer Academic Publishers.

Blackmore, J. (1996c) Doing emotional labour in the education market place: stories from the field of women in management, *Discourse*, 17(3), 337–50.

Blackmore, J., Bigum, C., Hodgens, J. and Laskey, L. (1996) Managed change and self-management in Schools of the Future, *Leading and Managing*, 2(3), 195–220.

Bolick, C. (1990) *A Primer on Choice in Education, Part 1. How Choice Works*. Washington, DC: Heritage Foundation.

Bottery, M. (1992) *The Ethics of Educational Management*. London: Cassell.

Bowe, R. and Ball, S. J. with Gold, A. (1992) *Reforming Education and Changing Schools: Case Studies in Policy Sociology*. London: Routledge.

Boyne, R. and Rattansi, A. (eds) (1990) *Postmodernism and Society*. London: Macmillan.

Boyson, R. (1990) Review of T. Edwards, J. Fitz and G. Whitty, *The State and Private Education*, *Times Higher Education Supplement*, 18 May.

Brennan, M. (1993) Reinventing square wheels: planning for schools to ignore realities. In J. Smyth (ed.) *A Socially Critical View of the Self-managing School*. London: Falmer Press.

Bridges, S. (1993) *Working in Tomorrow's Schools: Effects on Primary Teachers*. Christchurch, NZ: University of Canterbury.

Brighouse, T. (1996) *A Question of Standards: the Need for a Local Democratic Voice*. London: Politeia.

Broadbent, J., Laughlin, R., Shearn, D. and Dandy, N. (1993) Implementing local management of schools: a theoretical and empirical analysis, *Research Papers in Education*, 8(2), 149–76.

Broadfoot, P. M. (1996) *Education, Assessment and Society*. Buckingham: Open University Press.

Brooks, C. St J. and Hirsch, D. (1995) *Schools under Scrutiny: Strategies for the Evaluation of School Performance*. Paris: Organization for Economic Cooperation and Development.

Bryk, A. S., Lee, V. E. and Holland, P. B. (1993) *Catholic Schools and the Common Good*. Cambridge, MA: Harvard University Press.

Bryk, A. S., Easton, J. Q., Luppescu, S. and Thum, Y. M. (1994) Measuring achievement gains in the Chicago public schools, *Education and Urban Society*, 26(3), 306–19.

Bullock, A. and Thomas, H. (1994) *The Impact of Local Management of Schools: Final Report*. Birmingham: University of Birmingham.

Bush, T., Coleman, M. and Glover, D. (1993) *Managing Autonomous Schools: the Grant-maintained Experience*. London: Paul Chapman.

Caldwell, B. J. and Spinks, J. M. (1988) *The Self-managing School*. London: Falmer Press.

Caldwell, B. J. and Spinks, J. M. (1992) *Leading the Self-managing School*. London: Falmer Press.

Callinicos, A. (1989) *Against Postmodernism: a Marxist Critique*. Cambridge: Polity Press.

Campbell, J. and Neill, S. (1994) *Curriculum at Key Stage 1: Teacher Commitment and Policy Failure*. Harlow: Longman.

Capper, P. (1994) *Participation and Partnership: Exploring Shared Decision-making in Twelve New Zealand Secondary Schools*. Wellington: New Zealand Post Primary Teachers' Association.

Carl, J. (1994) Parental choice as national policy in England and the United States, *Comparative Education Review*, 38(3), 297–301.

Carnoy, M. (1993) School improvement: is privatization the answer? In J. Hannaway and M. Carnoy (eds) *Decentralization and School Improvement: Can We Fulfill the Promise?* San Francisco: Jossey-Bass.

Catherall, S. (1995) Ministers may look to New Zealand model, *Times Educational Supplement*, 1 September, 6.

Cawelti, G. (1994) *High School Restructuring: a National Study*. Arlington, VA: Educational Research Service.

Chadbourne, R. (1992) *The National Schools Project at Belmont Senior High School: a Formative Review of the First Nine Months*. Perth, Western Australia: International Institute for Policy and Administrative Studies.

Chapman, J. (1988) Teacher participation in the decision making of schools, *Journal of Educational Administration*, 26(1), 39–72.

Chapman, J., Boyd, W. L., Lander, R. and Reynolds, D. (1996) Introduction and overview. In J. Chapman, W. L. Boyd, R. Lander and D. Reynolds (eds) *The Reconstruction of Education: Quality, Equality and Control*. London: Cassell.

Chicago Panel on School Policy (1995) Chronicles of reform, *Reform Report*, V, 4 September.

Chubb, J. and Moe, T. (1988) Politics, markets and the organization of schools, *American Political Science Review*, 82(4), 1065–87.

Chubb, J. and Moe, T. (1990) *Politics, Markets and America's Schools*. Washington, DC: Brookings Institution.

Chubb, J. and Moe, T. (1992) *A Lesson in School Reform from Great Britain*. Washington, DC: Brookings Institution.

Clarke, J. (1995) Doing the right thing: managerialism and social welfare. Paper presented to the ESRC seminar, Professionals in Late Modernity, Imperial College, London, 26 June.

Clarke, J. and Newman, J. (1992) Managing to survive: dilemmas of changing re-organisational forms in the public sector. Paper presented to the Social Policy Association, University of Nottingham, July.

Clewell, B. C. and Joy, M. F. (1990) *Choice in Montclair, New Jersey*. Princeton, NJ: Education Testing Service.

Codd, J. A. (1993) Managerialism, market liberalism and the move to self-managing schools in New Zealand. In J. Smyth (ed.) *A Socially Critical View of the Self-managing School*. London: Falmer Press.

Codd, J. A. (1995) Educational reform and the contradictory discourses of evaluation, *Evaluation and Research in Education*, 8(172), 41–54.

Codd, J. A. (1996) Professionalism versus managerialism in New Zealand schools: educational leadership and the politics of teachers' work. Paper presented at the British Educational Research Association Annual Conference, University of Lancaster, 12–15 September.

Cohen, J. and Rogers, J. (eds) (1995) *Associations and Democracy*. London: Verso.

Coleman, J. S., Hoffer, T. and Kilgore, S. (1982) *High School Achievement: Public, Catholic and Private Schools*. New York: Basic Books.

CCSR (undated) *Charting Reform: the Teachers' Turn*, Report no 1 on a survey of CPS elementary school teachers. Chicago: Consortium on Chicago School Research.

Cookson, P. W. (1995) Goals 2000: framework for the new educational federalism, *Teachers College Record*, 96(3), 405–17.

Cooper, B. (1994) Administrative and economic efficiency in education: using school-site ratio analysis. Paper presented at the American Educational Research Association Annual Meeting, New Orleans, 4–8 April.

Crump, S. and Nytell, U. (1996) Schools, communities and the state in Australia and Sweden. Paper presented to the Ninth World Congress of Comparative Education Societies, University of Sydney, 1–6 July.

Curtain, R. and Hayton, G. (1995) The use and abuse of a competency standards framework in Australia: a comparative perspective, *Assessment in Education: Principles, Policy and Practice*, 2(2), 205–24.

Dale, R. (1989) *The State and Education Policy*. Milton Keynes: Open University Press.

Dale, R. (1992) Recovering from a pyrrhic victory? Quality, relevance and impact in the sociology of education. In M. Arnot and L. Barton (eds) *Voicing Concerns: Sociological Perspectives on Contemporary Education Reforms*. Wallingford: Triangle Books.

Dearing, R. (1993) *The National Curriculum and its Assessment: Interim Report*. York/London: NCC/SEAC.

Dearing, R. (1994) *The National Curriculum and its Assessment: Final Report*. London: SCAA.

Deem, R., Brehony, K. and Heath, S. (1995) *Active Citizenship and the Governing of Schools*. Buckingham: Open University Press.

Delfattore, J. (1992) *What Johnny Shouldn't Read*. New Haven, CT: Yale University Press.

DfE (1992a) *Choice and Diversity*. London: HMSO.

DfE (1992b) *Initial Teacher Training (Secondary Phase) (Circular 9/92)*. London: Department for Education.

DfE (1994) *Our Children's Education: the Updated Parent's Charter*. London: HMSO.

DfEE (1996) *Self-government for Schools*. London: HMSO.

Department of Trade (1987) *Australia Reconstructed*. Canberra: Australian Government Publishing Service.

Dianda, M. C. and Corwin, R. G. (1994) *Vision and Reality: a First Year Look at California's Charter Schools*. Los Alamitos, CA: Southwest Regional Laboratory.

Domanico, R. J. (1990) *Restructuring New York City's Public Schools: the Case for Public School Choice*. Education Policy Paper no. 3. New York: Manhattan Institute for Policy Research.

Dominelli, L. (1996) De-professionalizing social work: anti-oppressive practice, competencies and postmodernism, *British Journal of Social Work*, 26(2), 153–75.

Donzelot, J. (1975) *The Policing of Families*. London: Hutchinson.

Durham, M. (1996) Admen to sell sweets and videos in schools, *Observer*, 7 July, 1.

Edwards, T., Fitz, J. and Whitty, G. (1989) *The State and Private Education: an Evaluation of the Assisted Places Scheme*. London: Falmer Press.

Elmore, R. F. (1991) Foreword. In G. A. Hess, *School Restructuring, Chicago Style*. Newbury Park, CA: Corwin Press.

Englund, T. (1993) Education for public or private good. In G. Miron (ed.) *Towards Free Choice and Market-oriented Schools: Problems and Promises*. Stockholm: Institute of International Education, Stockholm University.

Epstein, D. and Kenway, J. (1996) Introduction: the marketisation of school education: feminist studies and perspectives, *Discourse*, 17(3), 301–14.

Evetts, J. (1996) The new headteacher: budgetary devolution and the work culture of secondary headship. In C. J. Pole and R. Chawla-Duggan (eds) *Reshaping Education in the 1990s: Perspectives on Secondary Schooling*. London: Falmer Press.

Feintuck, M. (1994) *Accountability and Choice in Schooling*. Buckingham: Open University Press.

Fiske, J., Hodge, B. and Turner, G. (eds) (1987) *Myths of Oz*. Sydney: Allen and Unwin.

Fitz, J., Halpin, D. and Power, S. (1993) *Grant Maintained Schools: Education in the Market Place*. London: Kogan Page.

Fitz, J., Halpin, D. and Power, S. (1997) Between a rock and a hard place: diversity, institutional autonomy and grant-maintained schools, *Oxford Review of Education*, 23(1), 17–30.

Flax, J. (1987) Postmodernism and gender relations in feminist theory, *Signs*, 12(4), 621–43.

Flew, A. (1991) Educational services: independent competition or maintained monopoly. In D. G. Green (ed.) *Empowering the Parents: How to Break the Schools Monopoly*. London: Institute of Economic Affairs.

Fliegel, S. with Macguire, J. (1990) *Miracle in East Harlem: the Fight for Choice in Public Education*. New York: Random House.

Ford, D. J. (1992) Chicago principals under school-based management: new roles and realities of the job. Paper presented at the American Educational Research Association Annual Meeting, San Francisco, 20–4 April.

Foster, P., Gomm, R. and Hammersley, M. (1996) *Constructing Educational Inequality: an Assessment of Research on School Processes*. London: Falmer Press.

Foucault, M. (1988) *Politics/Philosophy/Culture* (ed. L. D. Kritzman). New York: Routledge.

Fowler, F. C. (1994) The international arena: the global village, *Journal of Education Policy*, 9(5&6), 89–102.

Fowler, M. (1993) *Factors Influencing Choice of Secondary Schools*. Christchurch, NZ: University of Canterbury.

Fraser, N. (1997) *Justice Interruptus: Critical Reflections on the 'Postsocialist' Condition*. New York: Routledge.

Fullan, M. (1991) *The New Meaning of Educational Change*. London: Cassell.

Fuller, B. and Elmore, R. F. with Orfield, G. (eds) (1996) *Who Chooses? Who Loses? Culture, Institutions and the Unequal Effects of School Choice*. New York: Teachers College Press.

Furlong, J., Whitty, G., Whiting, C., Miles, S., Barton, L. and Barrett, E. (1996) Redefining partnership: revolution or reform in initial teacher education, *Journal of Education for Teaching*, 22(1), 39–55.

Gamble, A. (1983) Thatcherism and Conservative politics. In S. Hall and M. Jacques (eds) *The Politics of Thatcherism*. London: Lawrence and Wishart.

Gamble, A. (1988) *The Free Economy and the Strong State*. London: Macmillan.

Geddes, M. (1996) *Extending Democratic Practice in Local Government*. Greenwich: Campaign for Local Democracy.

Gerstner, L. V., Semerad, R. D., Doyle, D. P. and Johnston, W. B. (1994) *Reinventing Education: Entrepreneurship in America's Public Schools*. New York: Dutton.

Gewirtz, S. and Ball, S. J. (1995) Schools, signs and values: the impact of market forces on education provision in England. Paper presented at the American Educational Research Association Annual Meeting, San Francisco, 18–22 April.

Gewirtz, S. and Ball, S. J. (1996) From welfarism to new managerialism: shifting discourses of school leadership in the education quasi-market. Paper presented to Fourth ESRC Quasi-markets Seminar, University of Bristol, 25–6 March.

Gewirtz, S., Ball, S. J. and Bowe. R. (1992) Parents, privilege and the educational market place. Paper presented at British Educational Research Association Annual Conference, University of Stirling, 31 August.

Gewirtz, S., Ball, S. J. and Bowe, R. (1995) *Markets, Choice and Equity in Education*. Buckingham: Open University Press.

Gibbs, G. J. (1991) School-based management: are we ready? *IDRA Newsletter*, 18(4).

Giddens, A. (1991) *Modernity and Self-identity: Self and Society in the Late Modern Age*. Cambridge: Polity Press.

Giddens, A. (1994) Living in a post-traditional society. In U. Beck, A. Giddens and S. Lash (eds) *Reflexive Modernization: Politics, Tradition and Aesthetics in the Modern Social Order*. Cambridge: Polity Press.

Gillman, D. A. and Reynolds, L. L. (1991) The side effects of statewide testing, *Contemporary Education*, 62, 273–8.

Gitlin, A. and Margonis, F. (1995) The political aspect of reform: teacher resistance as good sense, *American Journal of Education*, 103, 377–405.

Glatter, R. (1993) Partnership in the market model: is it dying? Paper presented at the British Educational Management and Administration Society Annual Conference, Edinburgh, 10–12 September.

Glatter, R., Woods, P. A. and Bagley, C. (1997) Diversity, differentiation and hierarchy: School choice and parental preference. In R. Glatter, P. A. Woods and C. Bagley (eds) *Choice and Diversity in Schooling: Perspectives and Prospects*. London: Routledge.

Glennerster, H. (1991) Quasi-markets for education?, *Economic Journal*, 101, 1268–76.

Golby, M. and Brigley, S. (1989) *Parents as School Governors*. Tiverton: Fairway Publications.

Goldstein, H., Rasbash, J., Yang, M., Woodhouse, G., Pan, H. Q., Nuttall, D. and Thomas, S. (1996) A multilevel analysis of school examination results, *Oxford Review of Education*, 19(4), 425–33.

Gordon, L. (1992) The New Zealand state and education reforms: competing interests. Paper presented at the American Educational Research Association Annual Meeting, San Francisco, 20–24 April.

Gordon, L. (1993) *A Study of Boards of Trustees in Canterbury Schools*. Christchurch, NZ: University of Canterbury.

Gordon, L. (1994a) 'Rich' and 'poor' schools in Aotearoa, *New Zealand Journal of Educational Studies*, 29(2), 113–25.

Gordon, L. (1994b) Is school choice a sustainable policy for New Zealand? A review of recent research findings and a look to the future, *New Zealand Annual Review of Education*, 4, 9–24.

Gordon, L. (1995) Controlling education: agency theory and the reformation of New Zealand schools, *Educational Policy*, 9(1), 55–74.

Gordon, L. and Pearce, D. (1993) Why compare? A response to Stephen Lawton, *Journal of Education Policy*, 8(2), 175–81.

Gordon, L. and Wilson, K. (1992) Teacher unions in New Zealand. In B. Cooper (ed.) *Labor Relations in Education: an International Perspective*. Westport, CT: Greenwood Press.

Grace, G. (ed.) (1984) *Education and the City: Theory, History and Contemporary Practice*. London: Routledge.

Grace, G. (1991) Welfare labourism versus the New Right, *International Studies in Sociology of Education*, 1(1), 37–48.

Grace, G. (1993) On the study of school leadership: beyond education management, *British Journal of Educational Studies*, 41(4), 353–65.

Grace, G. (1995) *School Leadership: Beyond Education Management. An Essay in Policy Scholarship*. London: Falmer Press.

Granström, K. (1996) Decentralization and teachers: professional status cannot be granted it has to be acquired. In J. Chapman, W. L. Boyd, R. Lander and D. Reynolds (eds) *The Reconstruction of Education: Quality, Equality and Control*. London: Cassell.

Gray, J. and Wilcox, B. (1995) *'Good School, Bad School': Evaluating Performance and Encouraging Improvement*. Buckingham: Open University Press.

Gray, J., Jesson, D., Goldstein, H., Hedger, K. and Rasbash, J. (1995) A multilevel analysis of school improvement: changes in schools' performance over time, *School Effectiveness and School Improvement*, 6(2), 97–114.

Green, A. (1990) *Education and State Formation*. London: Macmillan.

Green, A. (1994) Post-modernism and state education, *Journal of Education Policy*, 9(1), 67–83.

Green, A. (1996) Education, globalization and the nation state. Paper presented to the Ninth World Congress of Comparative Education Societies, University of Sydney, 1–6 July.

Greene, J. P. and Peterson, P. E. (1996) School choice data rescued from bad science, *The Wall Street Journal*, 14 August.

Greenwald, R., Hedges, L. V. and Laine, R. D. (1996a) The effect of school resources on student achievement, *Review of Educational Research*, 66(3), 361–96.

Greenwald, R., Hedges, L. V. and Laine, R. D. (1996b) Interpreting research on school resources and student achievement: a rejoinder to Hanushek, *Review of Educational Research*, 66(3), 411–16.

Grutzik, C., Bernal, D., Hirshberg, D. and Wells, A. S. (1995) Resources and access in California charter schools. Paper presented at the American Educational Research Association Annual Meeting, San Francisco, 18–22 April.

Hall, S. and Jacques, M. (1989) Realignment of politics – manifesto for new times. In S. Hall and M. Jacques (eds) *New Times: the Changing Face of Politics in the 1990s*. London: Lawrence and Wishart.

Hall, V. (1993) Women in educational management: a review of research in Britain. In J. Ouston (ed.) *Women in Education Management*. Harlow: Longman.

Hall, V. (1996) *Dancing on the Ceiling: a study of Women Managers in Education*. London: Paul Chapman.

Halpin, D. (1997) Fragmentation into different types of school: diversifying into the past? In R. Pring and G. Walford (eds) *Affirming the Comprehensive Ideal*. London: Falmer Press.

Halpin, D., Fitz, J. and Power, S. (1994) Self-governance, grant-maintained schools and educational identities. End of Award Report to the Economic and Social Research Council (R000233911501), Swindon.

Halpin, D., Power, S. and Fitz, J. (1991) Grant-maintained schools: making a difference without being really different, *British Journal of Educational Studies*, 39(4), 409–24.

Halpin, D., Power, S. and Fitz, J. (1993) Opting into state control? Headteachers and the paradoxes of grant-maintained status, *International Studies in the Sociology of Education*, 3(1), 3–23.

Halpin, D., Power, S. and Fitz, J. (1997a) Opting into the past? Grant maintained schools and the reinvention of tradition. In R. Glatter, P. A. Woods and C. Bagley (eds) *Choice and Diversity in Schooling: Perspectives and Prospects*. London: Routledge.

Halpin, D., Power, S. and Fitz, J. (1997b) In the grip of the past? Tradition, traditionalism and contemporary schooling, *International Studies in Sociology of Education*, 7(1), 3–19.

Hanushek, E. A. (1994) *Making Schools Work: Improving Performance and Controlling Costs*. Washington, DC: Brookings Institution.

Hanushek, E. A. (1996) A more complete picture of school resource policies, *Review of Educational Research*, 66(3), 397–409.

Hargreaves, A. (1994) *Changing Teachers, Changing Times: Teachers' Work and Culture in the Postmodern Age*. London: Cassell.

Hargreaves, D. (1994a) *The Mosaic of Learning: Schools and Teachers for the Next Century*. London: Demos.

Hargreaves, D. (1994b) Another radical approach to the reform of initial teacher training, *Westminster Studies in Education*, 13, 5–11.

Harris, K. (1993) Power to the people? Local management of schools, *Education Links*, 45, 4–8.

Harris, K. (1996) The corporate invasion of schooling: some implications for pupils, teachers and education, *ACER SET: Research Information for Teachers*, 2.

Harty, S. (1994) Pied Piper revisited. In D. Bridges and T. H. McLaughlin (eds) *Education and the Market Place*. London: Falmer Press.

Harvey, D. (1989) *The Condition of Postmodernity: an Enquiry into the Origins of Cultural Change*. Oxford: Basil Blackwell.

Hatcher, R. (1994) Market relationships and the management of teachers, *British Journal of Sociology of Education*, 15(1), 41–62.

Hatcher, R. (1996) The limitations of the new social democratic agendas. In R. Hatcher and K. Jones (eds) *Education after the Conservatives*. Stoke on Trent: Trentham Books.

Held, D. (1987) *Models of Democracy*. Cambridge: Polity Press.

Held, D. (1989) The decline of the nation state. In S. Hall and M. Jacques (eds) *New Times: the Changing Face of Politics in the 1990s*. London: Lawrence and Wishart.

Held, D. (1995) *Democracy and the Global Order*. Cambridge: Polity Press.

Henig, J. R. (1994) *Rethinking School Choice: Limits of the Market Metaphor*. Princeton, NJ: Princeton University Press.

Hess, G. A. (1990) *Chicago School Reform: How It Is and How It Came To Be*. Chicago: Chicago Panel on Public School Policy and Finance.

Hess, G. A. (1991) *School Restructuring, Chicago Style*. Newbury Park, CA: Corwin Press.

Hess, G. A. (1992) Midway through school reform in Chicago, *International Journal of Educational Reform*, 1(3), 270–84.

Hickox, M. (1995). Situating vocationalism, *British Journal of Sociology of Education*, 16(2), 153–63.

Hill, P. T., Foster G. E. and Gendler, T. (1990) *High Schools with Character*. Santa Monica, CA: RAND.

Hill, R. (1992) *Managing Today's Schools: the Case for Shared Decision-making*. Wellington: NZ Institute for Social Research and Development.

Hill, T. (1994) Primary headteachers' careers: a survey of primary school heads with particular reference to women's career trajectories, *British Educational Research Journal*, 20(2), 197–209.

Hillgate Group (1987) *The Reform of British Education*. London: Claridge Press.

Hillgate Group (1989) *Learning to Teach*. London: Claridge Press.

Hirsch, D. (1995) The other school choice – how should over-subscribed schools select their pupils? Open lecture at the Institute of Education, University of London, 31 May.

Hirsch, D. (1997) Policies for school choice: what can Britain learn from abroad? In R. Glatter, P. A. Woods and C. Bagley (eds) *Choice and Diversity in Schooling: Perspectives and Prospects*. London: Routledge.

Hirst, P. Q. (1993) Associational democracy. In D. Held (ed.) *Prospects for Democracy*. Cambridge: Polity Press.

Hirst, P. Q. (1994) *Associative Democracy: New Forms of Economic and Social Governance*. Cambridge: Polity Press.

Hirst P. Q. (1995) Can secondary associations enhance democratic governance? In J. Cohen and J. Rogers (eds) *Associations and Democracy*. London: Verso.

Hirst, P. Q. and Thompson, G. (1996) *Globalization in Question: the International Economy and the Possibilities of Governance*. Cambridge: Polity Press.

Hoyle, E. (1974) Professionality, professionalism and control in teaching, *London Education Review*, 3(2), 13–19.

Hughes, M. (1997) The National Curriculum in England and Wales: a lesson in externally-imposed reform?, *Educational Administration Quarterly*, 33(2), 183–97.

Hutton, W. (1995) *The State We're In*. London: Jonathan Cape.

Jessop, B., Bonnett, K., Bromley, S. and Ling, T. (1987) Popular capitalism, flexible accumulation and left strategy, *New Left Review*, 165, 104–23.

Johnson, R. (1989) Thatcherism and English education: breaking the mould or continuing the pattern?, *History of Education*, 18(2), 91–121.

Jones, L. and Moore, R. (1993) Education, competence and the control of expertise, *British Journal of Sociology of Education*, 14, 385–97.

Kallos, D. and Lundahl-Kallos, L. (1994) Recent changes in teachers' work in Sweden: professionalization or what? In D. Kallos and S. Lindblad (eds) *New Policy Contexts for Education: Sweden and United Kingdom*. Umeå, Sweden: Umeå University.

Kenway, J. (1993) Marketing education in the postmodern age, *Journal of Education Policy*, 8(1), 105–22.

Kerchner, C. and Mitchell, D. (1988) *The Changing Idea of a Teachers' Union*. London: Falmer Press.

Knight, J. (1993) Delegated financial management and school effectiveness. In C. Dimmock (ed.) *School-based Management and School Effectiveness*. London: Routledge.

Knight, J., Bartlett, L. and McWilliam, E. (eds) (1993a) *Unfinished Business: Reshaping the Teacher Education Industry for the 1990s*. Rockhampton: University of Central Queensland.

Knight, J., Lingard, B. and Porter, P. (1993b) Restructuring schooling towards the 1990s. In B. Lingard, J. Knight and P. Porter (eds) *Schooling Reform in Hard Times*. London: Falmer Press.

Labaree, D. F. and Pallas, A. M. (1996) Dire straits: the narrow vision of the Holmes Group, *Educational Researcher*, 25(5), 25–8.

Lash, S. (1990) *Sociology of Postmodernism*. London: Routledge.

Lauder, H., Hughes, D., Waslander, S., Thrupp, M., McGlinn, J., Newton, S. and Dupuis, A. (1994) *The Creation of Market Competition for Education in New Zealand*. Smithfield Project. Wellington: Victoria University of Wellington.

Lauder, H., Hughes, D., Watson. S., Simiyu, I., Strathdee, R. and Waslander, S. (1995) *Trading in Futures: the Nature of Choice in Educational Markets in New Zealand*. Smithfield Project. Wellington: Victoria University of Wellington.

Lauglo, J. (1996) Forms of decentralization and the implications for education. In J. Chapman, W. L. Boyd, R. Lander and D. Reynolds (eds) *The Reconstruction of Education: Quality, Equality and Control*. London: Cassell.

Lawlor, S. (1990) *Teachers Mistaught: Training in Theories or Education in Subjects?* London: Centre for Policy Studies.

Lawn, M. and Ozga, J. (1986) Unequal partners: teachers under indirect rule, *British Journal of Sociology of Education*, 7(2), 225–37.

Lawton, S. (1990) Why restructure? An international survey of the roots of reform, *Journal of Education Policy*, 8(2), 139–54.

Le Grand, J. (1987) The middle class use of the British social services. In R. Gooding and J. Le Grand, *Not Only the Poor: the Middle Classes and the Welfare State*. London: Allen and Unwin.

Le Grand, J. and Bartlett, W. (eds) (1993) *Quasi-markets and Social Policy*. London: Macmillan.

Lee, V. E. and Bryk, A. S. (1993) Science or policy argument? In E. Rasell and R. Rothstein (eds) *School Choice: Examining the Evidence*. Washington, DC: Economic Policy Institute.

Levačić, R. (1995) *Local Management of Schools: Analysis and Practice*. Buckingham: Open University Press.

Levin, H. M. (1990) The theory of choice applied to education. In J. Witte and J. Clune (eds) *Choice and Control in American Education, Volume 1. The Theory of Choice, Decentralisation and School Restructuring*. London: Falmer Press.

Levitas, R. (1990) *The Concept of Utopia*. London: Phillip Allan.

Lewis, D. A. and Nakagawa, K. (1995) *Race and Educational Reform in the American Metropolis: a Study of School Decentralization*. Albany, NY: SUNY Press.

Livingstone, I. (1994) *The Workloads of Primary School Teachers – a Wellington Region Survey*. Wellington, NZ: Chartwell Consultants.

Louis, K. S. and Miles, M. B. (1992) *Improving the Urban High School: What Works and Why*. London: Cassell.

Lowe, R. (1988) *Education in the Post-war Years*. London: Routledge.

Lundgren, U. P. (undated) The knowledge base for national education policy-making: the case of Sweden. Mimeo, National Agency for Education, Sweden.

Mac an Ghaill, M. (1992) Teachers' work: Curriculum restructuring, culture, power and comprehensive schooling, *British Journal of Sociology of Education*, 13(2), 177–200.

McKenzie, J. (1993) Education as a private problem or a public issue? The process of excluding 'education' from the 'public sphere'. Paper presented at the International Conference on the Public Sphere, Manchester, 8–10 January.

McLean, M. (1992) *The Promise and Perils of Educational Comparison*. London: Tufnell Press.

McLean, M. (1995) *Education Traditions Compared: Content, Teaching and Learning in Industrialized Countries*. London: David Fulton.

MacLeod, D. (1995) School meals reveal 'sham' of equality, *Guardian*, 5 June.

MacLeod, D. (1996) Would you sign this?, *Education Guardian*, 15 October.

Maclure, S. (1993) Fight this tooth and nail, *Times Educational Supplement*, 18 June.

Macpherson, R. J. S. (1991) The politics of Australian curriculum: the third coming of a national curriculum agency in a neo-pluralist state. In S. H. Fuhrman and B. Malen (eds) *The Politics of Curriculum and Testing*. London: Falmer Press.

Mahony, P. and Hextall, I. (1996) Trailing the TTA. Paper delivered at the British Educational Research Association Annual Conference, University of Lancaster, 12–15 September.

Malen, B. (1994) Enacting site-based management: a political utilities analysis, *Educational Evaluation and Policy Analysis*, 16(3), 249–67.

Marginson, S. (1993) *Education and Public Policy in Australia*. Cambridge: Cambridge University Press.

Marks, H. M. and Louis, K. S. (1995) Does teacher empowerment affect the classroom? The implications of teacher empowerment for teachers' instructional practice and student academic performance. Paper prepared for the Center on Organization and Structuring of Schools, Wisconsin Centre for Education Research, Madison, WI.

Marks, J. (1992) *The Assisted Places Scheme*. London: Independent Schools Information Service.

Marquand, D. (1989) Beyond left and right: the need for a new politics. In S. Hall and M. Jacques (eds) *New Times: the Changing Face of Politics in the 1990s*. London: Lawrence and Wishart.

Marquand, D. (1995) Flagging fortunes, *The Guardian*, 3 July.

Marren, E. and Levačić, R. (1994) Senior management, classroom teacher and governor responses to local management of schools, *Educational Management and Administration*, 22(1), 39–53.

Maychell, K. (1994) *Counting the Cost: the Impact of LMS on Schools' Patterns of Spending*. Slough: National Foundation for Educational Research.

Medler, A. and Nathan, J. (1995) *Charter Schools: What Are They up to?*. Denver, CO: Education Commission of the States.

Menter, I., Muschamp, Y., Nicholls, P., Ozga, J. with Pollard, A. (1997) *Work and Identity in the Primary School: a Post-Fordist Analysis*. Buckingham: Open University Press.

Mickelson, R. (1996) A critical examination of business leadership of American school reform. Paper presented at the Comparative and International Education Society Conference, Williamsburg, VA, 6–10 March.

Minister of Education (1988) *Tomorrow's Schools: the Reform of Education Administration in New Zealand*. Wellington, NZ: Government Printer.

Miron, G. (1993) *Choice and the Use of Market Forces in Schooling: Swedish Education Reforms for the 1990s*. Stockholm: Institute of International Education, Stockholm University.

Moe, T. (1994) The British battle for choice. In K. L. Billingsley (ed.) *Voices on Choice: the Education Reform Debate*. San Francisco: Pacific Institute for Public Policy.

Mohrman, S. A., Wohlstetter, P. and associates (1994) *School-based Management: Organizing for High Performance*. San Francisco: Jossey-Bass.

Molnar, A. (1996) *Giving Kids the Business: the Commercialization of America's Schools*. Boulder, CO: Westview Press.

Mortimore, P., Sammons, P., Stoll, L., Lewis, D. and Ecob, R. (1988) *School Matters: the Junior Years*. Wells: Open Books.

Mouffe, C. (1989) Toward a radical democratic citizenship, *Democratic Left*, 17, 6–7.

Murfitt, D. (1995) The implementation of New Right reform in education: teachers and the intensification of work. Unpublished masters thesis, Education Department, University of Canterbury, Christchurch, New Zealand.

Murphy, J. (1994) *Principles of School-based Management*. Chapel Hill, NC: Educational Policy Research Center.

Murphy, J. and Beck, L. G. (1995) *School-based Management as School Reform: Taking Stock*. Thousand Oaks, CA: Corwin Press.

Nash, R. (1989) Tomorrow's schools: state power and parent participation, *New Zealand Journal of Educational Studies*, 24(2), 113–28.

Nathan, J. (1996) *Charter Schools: Creating Hope and Opportunity for American Education*. San Francisco: Jossey-Bass.

National Consumer Council (1996) *Sponsorship in Schools*. London: National Consumer Council.

Neave, G. (1988) On the cultivation of quality, efficiency and enterprise: an overview of recent trends in higher education in Western Europe, 1968–1988, *European Journal of Education*, 23(1/2), 7–23.

Newmann, F. (1993) Beyond common sense in educational restructuring: the issues of content and leadership, *Educational Researcher*, 22(2), 4–13.

Nixon, J., Martin, J., McKeown, P. and Ranson, S. (1997) Confronting 'failure': towards a pedagogy of recognition, *International Journal of Inclusive Education*, 1(2), 121–41.

Nozick, R. (1974) *Anarchy, State and Utopia*. Oxford: Basil Blackwell.

Odden, A. (1995) Decentralized school management in Victoria, Australia. Paper prepared for the World Bank, Consortium for Policy Research in Education, Madison, WI.

Odden, E. R. and Wohlstetter, P. (1995) Making school-based management work, *Educational Leadership*, 52(5), 32–6.

OECD (1994) *School: a Matter of Choice*. Paris: OECD/CERI.

OECD (1995a) *Reviews of National Policies for Education: Sweden*. Paris: OECD.

OECD (1995b) *Decision-making in 14 OECD Education Systems*. Paris: OECD.

Offe, C. (1975) The theory of the capitalist state and the problem of policy-formation. In L. Lindberg, R. Alford, C. Crouch and C. Offe (eds) *Stress and Contradiction in Modern Capitalism*. Lexington, MA: Lexington Books.

Offe, C. (1984) *Contradictions of the Welfare State*. London: Hutchinson.

Offe, C. (1996) *Modernity and the State: East, West*. Cambridge: Polity Press.

Ofsted (1994) *Primary Matters: a Discussion of Teaching and Learning in Primary Schools*. London: Ofsted.

Ogawa, R. T. and White, P. A. (1994) School-based management: an overview. In S. A. Mohrman, P. Wohlstetter and associates *School-based Management: Organizing for High Performance*. San Francisco: Jossey-Bass.

Ouston, J. (1993) Women as managers. In J. Ouston (ed.) *Women in Education Management*. Harlow: Longman.

Ozga, J. (1990) Policy research and policy theory: a comment on Fitz and Halpin, *Journal of Education Policy*, 5(4), 359–62.

Ozga, J. (1993) Teacher de-professionalization: hard lessons from England. Paper presented at the Annual Conference of the Australian Association for Research in Education, Fremantle, Western Australia, November.

Parsons, C. (1996) Exclusions from schools in England in the 1990s: trends, causes and responses. *Children and Society*, 10, 177–86.

Pauly, E. (1991) *The Classroom Crucible: What Really Works, What Doesn't, and Why*. New York: HarperCollins.

Pearce, D. (1996) Two years of peace? The Schools Consultative Group and the state in New Zealand. Unpublished PhD thesis, University of Canterbury, Christchurch, New Zealand.

Pennell, H. and West, A. (1995) *Changing Schools: Secondary Schools' Admissions Policies in Inner London in 1995* (Clare Market Papers no. 9). London: London School of Economics and Political Science.

Phillips, A. (1993) *Democracy and Difference*. Cambridge: Polity Press.

Phillips, A. (1995) *The Politics of Presence*. Oxford: Oxford University Press.

Picot, B. and members of the Taskforce to Review Educational Administration (1988) *Administering for Excellence* (Picot Report). Wellington, NZ: Government Printer.

Plank, S., Schiller, K. S., Schneider, B. and Coleman, J. S. (1993) Effects of choice in education. In E. Rasell and R. Rothstein (eds) *School Choice: Examining the Evidence*. Washington, DC: Economic Policy Institute.

Pollard, A., Broadfoot, P., Croll, P., Osborn, M. and Abbott, D. (1994) *Changing English Primary Schools? The Impact of the Education Reform Act at Key Stage One*. London: Cassell.

Pollard, S. (1995) *Schools, Selection and the Left*. London: Social Market Foundation.

Power, S. (1992) Researching the impact of education policy: difficulties and discontinuities, *Journal of Education Policy*, 7, 493–500.

Power, S. (1995) The detail and the 'bigger picture': the use of state-centred theory in explaining education policy and practice, *International Studies in Sociology of Education*, 5(1), 77–92.

Power, S. (1996) *The Pastoral and the Academic: Conflict and Contradiction in the Curriculum*. London: Cassell.

Power, S., Fitz, J. and Halpin, D. (1994) Parents, pupils and grant maintained schools, *British Educational Research Journal*, 20(2), 209–26.

Power, S., Halpin, D. and Fitz, J. (1996) Back to the future? The rise of educational fundamentalism. Paper presented at the Annual Conference of the British Sociological Association, University of Reading, April.

Power, S. and Whitty, G. (1996) Teaching new subjects: the hidden curriculum of marketised education systems, *Melbourne Studies in Education*, 37(2), 1–22.

Preston, B. and Walker, J. C. (1993) Competency-based standards in the professions and higher education. In C. Collins (ed.) *Competencies: the Competencies Debate in Australian Education and Training*. Canberra: Australian College of Education.

Pride, R. A. and Woodard, J. D. (1985) *The Burden of Busing: the Politics of Desegregation in Nashville, Tennessee*. Knoxville: University of Tennessee Press.

Pryke, R. (1996) Positioning the LEA in LEArning, *Education Journal*, 6, 21.

Pusey, M. (1991) *Economic Rationalism in Canberra*. Cambridge: Cambridge University Press.

Raab, C. D., Munn, P., McAvoy, L., Bailey, L., Arnott, M. and Adler, M. (1997) Devolving the management of schools in Britain, *Educational Administration Quarterly*, 33(2), 140–57.

Rafferty, F. (1994) Alarm at growth of 60–hour week, *Times Educational Supplement*, 5 August.

Rafferty, F. (1996) Working week grows longer, *Times Educational Supplement*, 9 August, 1.

Ranson, S. (1993) Renewing education for democracy. Paper contributed to an Institute of Public Policy Research Seminar on Alternative Education Policies, London, 25–6 March.

Raywid, M. A. (1994a) Focus Schools: a Genre to Consider. Urban Diversity Series no. 106. New York: ERIC Clearinghouse on Urban Education.

Raywid, M. A. (1994b) Alternative schools: the state of the art, *Educational Leadership*, 52(1), 26–31.

Reich, R. (1991) *The Work of Nations: Preparing Ourselves for 21st Century Capitalism*. London: Simon and Schuster.

Riddell, P. (1992) Is it the end of politics?, *The Times*, 3 August.

Riley, D. (1990) Should market forces control educational decision making?, *American Political Science Review*, 84(2), 549–58.

Roberts, P. (1994) Business sponsorship in schools: a changing climate. In D. Bridges and T. H. McLaughlin (eds) *Education and the Market Place*. London: Falmer Press.

Robertson, D. B. and Waltman, J. L. (1993) The politics of policy borrowing. In D. Finegold, L. Macfarland and W. Richardson (eds) *Something Borrowed, Something Learned? The Transatlantic Market in Education and Training Reform*. Washington, DC: Brookings Institution.

Robertson, P. J., Wohlstetter, P. and Mohrman, S. A. (1995) Generating curriculum and instructional innovations through school-based management, *Educational Administration Quarterly*, 31(3), 375–404.

Robertson, R. (1991) Social theory, cultural relativity and the problem of globality. In A. D. King (ed.) *Culture, Globalization and the World-System*. London: Macmillan.

Robertson, S. L. (1993) The politics of devolution, self-management and post-Fordism in schools. In J. Smyth (ed.) *A Socially Critical View of the Self-managing School*. London: Falmer Press.

Robertson, S. L. (1995) 'Free capitalism' and 'fast schools': new realities and new truths. Paper presented at the American Educational Research Association Annual Meeting, San Francisco, 18–22 April.

Robertson, S. L. (1996a) Teachers' work, restructuring and post-Fordism: constructing the new 'professionalism'. In I. F. Goodson and A. Hargreaves (eds) *Teachers' Professional Lives*. London: Falmer Press.

Robertson, S. L. (1996b) Markets and teacher professionalism: a political economy analysis. Paper presented to the Ninth World Congress of Comparative Education Societies, University of Sydney, 1–6 July.

Robertson, S. L. and Soucek, V. (1991) Changing social realities in Australian schools: a study of teachers' perceptions and experiences of current reforms. Paper presented at the Comparative and International Education Society Conference, Pittsburgh, PA, 14–17 March.

Robins, K. (1991) Tradition and translation: national culture in its global context. In J. Corner and S. Harvey (eds) *Enterprise and Heritage: Crosscurrents of National Culture*. London: Routledge.

Robinson, V. and Timperley, H. (1996) Learning to be responsive: the impact of school choice and decentralization, *Educational Management and Administration*, 24(1), 65–78.

Rogers, M. (1992) *Opting out: Choice and the Future of Schools*. London: Lawrence and Wishart.

Rose, N. and Miller P. (1992) Political power beyond the state: problematics of government, *British Journal of Sociology*, 43(2), 173–205.

Rose R. (1991) Comparing forms of comparative analysis, *Political Studies*, XXXIX, 446–62.

Rossell, C. H. and Glenn, C. L. (1988) The Cambridge controlled choice plan, *Urban Review*, 20(2), 75–94.

Rutter, M., Maughan, B., Mortimore, P. and Ouston, J. (1979) *Fifteen Thousand Hours: Secondary Schools and Their Effects on Children*. London: Open Books.

Ryan, B. (1993) 'And your corporate manager will set you free . . . ': Devolution in South Australian education. In J. Smyth (ed.) *A Socially Critical View of the Self-managing School*. London: Falmer Press.

Sammons, P., Hillman, J. and Mortimore, P. (1995) *Key Characteristics of Effective Schools: a Review of School Effectiveness Research*. London: Ofsted and Institute of Education, University of London.

SCAA (1996) *Consultation on Values in Education and the Community*. London: School Curriculum and Assessment Authority.

Scott, B. (1989) *Schools Renewal: a Strategy to Revitalise Schools within the New South Wales Education System, Management Review*. Milsons Point: NSW Educational Portfolio.

Sebring, P. B., Bryk, A. S. and Easton, J. Q. (1995) *Charting Reform: Chicago Teachers Take Stock*. Chicago: Consortium on Chicago School Research.

Seddon, T. (1994) Decentralisation and democracy. Paper presented at the Teachers and Decentralisation Seminar, National Industry Education Forum, Melbourne, 26 August.

Seddon, T., Angus, L. and Poole, M. (1991) Pressures on the move to school-based decision-making and management. In J. Chapman (ed.) *School-based Decision-making and Management*. London: Falmer Press.

Sexton, S. (1987) *Our Schools – a Radical Policy*. Warlingham: Institute of Economic Affairs, Education Unit.

Shakeshaft, C. (1993) Women in educational management in the United States. In J. Ouston (ed.) *Women in Education Management*. Harlow: Longman.

Shilling, C. (1991) Are all teachers equally free to be professionals?, *Gender and Education*, 3(1), 61–80.

Simon, B. (1994) *The State and Educational Change*. London: Lawrence and Wishart.

Sinclair, J., Ironside, M. and Seifert, R. (1993) Classroom struggle? Market oriented education reforms and their impact on teachers' professional autonomy, labour intensification and resistance. Paper presented to the International Labour Process Conference, 1 April.

Slattery, L. (1989) Goals set for nation's schools, *The Age*, 15 April, 1.

Smith, K. B. and Meier, K. J. (1995) *The Case against School Choice: Politics, Markets and Fools*. Armonk, NY: M E Sharpe.

Smith, T. and Noble, M. (1995) *Education Divides: Poverty and Schooling in the 1990s*. London: Child Poverty Action Group.

Smyth, J. (1993a) *Schools of the Future and the Politics of Blame*, PSMI Working Paper 34. Melbourne: Monash University.

Smyth, J. (1993b) Introduction. In J. Smyth (ed.) *A Socially Critical View of the Self-managing School*. London: Falmer Press.

Soucek, V. (1996a) Sociology of teachers' work in a global context. Paper presented at the International Sociological Association Mid-term Conference on Urban Education, University of California, Los Angeles, 20–22 June.

Soucek, V. (1996b) Education policy formation in the post-Fordist era and its impact on the nature of teachers' work. Unpublished PhD thesis, University of Alberta, Canada.

Stearns, K. (1996) *School Reform: Lessons from England*. Princeton, NJ: Carnegie Foundation.

Steffy, B. E. and English, F. W. (1995) Radical legislated school reform in the United States. In D. S. G. Carter and M. H. O'Neill (eds) *Case Studies in Educational Change: an International Perspective*. London: Falmer Press.

Sullivan, K. (1994) The impact of education reform on teachers' professional ideologies, *New Zealand Journal of Educational Studies*, 29(1), 3–20.

Swedish Institute (1995) *Factsheets*, www.si.se/english/factsheets/school.html, Swedish Institute.

Tan, N. (1990) *The Cambridge Controlled Choice Program: Improving Educational Equity and Integration*. Education Policy Paper no. 4. New York: Manhattan Institute for Policy Research.

Taylor, C. (1994) The politics of recognition. In A. Gutmann (ed.) *Multiculturalism: Examining the Politics of Recognition*. Princeton, NJ: University of Princeton Press.

Thomas, H. and Martin, J. (1996) *Managing Resources for School Improvement: Creating a Cost-effective School*. London: Routledge.

Thompson, K. (1992) Social pluralism and postmodernity. In S. Hall, D. Held and T. McGrew (eds) *Modernity and Its Futures*. Cambridge: Polity Press.

Toch, T. (1991) *In the Name of Excellence: the Struggle to Reform the Nation's Schools, Why It Is Failing, and What Should Be Done*. New York: Oxford University Press.

Tooley, J. (1995) Markets or democracy? a reply to Stewart Ranson, *British Journal of Educational Studies*, 43(1), 31–4.

Tooley, J. (1996a) *Education without the State*. London: Institute of Economic Affairs.

Tooley, J. (1996b) Depoliticising schooling: education, markets and civil society. The Second Aske's Education Lecture, Barber-Surgeons' Hall, London, 15 October.

Troman, G. (1996) The rise of the new professionals: the restructuring of primary teachers' work and professionalism, *British Journal of Sociology of Education*, 17(4), 473–87.

Troyna, B. (1992) 'The hub' and 'the rim': how LMS buckles antiracist education. Paper presented to the Education Reform Act Research Network, University of Warwick, 12 February.

Urahn, S. and Stewart, D. (1994) *Minnesota Charter Schools: a Research Report*. St Paul: Research Department, Minnesota House of Representatives.

Usher, R. and Edwards, R. (1994) *Postmodernism and Education*. London: Routledge.

Vincent, C., Evans, J., Lunt, I. and Young, P. (1995) Policy and practice: the changing nature of special educational provision in schools, *British Journal of Special Education*, 22(1), 4–11.

Walford, G. (1992a) *Selection for Secondary Schooling*. National Commission on Education Briefing Paper 7. London: National Commission on Education.

Walford, G. (1992b) Educational choice and equity in Great Britain. In P. W. Cookson (ed.) *The Choice Controversy: Current Debates and Research*. Newbury Park, CA: Corwin Press.

Walford, G. (1995) *Educational Politics: Pressure Groups and Faith-based Schools*. Aldershot: Avebury.

Walford, G. (1997) Diversity, choice and selection in England and Wales, *Educational Administration Quarterly*, 33(2), 158–69.

Walford, G. and Miller, H. (1991) *City Technology College*. Milton Keynes: Open University Press.

Waring, S. (1992) Women teachers' careers: do governors hold the key?, *Management in Education*, 6(4), 14–16.

Waslander, S. and Thrupp, M. (1995) Choice, competition and segregation: an empirical analysis of a New Zealand secondary school market 1990–1993, *Journal of Education Policy*, 10(1), 1–26.

Watkins, P. (1993) Pushing crisis and stress down the line: the self-managing school. In J. Smyth (ed.) *A Socially Critical View of the Self-managing School*. London: Falmer Press.

Watkins, P. and Blackmore, J. (1993) The development of representative committees in

Victorian schools: new structures in the democratization of educational administration? In B. Lingard, J. Knight and P. Porter (eds) *Schooling Reform in Hard Times*. London: Falmer Press.

Webb, A. (1991) Governors' perceptions of training needs. In M. Leicester (ed.) *Governor Training: Perspectives Post-ERA*. Coventry: University of Warwick Research Papers in Continuing Education.

Webb, R. and Vulliamy, G. (1996) A deluge of directives: conflict between collegiality and managerialism in the post-ERA primary school, *British Educational Research Journal*, 22(4), 441–59.

Weiler, H. N. (1983) Legalization, expertise and participation: strategies of compensatory legitimation in educational policy, *Comparative Education Review*, 27(2), 259–77.

Weiler, H. N. (1989) Education and power: the politics of educational decentralization in comparative perspective, *Educational Policy*, 3, 31–43.

Weiss, M. (1993) New guiding principles in educational policy: the case of Germany, *Journal of Education Policy*, 8(4), 307–20.

Welch, A. (1996) *Australian Education: Reform or Crisis?* St Leonards, NSW: Allen and Unwin.

Wells, A. S. (1990) *Public School Choice: Issues and Concerns for Urban Educators*, ERIC/CUE Digest no. 63. New York: ERIC Clearinghouse on Urban Education.

Wells, A. S. (1993a) *Time to Choose: America at the Crossroads of School Choice Policy*. New York: Hill and Wang.

Wells, A. S. (1993b) The sociology of school choice: why some win and others lose in the educational marketplace. In E. Rasell and R. Rothstein (eds) *School Choice: Examining the Evidence*. Washington, DC: Economic Policy Institute.

Wells, A. S. and Crain, R. L. (1992) Do parents choose school quality or school status? A sociological theory of free market education. In P. W. Cookson (ed.) *The Choice Controversy*. Newbury Park, CA: Corwin Press.

Wells, A. S., Grutzik, C. and Carnochan, S. (1996) The multiple meanings of US charter school reform: exploring the politics of deregulation. Paper presented at the British Educational Research Association Annual Conference, University of Lancaster, 12–15 September.

Wells, A. S. and Oakes, J. (1997) Tracking, detracking and the politics of educational reform: a sociological perspective. In C. Torres (ed.) *Emerging Issues in the Sociology of Education: Comparative Perspectives*. Albany, NY: SUNY Press.

Whiting, C., Whitty, G., Furlong, J., Miles, S. and Barton, L. (1996) *Partnership in Initial Teacher Education: a Topography*. London: Institute of Education.

Whitty, G. (1989) The New Right and the National Curriculum: state control or market forces?, *Journal of Education Policy*, 4(4), 329–41.

Whitty, G. (1992) Education, economy and national culture. In R. Bocock and K. Thompson (eds) *Social and Cultural Forms of Modernity*. Cambridge: Polity Press.

Whitty, G. (1997a) Creating quasi-markets in education: a review of recent research on parental choice and school autonomy in three countries, *Review of Research in Education*, 22, 3–47.

Whitty, G. (1997b) Social theory and education policy: the legacy of Karl Mannheim, *British Journal of Sociology of Education*, 18(2), 149–63.

Whitty, G., Edwards, T. and Gewirtz, S. (1993) *Specialisation and Choice in Urban Education: the City Technology College Experiment*. London: Routledge.

Whitty, G., Power, S. and Edwards, T. (1996) The role of the Assisted Places Scheme in privatisation and marketisation. Paper presented to the European Conference on Educational Research, Seville, Spain, 25–8 September.

Whitty, G., Rowe, G. and Aggleton, P. (1994) Subjects and themes in the secondary school curriculum, *Research Papers in Education*, 9, 159–81.

Wiener, M. J. (1981) *English Culture and the Decline of the Industrial Spirit 1850–1980*. Cambridge: Cambridge University Press.

Wilcox, B. and Gray, J. (1996) *Inspecting Schools: Holding Schools to Account and Helping Schools to Improve*. Buckingham: Open University Press.

Williams, E. (1994) The exclusion zone, *Search*, 21, 11–14.

Williams, F. (1991) The welfare state as part of a racially structured and patriarchal capitalism. In M. Loney, R. Bocock, J. Clarke, A. Cochrane, P. Graham and M. Wilson (eds) *The State or the Market*, 2nd edn. London: Sage.

Williams, R. (1983) *Towards 2000*. London: Chatto & Windus.

Williams, R. (1989) *Resources of Hope: Culture, Democracy, Socialism*. London: Verso.

Witte, J. F. (1990) Choice and control: an analytic overview. In W. H. Clune and J. F. Witte, (eds) *Choice and Control in American Education, Volume 1*. London: Falmer Press.

Witte, J. F., Thorn, C. A., Pritchard, K. and Claibourn, M. (1994) *Fourth Year Report: Milwaukee Parental Choice Program*. Madison, WI: Department of Public Instruction.

Witte, J. F., Thorn, C. A. and Pritchard, K. (1995a) *Private and Public Education in Wisconsin: Implications for the Choice Debate*. Madison, WI: University of Wisconsin.

Witte, J. F., Thorn, C. A. and Sterr, T. (1995b) *Fifth Year Report: Milwaukee Parental Choice Program*. Madison, WI: Department of Public Instruction.

Wohlstetter, P. (1995) Getting school-based management right: what works and what doesn't, *Phi Delta Kappan*, September, 22–6.

Wohlstetter, P. and Mohrman, S. A. (1993) *School-based Management: Strategies for Success*. New Brunswick, NJ: Consortium for Policy Research in Education.

Wohlstetter, P. and Odden, A. (1992) Rethinking school-based management policy and research, *Educational Administration Quarterly*, 28(4), 529–49.

Wohlstetter, P., Smyer, R. and Mohrman, S. A. (1994) New boundaries for school-based management: the high involvement model, *Educational Evaluation and Policy Analysis*, 16(3), 268–86.

Wohlstetter, P., Wenning, R. and Briggs, K. L. (1995) Charter schools in the United States: the question of autonomy, *Educational Policy*, 9(4), 331–58.

Woods, P. A. (1992) Empowerment through choice? Towards an understanding of parental choice and school responsiveness, *Educational Management and Administration*, 20(4), 329–41.

Wright, E. O. (1995) Preface to J. Cohen and J. Rogers (eds), *Associations and Democracy*. London: Verso.

Wylie, C. (1994) *Self Managing Schools in New Zealand: the Fifth Year*. Wellington: New Zealand Council for Educational Research.

Wylie, C. (1995a) Contrary currents: the application of the public sector reform framework in education, *New Zealand Journal of Educational Studies*, 20(2), 149–64.

Wylie, C. (1995b) The shift to school-based management in New Zealand – the school view. In D. S. G. Carter and M. H. O'Neill (eds) *Case Studies in Educational Change: an International Perspective*. London: Falmer Press.

Yeatman, A. (1994) *Postmodern Revisionings of the Political*. New York: Routledge.

Young, M. and Whitty, G. (eds) (1977) *Society, State and Schooling*. Lewes: Falmer Press.

INDEX

reform and, 80, 119
Sweden, 122, 125
United States, 80, 121, 122–3, 125
parents, 45
charter schools and, 97, 106
disadvantaged communities, 102
empowerment of, 103, 119
as governors, 95, 98, 103
grant-maintained schools and, 97–8
partnership role, 10, 95, 105–6
role (in education), 14, 102, 105–6
school management and, 103–4
as substitute teachers, 71
traditionalism and, 90
Parent's Charter, 105
Parsons, C., 90
Pauly, E., 86
Pearce, D., 43, 139
PEASE Academy (Minnesota), 96
Pennell, H., 120
performance, see school performance
Peterson, P. E., 123
Phillips, A., 136
Picot Report (1988), 21
Plank, S., 121
policy
convergence, 12, 31–6, 39–42
initiatives, 3, 4–5, 30
political approach, 126–42
science/scholarship (comparison), 5–6
politics
approach to policy, 126–42
challenge (of globalization), 46–7
reform and, 15, 33, 35–6, 47
Pollard, A., 87, 89
Pollard, S., 4, 41, 115
population distribution, 16–17, 81–2
post-Fordism, 12, 40–1, 42, 47, 71, 78
postmodernism, 12, 39, 40, 41–2, 46, 47, 76
poverty, 44, 131
Power, S., 5, 8, 90, 97, 118, 140
Preston, B., 78
Pride, R. A., 131
principals
role, 55–60, 62–3, 126
women, 60, 61–2
see also headteachers; school managers
priorities (management and educational), 57, 59–60
private schools, 53, 124, 127–8, 130
Australia, 24, 25, 96, 122, 123
choice, 122–3
England and Wales, 96, 117, 118, 122
New Zealand, 97
Sweden, 122, 123
United States, 25, 27, 96, 97, 122–3

privatization, 3, 46, 97, 127–8
'producer capture', 12
professional-contextualist conception of teaching, 65, 76
professionalism, 12–13, 64–5, 70, 71, 74–5, 76, 78, 112, 126, 127
progressive education, 89–90, 92
Protestant schools, 96
'provider capture', 72
Pryke, R., 129
public education (restructuring), 15–30
public schools (United States), 10, 27, 32, 121
'pump-priming' schemes, 45
pupils, see students
Pusey, M., 37

quasi-market, 3–4, 12, 36, 41, 128
Australia, 120, 122
community and, 95
contracts, 105
England and Wales, 115–20, 122
equity effects of, 115–22
New Zealand, 120–1
Sweden, 29, 122
United States, 121–3
see also free market; market
Queensland, 24, 68, 104

Raab, C. D., 59
racial segregation/desegregation policies, 121, 131
Rafferty, F., 67
Ranson, S., 119
Rattansi, A., 41
Raywid, M. A., 27, 96, 107
Reagan, Ronald, 8, 26
'real utopias' project, 135
reform, 5
academic excellence and, 119
appeal of, 41–2
community and, 93, 107
comparative approach, 6–14
equity effects, 115–22, 126–7
globalization, 6, 31–47, 137
Marxist critiques, 42, 132
parental choice and, 80, 119
politics and, 15, 33, 35–6, 47
professionalism and, 64–5, 78
regulation of, 80
responses to, 56–7, 133
restructuring policies, 15–30
terminology, 9–10
traditions and, 16
Reich, R., 46
representative committees, 24–5, 104–5
Republicanism, 9

neo-Marxist critiques, 132
paradox of, 131–4
regulation (changes), 43
role of, 46–7, 138–9
Stearns, K., 8
Steffy, B. E., 82
Stewart, D., 74, 86, 96
strategic evaluation, 36–7, 89
STRB (School Teachers' Pay Review Body), 67
Student Performance Standards, 24
students, 13
achievement, 83–4, 121
'at risk', 27, 106
commodification of, 105, 115
gifted, 90, 117
performance, 24, 80, 82, 113–14
'special needs', 90, 115, 116, 117, 118, 120
Stuyvesant High School, 27
Sullivan, K., 74
Sunday Times, 81
supermarket voucher schemes, 91
Sweden, 58
autonomy, 29, 30, 32–3
education system, 9, 15
National Curriculum, 29–30, 140
parental choice, 122, 125
population distribution, 16
private schools, 122, 123
quasi-market, 29, 122
research methods, 7
restructuring policies, 15, 28–30
teacher education, 78
teachers (role/work), 68, 74–5, 78
Swedish Institute, 28

Tan, N., 121
Targeted Individual Entitlement, 22
Taylor, C., 136
teacher education, 52, 75–8, 88
Teacher Training Agency (TTA), 76, 78
teachers
attitude to change, 75
decision-making, 74–5, 83
devolution (impact of), 70–5
education/training, 52, 75–8, 88
empowerment of, 64, 65–70, 85–6
as governors, 100
hours worked, 67
isolation of, 70
job satisfaction, 67
management participation, 73
parents as substitute, 71
professionalism, 12–13, 64–5, 70, 71, 74–5, 76–8, 112, 126, 127
relationships with headteachers, 68
'special needs', 90, 115
trade unions and, 70–5

work (changes), 64–78
see also headteachers; principals
technocratic-reductionist conception of teaching, 65, 76
terminology, 9–10, 53
Thatcher, Margaret, 8, 18, 39
Thomas, H., 58, 59, 66, 73, 83, 84, 100, 111, 114
Thompson, G., 6
Thompson, K., 41
Thrupp, M., 120, 121
Timperley, H., 102
Toch, T., 87
Tomorrow's Schools, 21, 40, 56
Tooley, J., 127, 128
Torres Strait Islanders, 16
Towards the 90s, 23–4
trade unions, 67, 70–5
traditionalism, 89–93
transformative strategies, 138
Troman, G., 70–1
Troyna, B., 88
TTA, (Teacher Training Agency), 76, 78
Tulasiewicz, W., 76

unions, 67, 70–5
'unit' curriculum, 23, 88
United States
autonomy, 26, 28, 32–3, 80–2, 84–6, 96–8, 102–3, 106, 112–13
charter schools, 17, 27–8, 30, 40, 47, 72–4, 95, 96, 97–8, 102, 106, 127
education system, 15
educational policy, 8
national curriculum, 39
parental choice, 80, 121, 122–3, 125
population distribution, 16
private schools, 25, 27, 96, 97, 122–3
public schools, 10, 27, 32, 121
quasi-market, 121–3
research methods, 7
restructuring policies, 15, 25–8
school managers, 55–6
site-based management initiatives, 69
terminology, 10
see also California; Chicago; Milwaukee programme; Minnesota
universalism, 52
university education (for teachers), 75, 76
Urahn, S., 74, 86, 96
Usher, R., 46
utopia (civil society), 135

Victoria (Australia), 60
representative committees, 24–5, 104–5
Schools of the Future programme, 24, 40, 56, 57, 61, 62, 64, 68–9